P9-CKO-668

IN THE EYE OF THE STORM

Contemporary Issues in the Middle East

IN THE EYE OF THE STORM

Women in Post-Revolutionary Iran

Edited by
MAHNAZ AFKHAMI and ERIKA FRIEDL

Syracuse University Press

;yracuse University Press,
3244–5160,
auris & Co. Ltd.

Britain

Library of Congress Cataloging-in-Publication Data

In the eye of the storm : women in post-revolutionary
Iran / edited by Mahnaz Afkhami and Erika Friedl.
p. cm. — (Contemporary issues in the Middle East)
ISBN 0–8156–2633–9. — ISBN 0–8156–2634–7 (pbk.)
1. Women—Iran. I. Afkhami, Mahnaz. II. Friedl, Erika.
III. Series.
HQ1735.2.I49 1994
305.4′0955′09048—dc20 93–49077
CIP

Typeset by The Midlands Book Typesetting Company,
Queens Road, Loughborough
Printed and bound in Great Britain by
WBC, Bridgend, Mid Glam.

Contents

Contributors

Mahnaz Afkhami	Foundation for Iranian Studies, Bethesda, Maryland
Akbar Aghajanian	Department of Social and Behavioral Sciences, Fayetteville State University, North Carolina
Haleh Esfandiari	Department of Near Eastern Studies, Princeton University, New Jersey
Erika Friedl	Department of Anthropology, Western Michigan University, Kalamazoo
Shahla Haeri	Department of Anthropology, Boston University, Massachusetts
Patricia J. Higgins	Department of Anthropology, State University of New York, Plattsburgh
Fatemeh E. Moghadam	Department of Economics, Hofstra University, Hempstead, New York
Azar Naficy	Department of English, Allameh Tabatabai University, Tehran
Hamid Naficy	Department of Art and Art History, Rice University, Houston, Texas
Pirouz Shoar-Ghaffari	Department of Communication, Denison University, Granville, Ohio

Foreword

Robin Morgan

The book you hold in your hands is not merely another well-intentioned, academic, analytic compendium about women in some distant society. It is a contribution toward understanding crucial dynamics that affect the majority of the human species—which happens to be female. And since the world is shrinking, the Women's Movement is growing, and *all* issues are 'women's issues,' this book is ultimately about you, whether you are female or male.

There is no way to address constructively our planet's crises—economic, political, social, environmental, or any other—unless and until we fully comprehend the female human condition.

Women are not only the majority of humanity but also the first and worst hit by every problem. Women and children comprise more than 90 per cent of all refugee populations; two-thirds of the world's illiterates are women (and while the male illiteracy rate is falling, the female rate is rising); women *are* the poor of every society (the 'feminization of poverty'); women outlive men in most cultures, so the problems of age are women's problems – and furthermore women are the primary caretakers both of the aged and of children in virtually all cultures, so ageism as well as childcare are each a 'woman's issue.' So is the environment—since toxic waste, nuclear leakage, and general pollution take their first toll as cancers of the female reproductive system, and in stillborn births and miscarriages. Most women on the planet desperately long for but are denied such basic human rights as reproductive freedom, freedom of sexual choice, the right to divorce, the right to child custody, the rights to education, land and property ownership, equality under the law, decently paid employment and labor conditions, respect for the enormous *un*paid work they perform ceaselessly, and an end to the daily, murderous, direct violence wreaked on their lives in the form of battery, rape, incest, female infanticide, genital mutilation, etc.

Women in the Islamic world—who they really are, and how and why they are being used on so many fronts—are central to any possibility of global political understanding. This is not only because the Middle East region and its environs are so geopolitically important and engaged in such upheaval, but also because Muslim women have borne the brunt of especially invidious stereotyping (by men of their own cultures, by westerners, and even, sadly, by western feminists). It is also because, contrary to those stereotypes, Muslim women are poised courageously on the cutting edge of change, both in their own societies and in the international Women's Movement. And among women in the Muslim world, the women of Iran are of particular importance, for many reasons. To cite only a few:

1. Iranian women have been the primary target of Islamic fundamentalism during a period when worldwide religious fundamentalism of all kinds (including Christian, Jewish, and Hindu) has been rising alarmingly.

2. Iranian women have virtually replaced Algerian women as the symbolic (yet poignantly real) victims of contemporary male-defined revolutions that classically betray the female people who support them; who can forget that outraged cry during the women's marches just after the fundamentalist revolution: 'At the dawn of freedom, where is *our* freedom?' Furthermore, Iranian women have been (again, classically) used as political 'footballs' in the cynical power games played between forces of the Right and the Left.

3. Iranian women must struggle not only against the economic, political, and social crises they face at home but also against ignorant misconceptions abroad that patronize the 'alien' complexity of their existence. Why cannot some western political activists understand that, for example, the forced inclosure of a woman in a *chador* is the other side of the coin from the forced exposure of a woman in pornography? In both cases the woman is objectified; in neither has she any real choice.

In this book—distinguished by its scholarship yet no less accessible for that—we glimpse the real female human beings the world calls 'Iranian women.' The voices are rich with intellectual rigor, and impassioned in their search for a self-defined reality. This is a window into the vibrant female culture buried *behind* the patriarchal culture so cowardly justified by 'cultural defense' arguments.

I call this a true voice of feminism. Because if feminism is defined solely in terms of western (or northern) women—or any one group of women, for that matter—it is doomed, and so are we all. Fortunately, a glad proliferation of feminisms is blossoming all over the world, and women cross-culturally have been learning to affirm our diversity while seeking our similarity. All the while we have been learning, listening to each other, daring to redefine everything from work to development to power to spirituality, and reinventing a new, non-simplistic solidarity. I believe that this profound and sophisticated politics, this plurality of feminisms, is in its deepest sense the politics of the twenty-first century. It will free (more than) half of humanity and, in so doing, save the other half. It will give voice and presence to the previously silenced and sequestered realities, talents, and pragmatic yet visionary solutions proposed by the global majority. This book, these voices, are one tiny, brilliant tile in the vast mosaic of that potential—a potential I believe could, without exaggeration or hyperbole, save the world.

Introduction

Mahnaz Afkhami and Erika Friedl

This book is based in part on the proceedings of a conference entitled 'Women in Post-Revolutionary Iran' which was organized and convened by the Foundation for Iranian Studies and the Middle East Center of the University of Pennsylvania at George Washington University in Washington, DC on October 5, 1991. At this unique conference, for the first time since the Iranian revolution scholars presented current research on the condition of Iranian women conducted in post-revolutionary Iran. The main goal of the conference was to transcend the stereotypes and plain misinformation that pervade discussions of the position of women in Iran today in the absence of well-documented scholarly research available for other parts of the Middle East.

Encouraged by the high quality of the presentations and by the audience's enthusiastic response, we decided to publish the papers. They form the core of this book. In addition, we asked other scholars with expertise in areas not covered at the conference to contribute to the project in order to present as many different theoretical and topical issues as possible. In its diversity, the resulting volume constitutes a serious effort to outline a frame of reference for the current study of Iranian women as well as to provide information on the often contradictory circumstances of life for women in the Islamic Republic. Each article in this collection focuses on a different aspect of women's lives today. Together, they trace a picture of a highly dynamic people who discover and invent ever more subtle and creative ways of self-expression as they contend with a modern theocratic regime which claims absolute authority for defining correct behavior in all aspects of life, and whose writ is theoretically unbounded.

The contributions to the book represent the different theoretical orientations and the professional expertise of their authors. They span a wide range of social scientific approaches, ranging from empirical analyses of census data to interpretive literary criticism. Underlying all of them is the assumption that the position of women can be evaluated in terms of the degree of women's participation in their society's institutions, in terms of women's access to available resources and services to fulfill their basic needs, and in terms of gender attributes that further or hinder participation and access and that are expressed in cultural texts such as in law, literature, philosophy and theology. Frequently, the authors suggest that conditions and practices affecting women adversely today are rooted deep in Iranian culture and therefore transcend the gender philosophies and gender policies of the Islamic Republic as they often transcended those of the Pahlavi governments earlier.

Robin Morgan, the keynote speaker at the conference, in the Foreword to this volume stresses the 'variety of feminisms' in the world today that reflect local ethnic and cultural traditions with their specific value systems, and the need for communicating and understanding the diverse backgrounds and concepts that inspire the various feminist movements.

Mahnaz Afkhami provides the book with its basic orientation in a historical sketch in which she explores the effects of the changes in the position of women in Iran on the development of this socially and culturally complex society. In it she places the interplay of cultural factors, political programs of the state, and religious proclamations over time into a global feminist discourse.

Patricia J. Higgins and Pirouz Shoar-Ghaffari's and Akbar Aghajanian's articles provide analyses of governmental census data pertaining to women. Higgins and Shoar-Ghaffari discuss the government's goals for education and the execution of educational policies as they affect women in Iran today and as they compare to the pre-revolutionary era. Aghajanian compares various indicators of the social status of women and female children in the 1976 and 1986 censuses, including access to jobs and survival rates, suggesting that women are discriminated against on most of these counts more so today than before.

Haleh Esfandiari's analysis of transcripts of recent debates in the parliament on women's issues provides a rare insight into the Islamic Republican law-makers' attitudes toward women's problems. She demonstrates the difficulties the few women representatives in parliament have with their male colleagues even when they try to articulate their women constituents' concerns within the parameters of the governmental gender philosophy.

Fatemeh E. Moghadam uses the model of commoditization to analyze laws and practices underlying the concept of female sexuality in the Islamic Republic. Historically inscribed in Iranian culture, and only partially modified before the revolution, the treatment of female sexuality as a commodity subject to contractually negotiated use by men has been reaffirmed in post-revolutionary marriage and divorce regulations as well as in the job participation of women.

Shahla Haeri combines textual interpretation and ethnographic information in a discussion of the formal re-institution of the custom of temporary marriage after the revolution. She analyzes the philosophy of sexuality in Islam generally and as expressed in the writings of ideologues of the revolutionary government, and discusses the effects of the institution on the women who use it.

Azar Naficy, in a critical analysis of the portrayal of women in Persian literature from its beginning to the present, suggests that the image of woman has shifted over time to one of a shadowy figure incapable of sustaining a creative dialogue with men. She concludes that this view of women and of gender relations mirrors the post-revolutionary society's insecurity about selfhood and about gender relationships.

Hamid Naficy analyzes the post-revolutionary film industry's dealings with governmental demands of sexual propriety. He describes the creative strategies male and female directors and actors have developed to cope with the new codes of gender modesty, which include not only codes for appropriate dress and action on screen but also a code for proper looking based on official tenets defining the subversive power of female sexuality.

Erika Friedl, addressing the seeming contradiction between public/legal curtailment of the power of women and their popularly ascribed domineering position within the family, examines the mechanisms and the consequences of different strategies women use to achieve a modicum of control over their own and others' affairs in an essentially male-defined and male-dominated society.

The Appendixes provide a translation of excerpts from 'The Legal Status of Women in the Family in Iran,' prepared by Sima Pakzad, and a selection of criminal laws pertaining to women in the Islamic Republic. The effects of laws depend on their applications and thus vary widely in Iran and elsewhere according to the ways in which individuals exercise rights, governments prosecute, and courts provide for meaningful defense and balanced judgment. Nevertheless, as these selections demonstrate, laws on the book give a good indication of the cognitive and behavioral boundaries within which women have to operate.

1· Women in Post-Revolutionary Iran: a feminist perspective

Mahnaz Afkhami

The study of Iranian women has advanced rapidly during the last two decades, producing an extensive body of descriptive and analytic literature. Most of these studies are methodologically social science oriented and ideationally pro-feminist, even though, usually, the feminist aspect is overshadowed by the political ideology that governs the text. Until recently, the ideology was mostly liberal or leftist, if produced within the academe, and doctrinal if produced within or in response to a variant of Islamic discourse. More recently, critical theory, specifically textual critical theory, has been applied to the study of Iranian women, but the practical consequences of this approach remain unclear.

In this chapter I will discuss the issue of women in post-revolutionary Iran as a practical feminist problem within a particular historical context. My discussion is conditioned by two intellectual premises. The first is the utility of making a conscious distinction between society and polity in any Third World country. I take contemporary Iranian society to be a product of years of unbalanced development that resulted in important cultural, social and economic contradictions, discontinuities and ruptures. Consequently, there has existed an inevitable duality between the Islamic Republic as a political–ideological system professing a self-consistent and unified vision of communal life and a multicultured Iranian society, composed of many social types, each exhibiting a different life-style, a variegated vision of the past, present, and future, and a complex and often self-contradictory set of values, beliefs, and aesthetic preferences. The second premise is that women everywhere constitute a special case and a special set of problems. I take this last proposition to be self-evident and therefore will place the issue of women in post-revolutionary Iran in a 'feminist' context.[1] In the course of the discussion, I will draw on my understanding of feminist philosophy, Shii Islam as practical culture rather than esoteric doctrine, history as basic to the production, preservation, and destruction of values and norms, and my own experiences as a secretary general of the former Women's Organization of Iran.

The history of Iranian women is bound inextricably to the history of Shii Islam and to the myths that emotionally and intellectually sustain it. As a practical philosophy of life, contemporary Shii Islam is a product of a historical process and, like all historical processes, has gone through many changes. The ruling clerics, however, present it as timeless dogma. By presenting it ahistorically, they suggest that Islam is qualitatively different from other religions. Islam, they argue, defines all aspects of life and the Quran, as God's Word, prescribes for all time the proper pattern of relationships within and among all social institutions. Furthermore, what Islam has prescribed as the word of God, they say, corresponds to the order of nature.[2] This is particularly stressed in the case of women and their position relative to men in the household and in society. Major Islamic 'myths'—the *sunna* or the custom of the Prophet and the *hadith*, the compiled sayings of the Prophet and Imams[3]—were designed to uphold this particular interpretation of 'reality' and in the course of time the interpretation itself, as content and process, was established as the center of historical reality. Consequently, Shiism is now what the Shii clerics who dispose of political and moral power say it is.

The ulema defined early and, over the years, precisely the proper place of woman in Iranian society. The late Ayatollah Morteza Motahhari (d. 1979), one of the more enlightened Iranian Shii clerics and probably the foremost authority on contemporary Shii jurisprudence regarding women, provides a modern example of the Shii formulation of woman's proper place. He argues the *naturalness* of the differences between the sexes and the conformity of Islamic law with the purpose of divine (natural) creation.[4] From the idea of purpose and order in the process of divine creation he deduces, among others, formally structured criteria of justice and beauty and concludes what amounts to the proposition that God, in His encompassing wisdom and justice, formally wills woman's subordinate position in accordance with the requirements of nature.

This 'natural' position for women has been asserted by all patriarchal religions throughout history. Indeed, the process of the subjugation of women appears remarkably similar in all cultures. The originary myth usually treats man and woman more equitably, but once the historical process begins, woman is reduced to a vehicle of procreation—the axis around which woman's history as myth or religion is organized.[5]

The theology of procreation emphasizes the family. Within the family, woman achieves value primarily as mother, and secondarily as wife, daughter, or sister. The more society grows, differentiates, and becomes structured, the more the originary concepts yield to systems of mores and regulations that define woman's subordinate place in increasing detail. In time, her contact with the larger society is totally mediated by man.

In the originary Zoroastrian sources, for example, the *Gatha*, the *Yashts* and other early religious texts as well as in parts of the *Matikan-e Hazar Datastan* (*The Digest of a Thousand Points of Law*), a later text compiled during the Sasanian period, woman is treated with respect, if not quite as an equal of man.[6] Women in Iranian epics—Sindokht, Rudabeh, Tahmineh, Gordafarid, Manijeh, and a host of others whose names are perpetuated in the *Shahnameh*—are invariably brave, aggressive, and full of initiative.[7] By the middle of the Sasanian period, however, under a dominant Zoroastrian clergy, women had lost many of their rights and privileges.[8]

Abrahamic religions also accord woman an important position in originary sources. Genesis, in fact, seems to treat Eve as the more resourceful of the first pair, man and woman, created in God's image. If human history is said to have begun with the fall of Adam, then Eve, in the act of leading Adam to the forbidden fruit, may be said to have taken upon herself the burden of a civilizing mission. In the Talmudic tradition, however, the laws apply only to men because in the course of time the Israelite woman was relegated to 'a dependent existence derived from that of her father or her husband.'[9] In the Gospels, the very 'idea' of Christ suggests a leveling of inequities that to be meaningful must have included women. After Paul, however, Christianity steadily moved toward the affirmation of patriarchy and by the second Christian century the patriarchal interpretation had become, for all practical purposes, established dogma.[10]

This pattern is repeated in Islam. In few religions have women played so significant a role for or against prophetic pronouncements as in early Islam. Two of Mohammad's wives, Khadija and Ayesha, were as important actors in giving shape to the Muslim community as any of

Mohammad's male followers.[11] Hind, Abu Sufiyan's aristocratic wife, was one of the most effective opponents the Prophet confronted.[12] Zaynab, the Prophet's granddaughter, bravely confronted Yazid, the powerful Umayyad caliph under whose order the house of Hosayn had been martyred in Karbala, in order to save the life of Hosayn's son Ali Zayn al-Abedin. The first part of the revealed text, the Meccan verses, spoke for equality. Knowledge was to be gained by both man and woman. Women attended the mosque and participated in the debate and fought on the battlefield alongside the men. In time, however, a combination of authoritative statements by the Prophet and his successors, economic and political inequities, and law and custom supporting a patriarchal hierarchy within the family increasingly separated women from the business of society. Woman's insulation was legitimated by an effective socialization process that inculcated in her the idea that she was created to serve God and Man by being an obedient wife and a good mother. Thus, over the centuries, women were effectively reconciled to their lot by an ethics of womanhood, derived from the presumed pronouncements of the Prophet and Imams and codified within an impenetrable discourse, created by an elite of male clerics and guarded by a system of exclusive rules. Thousands of *hadith*, whose authenticity is determined by a set of arcane rules on most of which there is no solid agreement, are adduced to keep women in their place. Examples of such sayings are legion. A prototypical prophetic *hadith* states that 'A woman does not have one-hundredth of the rights that a husband has over his wife.' And, according to another, the Prophet declares, 'If I could order any person to prostrate [*sujdeh*] before anyone except God, I would command that women prostrate before their husbands.'[13]

Major challenges to the Shii institution in Iran originated outside the Islamic tradition in response to secular trends that began and grew in the West and in time confronted not only Christianity, but also other religions in other societies. Secularism was closely bound to the idea of social contract, an important function of which is to present society not as a natural or divinely ordained phenomenon, but rather as an artifact of human will. By emphasizing the individual and challenging the notion of a religion-based community, secularism weakened the legal and ethical web that bound women to the patriarchal norms. The Enlightenment's ethos encouraged male and female equality, despite the prevailing socioeconomic conditions and cultural and religious tradition that opposed it. In time, its central political ideas—the 'consent of the governed,' which was derived from the notion of social contract, and the 'inalienable human rights,' on which stood the individual's legal, moral, and philosophical right to participate in the social contract—were claimed for women as well.[14] From Mary Wollstonecraft's *A Vindication of the Rights of Woman* to John Stuart Mill's *The Subjection of Women* to suffragette movements in England, the United States and on the continent, the idea of women's rights gained ground—in retrospect, inevitably.[15]

During the nineteenth century western ideas entered Iran as a feature of the colonial process. Equality, freedom, human rights, economic development, social change, and other such positive concomitants of modernization mingled with the other feature of colonialism—the harsh reality of material and moral exploitation—to produce a schizophrenic response to the West and the values it stood for. Initially, western power stimulated in the Iranian elite a sense of admiration and a desire for emulation. *Tajaddod*, or modernity, defined in terms of politics, education, law, custom, and culture, and including some leeway for women to participate in the society, gained favor with some of the upper and middle classes as well as with most of the intellectuals.[16] Since the Shii clerical establishment controlled the fundamental aspects of culture (facts, values, norms, aesthetics, rules of rational discourse, etc), there evolved inevitably a dialectical tension between religion and modernism. At the center of this dialectic was the structure of social relations, with woman as mother and wife as its strongest symbol.[17] Despite these influences and tensions, however, traditional Iranian society placed little emphasis on women's rights during the turmoil of the Constitutional Revolution of 1905–6, although women had participated significantly in the struggle.[18]

The first quarter of the twentieth century witnessed the emergence of a number of women leaders in Iran who demanded the most elemental social rights in a society that suppressed them at every level of the hierarchical social order.[19] This hierarchy was primarily, though not exclusively, supported by the clerical establishment and a formal structure of religious traditions on which the clerical pronouncements were based. Thus, the politics of women's liberation was closely allied with the politics of secularization, which gained momentum during and immediately after the Constitutional Revolution of 1905–6. To achieve a modicum of freedom and equality, women leaders found it axiomatic that religion be separated from government, as the small sphere of activity they had so laboriously carved out for themselves could be safeguarded only by government protection. There were, however, traditional 'ethical' boundaries to gender relations beyond which neither the women activists nor the government were willing to venture. Throughout the Reza Shah period, for example, government would not move beyond removing the veil and encouraging young girls to receive a modern education. But even these preliminary moves were strongly opposed by clerical leaders, who considered the unveiling a sacrilege and modern education for women a path to prostitution. Reza Shah's forceful presence kept the clergy at bay; it also imposed a certain behavioral etiquette on the small social sphere within which women could participate. To accommodate the patriarchal culture, for example, women were said to receive education in order to become better mothers in order to train better men in order that the country might progress. The physical veil was to be substituted by an impregnable internal veil of moral virtue. In places where new schools had been established and where parents allowed their daughters to attend, boys and girls studied in separate schools or classes. In matters of gender, as in many other matters, customary moral and ethical discipline was strictly enforced.

After Reza Shah's forced abdication in 1941, the discipline imposed by the government broke down. Social forces began to compete for control as the chaos of the war years encouraged many social and political tendencies to develop and a variety of opinions to be expressed. Some women, having been forced to unveil by the previous regime, reverted to the veil. Others, free from the discipline of the past period, adopted exaggerated versions of western dress and behavior, sometimes looking almost foreign to their own people. The women who opted for a middle ground, mostly teachers and other professionals, formed the main axis around which a new set of demands for women's participation in the society took shape. By this time, also, some members of the political elite had come to support certain issues of women's rights. As a rule, however, support was not forthcoming unless demands were couched in a language acceptable to traditional sensibilities. It was imperative to take traditional sensibilities into account so as to nurture this support to grow strong enough to withstand clerical opposition, for without it women might not have reached the next stage in their progress, namely, to be recognized as citizens in their own right, rather than merely as trained mothers whose job is to raise competent men for the society.

During the 1940s and 1950s a number of women's groups and associations were established, among them Iran Women's Council, founded by Safieh Firuz in 1944, and the New Path Society, founded by Mehrangiz Dowlatshahi in 1946. In the 1950s 17 women's groups were active, mostly concentrating on education and charity work. In 1959, wishing to coordinate and consolidate their activities, these groups formed a federation called the High Council of the Women's Organizations of Iran and asked Princess Ashraf Pahlavi, the powerful twin sister of the Shah, to act as honorary chair of the council. In the late 1950s, the right to vote stood at the apex of the demands of the women leaders.

Symbolically, the right to vote, achieved in 1963 as part of a reform package called the White Revolution, removed Iranian women from the category of minors, felons and the insane—a category formally denied the right to participate in the political process by virtue of some important biological, psychological, or moral impediment. Suffrage was a prologue to the acquisition of other rights as women began to exercise political power, meager though it was, in the major patriarchal institutions: the family, society, and state. It was the beginning of a serious struggle for women to reach beyond the traditional spheres to become involved in higher liberal and technical education, in the production and managerial job market, in law, in defining the ethics of family relations, and in the struggle to raise women's consciousness.

During the 1960s and 1970s women organized themselves in earnest.[20] They took advantage of the government's modernization programs to define women's issues and to promulgate them through appropriate legislation, budget allocation, and the provision of legal access to fields hitherto reserved exclusively for men. For the first time in their history, Iranian women found their way into the parliament, the cabinet, the armed forces, the legal profession, and a variety of fields in science and high technology.[21] They lobbied men and women in Iran and in other countries to bring about an international atmosphere supportive of women's rights everywhere. Through the provisions of the Family Protection Law, the Iranian woman finally achieved the right to participate significantly in her own marriage, divorce, and decisions about her children, particularly the custody of her children in case of her husband's death.[22] Women worked hard to educate male policy-makers in the basic feminist principles of freedom and equality of sexes and consciously sought to learn and use the method and the language that would make it possible for the government to pass the necessary legislation.[23] In short, the right to vote for Iranian women signified far more than the actual importance of voting as a vehicle of political influence; it initiated women into a process of politics that was specifically Iranian, and which they used efficiently to promote their right to participate in all spheres of society.

This process was reversed in the Islamic Republic. The Islamic leadership proposed to undo what women had accomplished by replacing the secular vision, from which women had drawn the moral and political force of their arguments, with the Islamic model, which rendered the feminist position irrelevant.[24] The Islamic model had its own definitions of value, which coopted the vocabulary that was central to the feminist argument: equality, freedom, respect for the human person, participation in the affairs of the society, denunciation of treating women as objects, etc. The Ayatollah Khomeini and others used these terms in profusion and, consciously or not, succeeded in confusing most of their liberal audience.

Once the Islamic Republic was firmly established, the government began to rewrite the laws and rules relating to women's recently acquired rights. The new regime tried to force women out of the job market in a variety of ways, including early retirement of government women employees, closing of childcare centers, segregating women and enforcing full Islamic cover (*hejab-e islami*) in offices and public places, and closing nearly 140 university fields of study to women.[25] But the problems arising from the enforcement of the veil and other Islamic tenets in the streets and homes showed clearly that there were limits in Iran to what a fundamentalist regime could do. Women fought seriously for their rights, making the strict enforcement of governmental intent costly. The regime succeeded in putting women back in the veil in public places, but not in resocializing them into fundamentalist norms. As the economy suffered after the revolution, women worked in villages and cities, often harder than men, to make ends meet. As the revolutionary elan subsided, women reasserted themselves in other domains: in the arts, in literature, in education and in politics,[26] creating an atmosphere of tension and contradiction that has propelled the issue of women's status to the center of the debate on the creation of an Islamic society in Iran. Needless to say, loss of governmental support has cost Iranian women dearly. In addition to the economic, social and cultural problems shared by all, women also lost significant ground in the struggle for gender equality.

What then is to be understood from this brief history?

First, traditional.patriarchal societies suppress women everywhere, regardless of social, cultural, or religious particularities. This point is important for the cause of Iranian women because it delegitimizes the clerical–patriarchal argument in favor of women's separate-but-equal position by introducing a sociohistorical and comparative dimension to confront and challenge the validity of the prophetic–eschatological discourse. The arguments adduced against women's rights in Islamic societies have been raised in the past in other religions, including Judaism, Christianity, Buddhism, and Hinduism.[27]

Second, Iranian women achieved the rights they possessed at the beginning of the Islamic revolution through their own hard and persistent effort. It took them almost a century to move from total public invisibility to a position of visible political, social, and economic presence. The rights they achieved during the Pahlavi regime were not a political ruse, as the Left has maintained in the past, nor were they offered to them on a silver platter, as pre-revolutionary state propaganda seemed to suggest. Both points are relevant to this discussion and need to be addressed.

In their struggle for equality and freedom, Iranian women received little help from the leftist movements. The Tudeh Party had helped raise women's consciousness during the 1940s; but from the 1950s on, and particularly after the initiation of women's suffrage, leftist organizations and groups subordinated women's interests to other demands of their ideology. Consequently, achievements in women's rights were routinely denigrated as superficial embellishments of an otherwise oppressive capitalist system.[28] The fact is that a 'modernizing' state in a traditional society is usually an ally of the women's movement against a majority in the society. The government's policy in pre-revolutionary Iran was to modernize the country. Women used this policy to promote their own cause. Government needed literate, skilled workers to expand industry, disseminate preventive care information, promote better nutrition standards, administer population control programs, and undertake a myriad of other policies that were open to the argument that women constitute half of the population and that without their participation there was no hope for the successful implementation of these policies. This was a chance for women to achieve, in a concerted effort, the right and the actual opportunity to participate in the policy planning process in order to establish and promote the foundations in law, economics, and politics necessary to the empowerment of women. Leftist critics subverted this chance with their refusal to participate on ideological grounds. Some supporters of the regime undermined the effort by disengaging from the process, putting their trust in the Pahlavi government's benevolence to set everything 'right' without their effort and weakened the movement by devaluing women's efforts in the process of achieving fuller participation in society.

Third, without the support of the modernizing state and its political organs, which were controlled by men, women's rights are unattainable in an Islamic society. The law as the expression of the will of the state was indispensable to the securing of women's rights in Iran. Governments and leaders, as we have seen, can make decisions in favor of women's rights as part of a general ideological or policy outlook that may entail no specific emotional, moral, or ideological commitment to the cause of women. Reza Shah ordered the unveiling of Iranian women, but, according to his daughter Princess Ashraf, he felt wretched the day his wife and daughters appeared in public unveiled.[29] Mohammad Reza Shah took pains to emphasize, whenever he had an opportunity, that he did not believe in women's equality with men.[30] Paradoxically, a government of men who would shrink at the slightest intimation of equality between the sexes became a lever of women's liberation. The women's movement was helped because the problem of women was not primarily the government, which could be coopted through effective use of its own arguments for progress and modernization, but rather the male-dominated society. By the end of the Pahlavi era, there remained, of course, a huge gap between the promise and the delivery, but it was the beginning of a political commitment formally made by the state to promote the rights of women in Iran.

Fourth, women achieved these rights outside the sphere of traditional Shii Islam and against the will of the Shii religious leaders. I have already mentioned the religious constraints under which Iranian women leaders worked. On the one hand, they needed to transcend the Shii discourse, which meant they had to internalize and implement values that were essentially exogenous to their culture. On the other hand, they had to reconcile these values with Islamic prescriptions, if they were to communicate successfully with the masses of women in villages and small towns and to enlist the support of at least a part of the political leadership. This problem was tackled, though not always successfully, by a two-pronged strategy: women took care to gild their demands with a veneer of Islamic probity; most religious leaders, for their part, chose to pretend, perhaps as a matter of *taqiyyeh*,[31] that they accepted the proposition in good faith. There was no practical alternative to this mode of interaction then and, in all likelihood, there will be none in the future, even if Iran achieves a political system based on a formal separation of church and state.

Fifth, once rights have been achieved, they settle in the society's collective psyche creating a new set of historical conditions and thereafter cannot be easily dislodged. The obverse of this statement is that lasting social change involves hard infrastructural transformation, resulting from persistent and diverse economic, social, and intellectual stimuli and support. The post-revolutionary experience in Iran clearly indicates that cultural change is not obtained by an exercise of will alone. Thus, the women's rights dilemma in Iran will not be solved merely by changing the rules of discourse. The discourse, however, is important because, as both the pre- and post-revolutionary experiences in Iran demonstrate, it defines the modality of politics, which is to say, the discourse is directly relevant to the achievement or loss of political power. Unless there exists significant political power in favor of secular human rights, the Shii clerical hierarchy is unlikely to condone women's rights as internationally understood.

In the final analysis, therefore, achieving women's rights in Iran depends on achieving and dispensing political power. On the other hand, Shiism lies at the core of Iranians' value system and no matter how fragmented or self-contradictory it may be rendered by history, it will nevertheless constitute an important aspect of Iranian popular culture. Thus, inevitably, the emotional attachment to Shiism and the recognition that it is unlikely for women to achieve meaningful human rights within its compass make for intellectual schizophrenia. How is it then possible for women to engage the religious dialogue without forgoing their human rights?

The universality of the feminine condition at present suggests the possibility of empathy among women on a global scale—a humanizing process that to succeed must be empowered to travel over time and space, as all successful discourses have historically done. Zoroastrianism, Buddhism, Judaism, Christianity, and Islam moved over many countries across many centuries, nourishing and receiving nourishment from the cultures they encountered. Saint Augustine was a Manichaean at first; Thomas Aquinas received Aristotle's teachings through the intermediary of Muslim scholars. During the nineteenth and twentieth centuries, as we have seen, secular ideas derived from the European Enlightenment traveled east and south. Each transmission produced contradiction, agony, and despair as well as hope. New and unfamiliar ideas broke into established systems and clashed with tradition, merging with indigenous thought, energizing it to overcome intellectual inertia and to produce new form and content that challenged and often changed the established norms and values.

Waging their struggle in the colonial environment, Third World feminist thinkers have achieved a multicultural ethical and intellectual formation and a plethora of experience relevant to the development of an internationally valid and effective discourse addressing women's condition on a global scale. The question is whether this foundation can become a springboard for a global discourse. By definition, such a discourse must transcend the boundaries of Christian, Jewish, Muslim, Buddhist, socialist, capitalist, or any other particular culture. It will be feminist rather than patriarchal, humane rather than ideological, balanced rather than extremist, critical as well as exhortatory.[32] The global feminist discourse recognizes that the problem of women constitutes an issue in its own right, not as a subsidiary of other ideologies, no matter how structurally comprehensive or textually promising they might seem to be. It insists in relating concepts to the historical contexts in which they are embedded.[33] Since 'traditional' concepts are by definition founded in patriarchal discourse, global feminism must be skeptical of propositions that present them as liberating. This feminism is not anti-man; rather, it sees the world in humane terms, that is, it seeks a redefinition of social, economic, and political principles of societal organization on the basis of non-paternalistic models. Realizing that such a feat cannot be accomplished without or against men's participation, it does not hesitate to engage men politically in favor of the feminist cause. On the other hand, given the present effects of the historical process, feminism will be critically aware of and fight against patriarchal structures and institutions.[34]

The global feminist discourse rejects the notion that 'East' and 'West' constitute mutually exclusive paradigms; rather, it looks at life as evolving for all and believes that certain humane and morally defensible principles can and should be applied in the West and in the East equally. The point is not that Iranian women should forget the problems that are obviously 'Iranian' and intensely present. It is, rather, that unless Iranian feminists think globally, they will neither be able to mobilize world opinion for their cause, nor succeed in breaking out of the boundaries of patriarchal discourse on their own, and, therefore, they will likely fail to address their problems in a way that will lead to their solution.[35]

At present, of course, reality belies the potential. The disparity in physical and material power between the developed and less-developed countries forces Third World women to withdraw to reactive positions, formulating their discourse in response to the West and its challenge. Consequently, they fail to think globally, that is, to move beyond the indigenous culture they have objectively outgrown. Their discourse remains nationalistic, parochial, fearful, tradition-bound, and rooted in the soil of patriarchy. The world, however, is undergoing a qualitative change, an important aspect of which may be the tumbling of nation-states qua culture boundaries. In the process, women may gain a chance to promote on a world scale the kinds of ideas that are applicable to women everywhere. If they do, Third World women will be able to critique women's condition in the West from a vantage point that transcends the cultures of Abraham, Buddha, and Confucius and thus will help the women of all 'worlds of development', including Iran.

I am not suggesting therefore that the West be taken as the standard for the evaluation of women's conditions in Iran. On the contrary, it seems to me that there are significant issues of commission and omission in the western discourse that can be addressed profitably only from the global feminist position. The virtue of the global position is that it partakes of the wisdom of all cultures and that it accommodates differences in the levels of economic and social development without succumbing to either the normlessness of cultural relativism or the self-righteous parochialism of any particular culture.

The heightened awareness of female human rights that exists today throughout the world makes possible a more unified and effective approach to the global feminist movement. Western feminists can help this process but only to an extent, because they are burdened by two severe handicaps. First, they carry the onus of historical western hegemony, even though they themselves are the victims of a taxing patriarchal order.[36] Second, their problems as women are often of a different order than the problems of women in Third World countries. Consequently, they appear alternately as self-righteous promoters of their own western culture, when they advocate principles and rights that differ with the tenets of Third World societies, or as self-deprecating defenders of atrociously anti-feminist conditions, when they explain away oppressive behavior in the developing world on the grounds of cultural relativism.

Non-western feminists can be instrumental in the development of a viable global feminism despite their historical handicap. As the world moves from a disjointed society of nation-states to an increasingly interconnected economic and technological system, and as the symmetry of the enclaves of poverty and backwardness in the developed and developing countries is increasingly apparent, it becomes easier for Third World feminists to develop a sense of empathy with their sisters in other parts of the globe. Indeed, unless such empathy is effected and expanded, patriarchal norms, for all practical purposes, will not be transcended and feminism, global or otherwise, will not fully succeed.

It is from this vantage point that the originary myth in the Shii lore may be successfully engaged. Here is a chance for Iranian women to transcend the parochial discourse. By showing at once the similarity in the historical treatment of women in all societies and the need for women to deny the legitimacy of the patriarchal order in all cultures, Iranian women can challenge the claim that there is something unique in Islam that separates it from other human experiences. The goal is to contest the right and legitimacy of Iran's patriarchal clerical order to be the sole interpreters of the values, norms, and aesthetic standards of Shii Islam—a religion that lies at the core of Iranian culture. The truth is that there is nothing sacred about a limited and highly protected discourse, developed over centuries by a society of zealous men in order to produce and maintain a regime of control, a major function of which is to keep women in bondage—for ever.

2· Women's Education in the Islamic Republic of Iran

Patricia J. Higgins
Pirouz Shoar-Ghaffari

In the Islamic Republic of Iran, as indeed in all contemporary societies, formal schooling is largely a state institution—established, maintained, and controlled in order to implement government policies concerning what may be broadly termed 'the development of human resources.' Typically, the state is interested in several aspects of human resources in its efforts to train and socialize the population. The state seeks to produce motivated and competent workers, with the range and diversity of skills necessary to build and maintain itself; socially responsible adults who more or less voluntarily care for one another in families and local communities and who willingly bear and rear the next generation; and good citizens generally supportive of the state and willing to play by its rules. Although limited by economic resources and by the impossibility of controlling every action of the thousands of people who typically carry out educational programs, government policies have a major impact on who gets educated and what is taught.

This is the basis for our approach to the subject of women's education in the Islamic Republic. Our study concerns women's education by itself as well as in relation to men's education, and includes a comparison with education during the Pahlavi era, from which education in the Islamic Republic has developed, and with the education of women internationally. Our research on these issues is restrained by the paucity of social science research generally in Iran during the last decade.[1]

Government Policies Concerning Women's Education

The educational policies of any government are shaped by the relative importance given to the development of different aspects of human resources. Whereas most other contemporary developing societies emphasize the need for trained workers, the Islamic Republic of Iran has given more emphasis to the need for socially responsible adults and for good citizens. This has been taken to mean, in effect, good Muslims.

All who have written about education in the Islamic Republic agree that its chief aim is the creation of an Islamic person or, in the case of recognized religious minorities, the development of commitment to one God.[2] The High Council of Education lists among the basic goals of education religious and spiritual ones first, followed by scientific and cultural, social, political, and finally economic goals.[3] This emphasis can also be seen in the embracing of the principles that purification and commitment take precedence over knowledge and skills[4] and that specialization without piety is more dangerous than piety without specialization.[5]

An integral part of Islam, as understood in Iran today, is the belief that males and females differ in fundamental ways that extend considerably beyond physical features and biological reproduction. Biological differences are thought to be accompanied by psychological and behavioral differences that prepare men and women to play somewhat different roles in the family and in society. This emphasis on the inherent distinctiveness of males and females is accompanied by a belief that the power of sexuality, if unregulated, can destroy society. Properly channelled, however, sexuality plays a very positive role and is highly valued.

Since the family is seen as key to Muslim society, being a good Muslim, a socially responsible adult, and a good citizen mean carrying out family responsibilities according to one's sex. Motherhood and the direct care and upbringing of children are seen as the primary role and major responsibility of women; the suitability of other activities can be judged more or less according to the degree to which they interfere with or draw women away from their family responsibilities. Men's family responsibilities, in contrast, focus on the provision of economic support and the articulation of the family with other public institutions. These family relationships, and society itself, are best protected from the potential disruptiveness of unregulated sexuality through segregation of the sexes in public environments.

These features of the Islamic world view and their expression in contemporary Iran are commonly recognized and discussed in the literature and need not be elaborated here. Their significance in the present context is that if males and females are thought to be inherently different and preparing for different roles in life, it is quite logical that their education too should be different. While the Constitution of the Islamic Republic establishes the government's responsibility for providing free education for all citizens up to the secondary level (Article 30), in discussing the rights of women the constitution specifies that these rights will be assured 'in conformity with Islamic criteria' (Article 21).[6] Similarly, one of the basic goals of education is 'protecting the sanctity and stability of family relations based on Islamic rights and morality.'[7]

Nevertheless, the formal structure and content of education for males and females in the Islamic Republic is essentially the same. While a few children attend kindergarten, schooling begins for most at age six with the five-year elementary cycle. This is followed by a three-year guidance cycle during which students are to be assisted in determining the appropriate future direction of their education. Those who continue at the secondary level do so in one of several specialties within the academic or vocational branches or in a rural teacher-training program. A few students from most of these specialties are able to continue their education at the college level. Although the schools are sex segregated through the high school level, there is no difference in the curriculum for boys and girls, and the same state-produced textbooks are used by all.

The leaders of the Islamic Republic have placed considerable importance on education in their ideological statements and planning documents.[8] Their support for education, especially elementary education, can be seen in the government's budgetary priorities as well. In a recent analysis, Robert Looney shows that while government expenditures on education have declined in absolute terms since the Pahlavi era, they were 3 per cent of the country's GDP (gross domestic product) in 1985, just as they had been in 1975.[9] Despite the expense and dislocations of the revolution and the war with Iraq, education received around 20 per cent of government expenditures throughout the period 1980–86, a considerably larger share of the budget than it received in the 1970s.[10] Looney's figures also show that the government has been willing to increase its deficit to maintain the level of instruction, especially with respect to primary education, and he predicts that education will receive an even larger proportion of the budget in the post-war years.[11] The government's recently approved five-year plan, which counts on an 8 per cent per annum growth in

GDP and aims at a lower fertility rate, calls for a major expansion of the school system.[12]

Women's Access to Education

The Islamic Republican government accepts responsibility for the education of women, but do Iranian women actually have equal access to education? In Iran, as in most countries of the world, women's education has long lagged behind that of men. A larger proportion of males than of females learned the rudiments of reading and writing in the traditional Islamic *maktab*. The first 'modern' school in the country, the Dar al-Fonun, which opened in 1851, was exclusively for males, and western-style elementary schools were established late in the nineteenth century, first for males and only later for females.[13] In the Pahlavi era considerable progress was made in enrolling both boys and girls in school, but female enrollment at all levels continued to lag behind that of males. By 1977, females made up 38 per cent of Iran's elementary enrollment and 36 per cent of its middle and secondary enrollment (see Table 2.1). The latest statistics indicate that female education continues to trail that of males in Iran. In 1990–91 women made up less than half of the enrollment at every educational level, although they were approaching parity at the elementary level. At each level one also finds a smaller proportion of females of that age group enrolled in school than is true of males (see Chapter 3, Table 3.3 in this volume).

The results of this history can be seen today in the gender gap in literacy. For the country as a whole, only 52 per cent of females aged six and over were literate in 1986, compared with 71 per cent of males. This gap is more pronounced in rural areas than in urban areas, and more pronounced in the middle generation than among youth (see Table 2.2). Literacy, it should be noted, is defined in both the 1976 and 1986 censuses as the ability to read and write a simple text, and all students, including those in the first grade and those enrolled in literacy campaign classes, are classified as literate.

On the other hand, comparison over time indicates that the situation has been improving during the decade of the Islamic Republic. The gender gap in literacy has decreased from 23 percentage points to 19 percentage points overall, and among youths of 15 to 19 years of age it has decreased from 26 percentage points to 16 percentage points (see Table 2.2). The female proportion of the school enrollment has also increased in the last 15 years, and figures for the last five years

Table 2.1 Female Proportion of Total School Enrollment

	1976–7		1986–7		1990–91	
	Total Enrollment	Percentage Female	Total Enrollment	Percentage Female	Total Enrollment	Percentage Female
Elementary	4,768,588	38	7,232,820	44	9,369,646	46
Middle (Total)	1,377,696	36	2,299,510	39	3,232,682	41
Guidance Cycle	1,368,910	36	2,299,510	39	3,232,682	41
Intro. Vocational	8,786	3				
Secondary (Total)	979,182	36	1,292,013	40	1,852,150	41
Academic Sec.	740,471	40	1,076,762	43	1,590,405	45
Vocational Sec.	192,332	20	201,159	23	230,061	20
Technical	98,518	2	106,829	.07	132,005	0.5
Business*	84,233	32	86,183	54	86,374	52
Agriculture**	9,581	5	8,147	0	11,682	0
Teacher Ed.***	46,025	49	14,092	8	32,684	33

*Services in 1976–7
**Rural Vocational in 1976–7
***Rural Teacher's Education in 1986–7 and 1990–91 (secondary level program). Postsecondary teacher education programs enrolled 72,633 students in 1990–91, 34 per cent of whom were female.
Source for 1976–7: Summary of Educational Statistics for the Academic Year 2535–6. (Tehran: Ministry of Education, 1977.)
Sources for 1986–7 and 1990–91: Iran Statistical Yearbook 1369 (March 1990–March 1991). (Tehran: Islamic Republic of Iran, Plan and Budget Organization, Statistical Center of Iran, 1992.)

Table 2.2 Literacy Rates by Sex, Rural-Urban Residence, and Selected Age Groups

	Total (6+)*			**Urban**			**Rural**		
	1966	**1976**	**1986**	**1966**	**1976**	**1986**	**1966**	**1976**	**1986**
Male	30.1	58.9	71.0	61.4	74.4	80.4	25.4	43.6	60.0
Female	17.9	35.5	52.1	38.3	55.6	65.4	4.3	17.3	36.3
Difference	12.2	23.4	18.9	23.1	18.8	15.0	21.1	26.3	23.7
	15–19 Age Group			**40–44 Age Group**			**65+ Age Group**		
	1966	**1976**	**1986**	**1966**	**1976**	**1986**	**1966**	**1976**	**1986**
Male	55.9	74.1	86.2	25.2	32.1	52.9	13.9	16.1	22.6
Female	27.8	47.6	70.2	7.1	10.8	24.1	1.8	3.5	7.3
Difference	28.1	26.4	16.0	18.1	21.3	28.8	12.1	12.6	15.3

*7+ for 1966

Source: Iran Statistical Yearbook 1396 (March 1990–March 1991). (Tehran: Islamic Republic of Iran, Plan and Budget Organization, Statistical Center of Iran, 1992.)

show that the increase has continued quite steadily under the Islamic Republic (see Table 2.1). If we consider the proportion of the school-age population in school, again we see that it has been increasing gradually for females as well as males at the elementary and middle school levels and that the gap between male and female school participation rates is declining (see Chapter 3, Table 3.3 in this volume).

Despite apparent gains in education for women, especially at the elementary level, it has been claimed that 'at the precollege level . . . the policies of the Islamic regime significantly decreased the access of lower class and minority women to education.'[14] No data on differential access to education by class or by minority status are given, however. As a preliminary test of this hypothesis we have compared the female proportion of school enrollment for the elementary age level (six through ten) and the proportion of literates who are female in each province for 1976 and 1986. When the provinces are ranked according to their degree of economic development in 1976, as calculated by Amirahmadi and Atash,[15] we find not surprisingly that females make up a smaller proportion of literates and of the six-through-ten-year-olds enrolled in school in the least developed provinces of the country (see Table 2.3). If we compare these figures over time, however, we find that the proportion of literates who are

*Table 2.3 Female Education by Province, Ranked by Degree of Economic Development**

	Female Proportion of School Enrollment (6–10 Age Group)			**Female Proportion of Literates**		
	1976	**1986**	**Increase**	**1976**	**1986**	**Increase**
Markazi**	46.1	48.4	2.3	40.8	44.5	3.7
Esfahan	41.2	47.8	6.6	35.6	42.5	6.9
Yazd	43.8	48.3	4.5	37.2	42.7	5.5
Khuzestan	42.6	43.4	0.8	38.4	40.0	1.6
Fars	42.5	46.7	4.2	37.1	41.8	4.7
Semnan	46.1	47.7	1.6	41.0	43.8	2.8
T. Most Developed†	*44.3*	*47.3*	*3.0*	*39.3*	*43.2*	*3.9*
Bakhtaran	38.3	41.9	3.6	33.7	37.2	3.5
Khorasan	39.2	45.5	6.3	33.6	41.0	7.4
E. Azarbayjan	33.9	42.2	8.3	29.1	36.5	7.4
Gilan	45.4	47.6	2.2	40.0	43.5	3.5
Hamadan	30.0	42.8	12.8	26.1	36.7	10.6
Kerman	43.9	47.1	3.2	38.9	43.2	4.3
Mazandaran	42.9	47.5	4.6	37.2	42.5	5.3
Bushehr	38.0	46.0	8.0	31.0	40.9	9.9
T, Medium Developed†	*39.4*	*45.1*	*5.7*	*34.1*	*40.3*	*6.2*
Char./Bakhtiari	34.9	44.8	9.9	27.7	37.7	10.0
Hormozgan	38.6	44.3	5.7	31.0	39.4	8.4
Kordestan	27.2	33.2	6.0	24.0	28.7	4.7
Ilam	34.7	42.6	7.9	27.2	36.5	9.3
W. Azarbayjan	37.8	39.4	1.6	32.0	35.8	3.8
Lurestan	36.7	43.1	6.4	31.5	37.9	6.4
Boir Ahmad/Kuh.	35.3	41.7	6.4	29.2	36.1	6.9
Sistan/Baluch.	38.8	38.6	–0.2	31.7	34.5	2.8
Zanjan	30.2	44.6	14.4	26.0	39.2	13.2
T. Least Developed†	*35.3*	*41.4*	*6.1*	*29.7*	*36.6*	*6.9*
Country Total	**41.0**	**45.4**	**4.4**	**36.3**	**41.1**	**4.8**

*Based on Amirahmadi and Atash 1987.
**Includes Tehran Province (listed separately in 1986 figures).
†Figures for *T. Most Developed*, *T. Medium Developed* and *T. Least Developed* and **Country Total** are averages of the respective provinces corrected for size of the population groups in question.
Sources: National Census of Population and Housing, November 1976, Ostan Reports. (Tehran: Statistical Center of Iran, 1980.) National Census of Population and Housing, October 1986. Selected Tables: Total Country. (Tehran: Statistical Center of Iran, 1990.) Iran Statistical Yearbook 1369 (March 1990–March 1991). (Tehran: Islamic Republic of Iran, Plan and Budget Organization, Statistical Center of Iran, 1992.)

female increased in every province between 1976 and 1986, and the increase was larger in the least developed provinces than it was in the most developed provinces. Similarly, the female proportion of elementary age school enrollment increased in every province save one (Sistan and Baluchestan), and the increase was greater in the least developed provinces.

An alternative way to interpret these figures is to assume that the goal is equal literacy rates and school enrollment for males and females and to determine the extent to which the gap between this goal and reality was closed in the period 1976–86. Since females make up 49 per cent of the population in Iran, this could be taken as a target figure. Using this approach, women in the most developed provinces could still be said to have the edge on their sisters in the least developed provinces. In the most developed provinces 64 per cent of the school enrollment parity gap and 40 per cent of the literacy parity gap were removed between 1976 and 1986, whereas in the least developed provinces only 45 per cent of the school enrollment parity gap and 36 per cent of the literacy parity gap were eliminated.

Similarly, if we distinguish 'ethnic' from 'Persian' provinces and compare enrollment and literacy figures, we find that the proportion of females among the six-through-ten-year-old age group enrolled in school was less in the ethnic provinces in both 1976 and 1986 than it was in the Persian provinces, as was the proportion of females in the literate population (see Table 2.4). Yet the proportion of females among the six-through-ten-year-olds enrolled in school grew more rapidly between 1976 and 1986 in the ethnic provinces than it did in the Persian or mixed provinces, as did the proportion of females among the literate population. Nevertheless, the parity gap in school enrollment and in literacy was reduced more in the Persian than in the ethnic provinces—69 per cent versus 45 per cent for school enrollment and 44 versus 34 per cent for literacy.[16]

If we compare indicators of women's access to elementary education in rural and urban areas over time we find that the literacy rate for rural women doubled between 1976 and 1986 (from 17.3 per cent to 36.3 per cent) while it increased by 9.8 percentage points for urban women (from 55.6 per cent to 65.4 per cent). The gender gap in literacy rates declined in both urban and rural areas, but the decline was larger in urban (3.8 percentage points) than in rural areas— 2.6 percentage points (see Table 2.2). Similarly, the elementary school enrollment rate for women increased by nearly 20 percentage points in rural areas between 1976 and 1986, and the difference between male and female enrollment rates declined by over one-third. The increase of 4.2 percentage points in elementary school enrollment rate for urban women had the effect of lowering the male–female difference by over 40 per cent.

The increase over this ten-year period in the proportion of literates who are female, in less developed, ethnic, and rural regions as well as in well developed and Persian provinces and urban areas, can be attributed at least partially to Pahlavi efforts of 1976–9 and earlier and to the gradual demise of a generation in which very few women were literate. The school enrollment figures, on the other hand, reflect the situation in 1986, after seven years of Islamic Republican rule. While the parity gap is not being closed as quickly in the least developed and the ethnic provinces as it is in the most developed and Persian provinces, females are making up a larger proportion of the elementary school population than earlier in virtually all these regions. Thus, the data currently at our disposal suggest that rather than experiencing decreased access to education, women in less developed, more ethnic, and rural regions of the country have greater access to at least elementary education in 1986 than they did in 1976.

Secondary schooling is not currently included in the educational program which the state has promised to provide free to all citizens (nor was it in the Pahlavi era), and differential access to education is more pronounced at this level. Although the female proportion of secondary enrollment increased from 36 to 40 per cent between 1976 and 1986 (see Table 2.1), the school enrollment rate—the proportion of women of that age group enrolled in school—actually declined 1.2 percentage points (see Chapter 3, Table 3.3 in this volume). The gap between male and female enrollment rates declined at the secondary level, as it did at the elementary and middle school levels, but this is because the enrollment rate for young men declined even more sharply. As Aghajanian notes, these gains for women relative to men must be seen in light of the overall decline in high school enrollment rates, which was especially pronounced in rural areas.

Specialization in Iranian education begins at the high school level, and here we see evidence of the channeling of women into fields of study considered more appropriate for their sex. In the vocational branch women make up more than half of the students in business fields, but they are virtually excluded from the technical and agricultural areas (see Table 2.1). In the academic branch of

*Table 2.4 Female Education by Province, Ranked by Linguistic Ethnicity**

	Proportion of Population Able to Speak Persian (1986)	Female Proportion of School Enrollment (6–10 Age Group)			Female Proportion of Literates		
		1976	1986	Increase	1976	1986	Increase
Persian Provinces	*Above 90*	*43.2*	*47.2*	*4.0*	*38.2*	*42.9*	*4.7*
Kerman	99.2	43.9	47.1	3.2	38.9	43.2	4.3
Semnan	99.2	46.1	47.7	1.6	41.0	43.8	2.8
Yazd	99.2	43.8	48.3	4.5	37.2	42.7	5.5
Esfahan	99.1	41.2	47.8	6.6	35.6	42.5	6.9
Fars	99.0	42.5	46.7	4.2	37.1	41.8	4.7
Bushehr	98.4	38.0	46.0	8.0	31.0	40.9	9.9
Chah./Bakhtiari	98.4	34.9	44.8	9.9	27.7	37.7	10.0
Markazi**	97.7	46.1	48.4	2.3	40.8	44.5	3.7
Hormozgan	97.0	38.6	44.3	5.7	31.0	39.4	8.4
Khorasan	96.6	39.2	45.5	6.3	33.6	41.0	7.4
Mixed Provinces	*75–90*	*41.9*	*45.6*	*3.7*	*36.9*	*41.3*	*4.4*
Mazandaran	87.4	42.9	47.5	4.6	37.2	42.5	5.3
Gilan	84.1	45.4	47.6	2.2	40.0	43.5	3.5
Khuzestan	81.7	42.6	43.4	0.8	38.4	40.0	1.6
Hamadan	80.7	30.0	42.8	12.8	26.1	36.7	10.6
Ethnic Provinces	*Below 75*	*35.1*	*41.4*	*6.3*	*30.0*	*36.4*	*6.4*
Lorestan	71.8	36.7	43.1	6.4	31.5	37.9	6.4
Bakhtaran	68.3	38.3	41.9	3.6	33.7	37.2	3.5
Sistan/Baluch.	66.6	38.8	38.6	–0.2	31.7	34.5	2.8
Zanjan	64.8	30.2	44.6	14.4	26.0	39.2	13.2

Table 2.4 (cont'd)

	Proportion of Population Able to Speak Persian (1986)	Female Proportion of School Enrollment (6–10 Age Group)			Female Proportion of Literates		
		1976	1986	Increase	1976	1986	Increase
Boir Ahmad/Kuh.	57.3	35.3	41.7	6.4	29.2	36.1	6.9
Ilam	52.5	34.7	42.6	7.9	27.2	36.5	9.3
E. Azarbayjan	40.7	33.9	42.2	8.3	29.1	36.5	7.4
W. Azarbayjan	39.1	37.8	39.4	1.6	32.0	35.8	3.8
Kordestan	38.9	27.2	33.2	6.0	24.0	28.7	4.7
Country Total	**82.7**	**41.0**	**45.4**	**4.4**	**36.3**	**41.1**	**4.8**

*See also Aghajanian 1983 and Amirahmadi 1987.

**Includes Tehran Province (listed separately in 1986 figures).

Sources: National Census of Population and Housing, November 1976, Ostan Reports. (Tehran: Statistical Center of Iran, 1980.) National Census of Population and Housing, October 1986. Selected Tables: Total Country. (Tehran: Statistical Center of Iran, 1990). Iran Statistical Yearbook 1369 (March 1990–March 1991). (Tehran: Islamic Republic of Iran, Plan and Budget Organization, Statistical Center of Iran, 1992.)

secondary education, which enrolls 86 per cent of all secondary students (93 per cent of female secondary students), enrollment figures by specialization are not available. If we look at the number of graduates by field, however, we see that women made up over half the 1989–90 graduates in the natural sciences, but only 23 per cent of those graduating in math and physics (see Table 2.5). If we compare the number of graduates from each of the academic fields in 1989–90 with 1975–6, we see that the proportion of females has increased in every academic field (save home-making, an all-female field which has been eliminated), and the proportion of women among the graduates in the academic division as a whole was essentially at parity by 1986. In the vocational area, female representation among graduates had nearly doubled in 14 years (from 17 per cent to 30 per cent), due to an increase in the proportion of females among the graduates in business. The proportion of women among graduates in the technical and agricultural fields has declined from 2 per cent to zero. The current total absence of female graduates from technical and agricultural fields could have a long-term negative impact on the status of women, but this should not obscure the fact that women have made gains in other areas.

At the post-secondary level women's access to even more fields of education has been officially constrained. By the end of the Pahlavi era, 26 universities, 50 colleges and 168 other institutions of higher education enrolled around 180,000 students. Competition for entrance into these institutions was keen. In 1976, 300,000 applicants took the unified national entrance exam hoping for one of only 34,000 freshman places. In 1979–80, 550,000 applicants took the test, and approximately 10 per cent were admitted.[17] The closure of the universities during 1980–83, while efforts were made to Islamicize the curriculum and staff, did little to relieve the enrollment pressure. In 1986–7, 586,086 applicants took the entrance exam, and 62,000 or 10.6 per cent were admitted.[18]

Faced with such a demand for scarce places, and operating on the principle that in a sex-segregated society highly trained women are especially needed in some areas while conditions of work preclude their employment in others, the government established a system barring women from some fields and admitting them in limited numbers to others.[19] There is lack of agreement in the literature on the number and identity of the fields from which women were excluded, apparently reflecting in part changes in the rules from year to year. It

Table 2.5 Secondary School Graduates by Sex and Field, 1975–6 and 1989–90

	1975–6				**1989–90**		
	Number of Grads	**Female Prop. of Grads**	**Prop. of Female Grads**		**Number of Grads**	**Female Prop. of Grads**	**Prop. of Female Grads**
Natural Science	65,965	41	64	Natural Science	60,550	56	45
Math	21,977	19	10	Math & Physics	18,041	23	6
Literature	9,437	43	9	Humanities	32,245	50	21
Homemaking	4,009	100	9				
				Econ. & Soc. Sci.	33,039	46	20
Total Academic	*101,388*	*39*	*92*	*Total Academic*	*143,874*	*49*	*92*
Technical	10,763	2	0.4	Technical	9,381	0	0
Rural Vocational	3,281	2	0.2	Agriculture	816	0	0
Service	4,767	43	7	Business	8,614	66	8
Total Vocational	*18,811*	*17*	*8*	*Total Vocational*	*18,811*	*30*	*8*
Total	**120,199**	**36**	**100**	**Total**	**162,685**	**46**	**100**

Sources: Summary of Educational Statistics for the Academic Year 2535–6. (Tehran: Ministry of Education, 1977). Iran Statistical Yearbook 1369 (March 1990–March 1991). (Tehran, Islamic Republic of Iran, Plan and Budget Organization, Statistical Center of Iran, 1992.)

appears that women were excluded from as many as 44 per cent of the majors, including veterinary medicine, geology, agrarian sciences, animal husbandry, and natural resources in the natural sciences, and ideological and political guidance training programs, accounting, commercial management, and security in the human sciences,[20] as well as a number of fields in mathematics and technical sciences such as mining, civil, chemical, industrial, mechanical, and material engineering.[21] On the other hand, men have been barred from some fields as well; in 1984–5 they could not study fashion design and sewing instructor training, and in 1989–90 'midwifery, dental hygiene, and family health were exclusively open to women.'[22] Men have also been excluded from gynecology and nursing.[23] Most of the restrictions and quotas on female enrollment were lifted in 1989, apparently as a result of lobbying by the Women's Cultural and Social Council.[24]

The actual enrollment patterns show some interesting changes in the distribution of students, both male and female, among fields as well as changes in the proportion of women within fields (see Table 2.6). Compared to 1977, a larger proportion of students were enrolled in education science and teacher education, health and medicine, and engineering in 1990–91, while a smaller proportion were enrolled in the humanities and theology and in most other fields. Women had increased their share of seats in education science and teacher training, mathematics and computer science, and mass communication, while their proportion had declined in other areas—most notably in law, but also in medicine and health and in commerce and business. The proportion of women among the students had declined from 32 per cent to 27 per cent, but the larger number of students meant that in absolute terms more women were enrolled in most fields in 1990–91 than in 1977. Of particular importance for the future education of women is that in 1990–91 five times as many women were preparing at the college level to work in education as had been in 1977. Similarly, three times as many women were training in mathematics and computer science, two and a half times as many in health and medicine, and one and a half times as many in engineering.

Since the revolution, access to higher education in Iran has been controlled and channeled not only according to the student's sex, but also through a political screening process and the establishment of quotas based on service to the state. In a study of such political screening for both college entrance and employment, Nader Habibi asserts that 'in recent years the redistribution of educational and economic opportunities in favor of the government supporters, particularly the war veterans and their families, has emerged as the prime objectives of P.S. (political screening) policies.'[25] The specific groups and the proportion of college openings allotted in each field have changed from year to year, but in 1988–9, 20 to 30 per cent of all college seats were reserved for members of such groups (up from 5 to 9 per cent in 1985).[26]

Habibi does not indicate whether this quota system, or other features of political screening, have any effect on the sex ratio in college enrollment. Some of the privileged categories, such as 'handicapped veterans' and 'volunteer war veterans' are probably constituted solely of males, but others, such as 'families of martyrs' and 'crusaders and literacy campaign workers,' could include women. Whatever the effect of these policies on the sex ratio of the college population, Habibi concludes that they are effective in redistributing educational opportunities away from the urban upper and middle class toward rural and urban lower-class populations.[27] A final area in which the relative access of women to education should be considered is in connection with adult literacy campaigns. In the Pahlavi era adult education programs had been in existence since at least the 1940s,[28] and members of the Literacy Corps, established in the 1960s, were expected to organize classes for adults as well as children. The Literacy Corps was abolished shortly after the revolution, but renewed efforts to eradicate adult illiteracy were initiated by the Islamic Republican government with the establishment of the Literacy Movement of Iran in 1979.[29] According to the *Iran Statistical Yearbook*, in the second half of 1990–91 there were 117,491 classes offered at various levels and 2,046,809 students enrolled. Of the 78,744 instructors, 60 per cent were women.[30] The breakdown of students by sex for 1990–91 is not given, but in 1989 over 65 per cent of the students were women.[31] By 1988 only 41 per cent of the students enrolled in previous years had received their certificates of completion, but women did so at a greater rate than did men (47 versus 30 per cent).[32] In a special Mass Mobilization Plan to Uproot Illiteracy initiated in 1990–91, women again participated at a higher rate; 80 per cent of the instructors were women as were 85 per cent of the urban students.[33] The majority of the literacy classes and the majority of the students have been in rural areas, reflecting both the higher rates of rural illiteracy and 'the priority

Table 2.6 University Enrollment by Sex and Field of Study 1976–7 and 1990–91

Field	1976–7			1990–91		
	Number of Students	Prop. of Total Students	Prop. of Students Female	Number of Students	Prop. of Total Students	Prop. of Students Female
Education Sci. & Teacher Ed.	11,992	7.6	27	43,570	14.0	39
Humanities & Theology	23,461	15.0	43	28,470	9.1	40
Fine Arts	1,516	1.0	50	4,398	1.4	43
Law	2,085	1.3	27	5,811	1.9	10
Social & Behav. Science	10,264	6.6	39	17,230	5.5	34
Commerce, Admin. & Manag.	9,302	6.0	33	11,735	3.8	21
Mass Communic.	1,171	0.6	48	901	0.3	53
Home Economics	556	0.4	57	0	0	0
Public Service	196	0.1	82	0	0	0
Natural Sciences	14,459	9.3	31	19,960	6.4	32
Math & Computer Science	9,992	6.4	20	13,047	4.2	27

Table 2.6 (cont'd)

Field	1976–7			1990–91		
	Number of Students	**Prop. of Total Students**	**Prop. of Students Female**	**Number of Students**	**Propor. of Total Students**	**Prop. of Students Female**
Medical & Health Sci.	21,386	13.7	55	76,440	24.5	42
Engineering	24,877	16.0	7	70,487	22.4	4
Architecture & Urban Planning	3,076	2.0	24	2,474	0.8	16
Trade, Craft & Industrial Prog.	1,234	0.8	18	0	0	0
Transportation & Communication	319	0.2	24	0	0	0
Agricul., Forestry & Fishing	6,811	4.4	17	16,260	5.2	5
Other & Not Specified	13,184	8.5	31	1,293	0.4	0
Total	**155,811**	**100**	**32**	**312,076**	**100**	**27**

Sources: 1977 from Shahidian (1991); 1991 from Iran Statistical Yearbook 1369 (March 1990–March 1991). (Tehran, Islamic Republic of Iran, Plan and Budget Organization, Statistical Center of Iran, 1992.)

given to villagers in the allocation of resources in postrevolutionary Iran.'[34]

Educational Content

Although women's access to some fields of higher education has been officially restricted, and females have been effectively excluded from some fields of secondary education and encouraged to pursue others, the formal structure and content of education is the same for males and females within educational programs and levels. Studies of US education have demonstrated, however, that males and females can learn different things even though they are presented with the same formal curriculum.[35] It is relevant, therefore, to examine the content of that common education, particularly in terms of what it teaches about men and women and their roles in society.

The primary expression of the curriculum at all levels in Iran is the textbook, one set of which is produced for use in all schools in the country. An indication of the importance of the textbook in Iranian education, as well as the significance given to education by the Islamic Republican government, is the speed with which the post-revolutionary government began to revise the Pahlavi textbooks. Significant changes had been made within the first year, and the books undergo continuous revision.[36]

Ministry of Education officials claim that the 'teaching programs and textbooks at the primary, guidance, and secondary levels have been fundamentally revised;'[37] in fact, the modifications are somewhat less far reaching. The changes have affected religion, social studies, and language and literature texts much more than science and mathematics, and even in those areas the books were more often revised than rewritten. Comparative content analysis of the elementary Persian language textbooks showed that 60 per cent of the Islamic Republican era lessons were identical to those of the Pahlavi era or differed only in the pictures, names of characters, or an isolated word or two.[38] Overall, only 10 per cent of the texts in use in the Islamic Republic are completely new.[39]

Whatever the subject, the major thrust of the changes has been to bring the books in line with the primary educational goal of creating knowledgeable and committed Muslims and supporters of the Islamic Republican government. Since appropriate sex role behavior is seen as an important part of maintaining an Islamic society, it is not surprising to find that the portrayal of women and their activities in the textbooks is an area of major concern. Two previous publications have focused on these aspects of the new textbooks.

Jacquiline Rudolph Touba analyzed the elementary-level Persian language, social studies, religion, and science textbooks in use in the first year after the revolution.[40] She compared the roles played by males and females in these texts to a list of traditional sex roles constructed by four Iranian family sociologists (two male and two female). On the basis of this analysis, Touba concluded that the books portrayed only men in most economic activities, including some activities traditionally performed by both sexes; women were seen only as agricultural workers and as teachers of girls. On the other hand, some scientific activities which were traditionally male were performed by both sexes in the textbooks, and women were also portrayed in some recreational, artistic, and political and social activities that they did not traditionally perform. Similarly, males were shown performing some traditional female tasks, such as caring for small children and helping mother in household activities. Over and above the particular activities performed, Touba found that women were never presented as assertive in the texts, whether in positive, innovative ways or in disruptive, deviant ones, and that many positive features traditionally characteristic of women or of both sexes were portrayed in the texts as characteristic only of males.

To determine the extent of change in the textbooks, we carried out a quantitative content analysis comparing Persian language textbooks in use in 1986–7 in grades one through four with those in use in 1969–70.[41] We found the dramatic change in dress and in the portrayal of sex segregation (especially in public settings) to be the most consistent modifications in these texts. These changes were accompanied by the somewhat lowered visibility of women. On the other hand, we found no significant change in the occupations in which women were portrayed, in the prominence given to family life, in the size or structure of the family, in the characteristics of sex roles within the family, or in selected stereotypically gendered behavioral characteristics.

Since children are thought to learn best from materials and models with which they can identify,[42] the lowered visibility of women may effectively restrict female access to education, even if young girls are present in school rooms. Given the potential significance of this variable, we attempted to measure the visibility of women in the texts by several means. Considering simply the presence or absence of males and females in each lesson, we found that females were included in pictures and/or text 80 per cent as often as males in the Pahlavi era, but they appear only 54 per cent as often as males in the Islamic Republican era textbooks. Virtually all of this decline occurs in lessons set in public; in private settings females are portrayed slightly more often than males in both the Pahlavi and the Islamic Republican era texts.

Considering the number rather than presence or absence of males and females in a lesson, we found again that females were underrepresented in both eras, and that this underrepresentation was most striking for adult females. While the proportion of characters pictured who were female was about the same in the two eras (declining slightly from 45 per cent to 43 per cent), the proportion of gender-specific characters in the text who were female declined from 41 per cent to 27 per cent. (The gender of characters mentioned in the text but not pictured was unspecified in 46 per cent of the cases in the Pahlavi era texts and in 56 per cent of the cases in the Islamic Republican era texts—a situation facilitated by the lack of distinction between 'he' and 'she' in the Persian language and the grammatical gender neutrality of such words as 'student', 'teacher', 'worker', and 'doctor'.) Similarly, while females were portrayed as students in the same number of lessons in the Pahlavi era, females are shown as students in only two-thirds as many lessons as are males in the Islamic Republican era textbooks.

The absence of significant changes in the roles of women in the post-revolutionary textbooks is due not so much to the liberalness of the Islamic Republican texts as to the conservative nature of the Pahlavi era texts. Despite the rhetoric of the Pahlavi era in support of women's increased involvement in a sex-integrated world of work and public affairs, the textbooks of that era portrayed women primarily as mothers, housewives, and teachers. Women were portrayed doing work of any kind in only 23 per cent of the Pahlavi and 17 per cent of the Islamic Republican era lessons involving people. In nearly half of these lessons women are doing housework, and in both eras three-quarters of the lessons portraying women at work outside the home showed them teaching. The remainder portrayed women in agricultural work. Males, not surprisingly, were portrayed at work in a larger proportion of lessons than were women, and they were portrayed in a wider variety of occupations in both eras. Hence, both sets of texts present the reader with a division of labor largely in keeping with the principles espoused by the Islamic Republic, and both provide few models and little encouragement for girls to consider non-traditional careers.

Family and family relationships have an important part in the elementary school textbooks of both eras; in contrast to our expectations, however, the proportion of lessons portraying family relationships actually declined from 50 per cent to 36 per cent in the Islamic Republican texts. In both eras, nearly all the family relationships portrayed are those within the nuclear family, and the number of children portrayed in the families remained low at about 1.5. The focal family in the first-grade textbooks continues to consist of one girl and one boy, both attending school, and their mother and father.

In both sets of texts behavior within families is gendered, but not to the extent that one might expect. Mothers are almost always portrayed as caretakers, nurturers, or instructors, but fathers also are often portrayed as caretakers or instructors, a tendency that is more pronounced in the Islamic Republican era texts. Similarly, in both eras approximately 20 per cent of the males displaying any of the personality characteristics we coded (emotionality, impulsiveness, dependency, rationality, independence, and assertiveness) displayed the stereotypically feminine characteristics of emotionality and/or dependency. Adult females also displayed stereotypically male characteristics, especially rationality, either alone or in combination with stereotypically female characteristics as often as they displayed the classically female characteristics alone.

In assessing the impact on readers of the underrepresentation of female characters and the skewed distribution of female characters in particular roles, the existence of a large number of gender-unspecified characters in the texts should be noted. These gender-neutral characters have increased in both number and proportion in the Islamic Republican era texts; they now constitute over half of all the characters represented. The impact of the decline in the proportion of lessons in which females are portrayed as students, for example, may be alleviated by the many references to students that do not specify gender, allowing both males and females to identify with these characters.

The most dramatic and noticeable changes in the texts are in dress. Western-style dress was depicted in 73 per cent of the Pahlavi era lessons in which dress was shown, and only 5 per cent displayed full Islamic-style dress; another 7 per cent displayed working clothes, which do tend to be loose fitting and concealing and therefore Islamically modest. In contrast, while western-style dress is hardly depicted in the Islamic Republican era lessons, and 56 per cent of the lessons showing dress clearly feature Islamic dress, another 36 per cent feature working-class (modest) attire. Similarly, while Pahlavi era lessons commonly showed children and children and adults in mixed sex groups, such portrayals are rare in the Islamic Republican era texts.

In other ways as well, the new texts are clearly more oriented toward the lower and lower-middle classes than are the Pahlavi era texts which focus more on the professional, urban, middle classes. Not only do a larger proportion of the lessons show working-class clothing, families in the new texts commonly sleep, eat, and visit on carpet-covered floors instead of on western-style furniture; fathers of school children are identified as craftsmen rather than office workers; and some of the families featured live in rural environments. To the extent that learning is enhanced by being able to identify with the textbook characters, the newer texts expand real educational access for rural and lower-class children.

Overall, the textbooks of the Islamic Republican era appear to present a more realistic picture of the social world of the students than did those of the Pahlavi era. Indeed, the Islamic Republican era texts do teach children that their traditional sex roles are normal,[43] but also that it is normal for lower-class and rural children, males and females, to attend school.

Context of Women's Education

One of the first educational changes initiated by the Islamic Republican government, along with the revision of textbooks, was to convert all coeducational schools into single-sex institutions and to establish Islamic dress codes in schools. These two features of Iranian education are often cited as contributing to a decline in the quantity or quality of education for women. One concern has been that in rural areas where facilities are lacking for parallel schools and separate female staff, girls will be prevented from obtaining an elementary education. At higher levels of education a shortage of female teachers, especially in science and mathematics, is taken to mean that 'girls automatically will receive no or inadequate training in "male" dominated fields'[44] and that women's access to technical education, in particular, has become more limited.[45] How the institution of *hejab* is thought to impact negatively on the elementary and secondary education of women has not been specified in the literature, but it is reported that the pressure of maintaining Islamically proper demeanor in coeducational colleges and universities hampers women's interaction with their male classmates.[46]

In evaluating the impact of these changes on female education in Iran it must be remembered that most schools in the Pahlavi era were single-sex institutions, that long-sleeved, knee-length smocks worn over pants already constituted a common school uniform for girls, and that many women habitually wore Islamically modest head coverings even when this was discouraged by the Pahlavi government. In addition, it has been reported that the Islamic Republican government has relaxed the rules of sex segregation to allow for mixed primary schools in rural areas[47] and for male instructors for female students in the absence of qualified female instructors, thus alleviating the negative effects of limited resources for girls' schools. At the same time, in a society in which sex segregation in public settings is customary, sex segregation in the schools can effectively increase the access of girls and women whose families would not allow them to attend coeducational schools.[48]

Numerous studies of educational equity in the USA and the UK provide convincing evidence that coeducational schools and classrooms are no guarantee of equal education for women. The books used in such schools often give males twice the visibility of females, depict males in many more occupations, and characterize females as dependent and nurturant.[49] Teachers talk to boys more, ask them more higher-order questions, and express more confidence in their abilities.[50] Teachers' differential behavior is generated in part by the different behavior of boys and girls in these classrooms. Boys regularly monopolize physical space, dominate linguistic space, and emphasize their masculinity by using girls as a negative reference.[51] Indeed, one researcher found sexual harassment of girls so pervasive in English coeducational secondary schools she concludes that 'mixed-sex groupings constitute a disaster area for girls.'[52] Nor does the typical staffing of coeducational schools provide equal encouragement and strong role models for girls, since administrative and leadership roles are much more often held by men even though the majority of teachers are women.[53]

Students who have been educated in mixed-sex settings select college majors and secondary courses in a gender-biased pattern quite similar to the patterns evident in Iranian schools. English boys enroll in physics, chemistry, general science, economics, mathematics, computer science, and design and technology at the secondary level in greater numbers than do girls, and more girls than boys enroll in biology, French, German, music, religion, sociology, English literature, art, and commercial subjects.[54] In the USA, women earned 31 per cent of all doctorates awarded in 1980–81, but only 12 per cent of the doctorates in the physical sciences, 10 per cent in computer science, 4 per cent in law, and 3 per cent in engineering.[55] While girls educated in single-sex institutions in the USA and the UK are still more likely to specialize in the humanities and social sciences rather than in physical sciences and mathematics, a larger proportion of such students specialize in traditionally male fields than do their coeducated sisters.[56]

Sex segregation in education can mean inferior facilities and opportunities for women, and it can mean a very different educational content, but it can also mean greater opportunity for women to express themselves in class, to observe women in leadership positions, and to pursue interests in traditionally male-dominated areas. To determine whether sex segregation (and *hejab*) by themselves have a negative effect on female education in Iran, much more information is needed—on the facilities of boys' and girls' schools; on the quality and preparation of male and female teachers; on the student–teacher ratio in male and female classrooms; on the nature of student–teacher interaction in male and female classrooms; and on messages about male and female qualities and potentials transmitted by means other than the textbooks used by both.

Conclusion

Discussions of Iranian education in western media and scholarly literature have been dominated by politically motivated critiques, often with little supporting data. This review of the policies and practices of the Islamic Republican government indicates that there has been considerable support for women's education, especially at the elementary level. Female access to education, while still less than that of males, has continued to expand at elementary and middle-school levels in virtually all regions of the country. At the high-school level, women's proportion of enrollment has increased, but in a context of declining enrollment rates for both males and females, especially in rural areas. While the war with Iraq and economic dislocations may be causes of the general decline in high-school enrollment rates, the decline for women may also be a result of cultural pressures toward early marriage and home-making activities. Restrictions on women's entry into certain fields of education, skewed enrollment patterns in others, and the content of textbooks all indicate that women are being educated to play a more limited role in the public sphere than are men.

While the education of women in the Islamic Republic may leave much to be desired, it is important for critics and potential reformers to have as accurate a perception as possible of the current situation. It is also useful to maintain a comparative perspective. Education has commonly been seen as a major route to advancement for women, and in other countries of the world women's rights movements have grown in settings of sex-segregated and limited-purpose education for women. In the Islamic Republic, too, even the basic and somewhat restricted education being afforded women may give women the tools to become more aware of their possibilities and more articulate about alternative social arrangements, and hence increase their basis for influence and independence.

3· The Status of Women and Female Children in Iran: an update from the 1986 census

Akbar Aghajanian

The concept of the status of women is widely used in the literature about women in developing countries including those of the Middle East.[1] A large array of components such as ideologies, legal and property rights, inheritance rules, material transactions, age at marriage, husband–wife age differentials, availability and use of contraceptives, arranged marriages, polygyny, women's attire, segregation, divorce rights, and temporary marriage have been used by various authors as indicators of the status of women. In recent years changes in the legal and social status of women and in women's roles in Iran have been widely explored in the literature.[2] This literature focuses on ideological components and legal rights and duties of women, but the concept of the status of women encompasses a range of 'objective' issues as well, such as economic participation and access to family and community resources.[3] The present chapter favors the use of an objective approach for the analysis of the status of women, concentrating on the changes in the objective socioeconomic indicators of the status of women relative to men, and utilizing data from the most recent census of Iran. Specifically, this chapter highlights the issues of relative access of women to education, women's economic participation, and nutrition and health resources of women.

Female Status and Relative Access to Education

Education is one of the most objective dimensions of the status of women in any society today. It is one of the scarce resources available to communities and families in many developing countries. Hence, social class and gender play important roles in the allocation of educational resources at the community level and within the family. Education is also important as it determines other dimensions of the status of women such as paid labor force participation and health status of women and female children.

The literacy rate is a good indicator of the relative educational status of women. Table 3.1 shows the literacy rate of males and females in the two most recent censuses in Iran. (The literacy rate is defined as the percentage of literate people in the total population six years of age and older.) The table shows lower literacy rates for women compared to men at both times and in both rural and urban areas.

Social reforms designed to improve the status of women peaked in 1976. Nevertheless, the census data still show a wide gap in the literacy rates of men and women. The literacy rate for men is 23 percentage points higher than for women. The gap in the literacy rate between men and women in urban areas is about 19 percentage points and thus considerably lower than in rural areas. Rural women have the lowest literacy rate: only about 17 per cent of the rural female population six years and older were literate in 1976. Considering the fact that more than 50 per cent of Iranian women lived in rural areas in 1976, this suggests an overall high illiteracy rate for women at the time.

According to the 1986 census, the literacy rate of men and women has increased significantly since 1976. Along with this change, the gap in literacy between men and women has also narrowed. In urban areas, the difference declined from 19 percentage points to 15 percentage points. The decline in rural areas was about 2 percentage points. While the literacy rate of rural women doubled during the period 1976–86, rural women still had the lowest literacy rate in 1986: less than half the rate for urban men.

Table 3.2 shows the literacy rate of men and women in different

Table 3.1 The Literacy Rate of Men and Women in Iran*

	Total		**Urban**		**Rural**	
	1976	**1986**	**1976**	**1986**	**1976**	**1986**
Male	58.6	71.0	74.4	80.4	43.6	60.0
Female	35.5	51.9	55.6	65.4	17.3	36.0
Difference	23.1	19.1	18.8	15.0	26.3	24.0

Source: Iran Statistical Center, 1990.
*Literacy rate is defined as the percentage of literates in the population six years and older.

provinces. It indicates that in some provinces the difference in the rates for men and women is much wider than in others, and compares this difference to the average difference for the country as a whole, stating it as deviation from the mean. A negative sign indicates that the gender gap in the literacy rate of the province is below the national level; no sign indicates that the gap is above the national level; zero indicates that the gap in this province is similar to the national average. The female–male difference in the literacy rate varies widely across different provinces: in Tehran province the gap is almost 8 percentage

Table 3.2 Literacy Rate of Men and Women in Different Provinces in Iran, 1986*

	Male	Female	Difference	Deviation from Mean*
Tehran	83.7	72.4	11.3	–7.8
Markazi	73.2	51.2	22.0	2.9
Mazandaran	73.4	57.9	15.5	–3.6
East Azarbayjan	72.4	54.3	18.1	–1.0
West Azarbayjan	64.6	39.1	25.5	6.4
Bakhtaran	59.3	34.3	25.0	5.9
Khuzestan	67.7	42.8	24.9	5.8
Fars	69.3	48.6	20.7	1.6
Kerman	74.6	56.0	18.6	–0.5
Khorasan	65.9	51.4	14.5	–4.6
Esfahan	78.5	62.7	15.8	–3.3
Sistan & Baluchestan	46.3	25.3	21.0	1.9
Kordestan	54.3	23.2	31.1	12.0
Hamadan	68.9	43.6	25.3	6.2
Chaharmahal & Bakhtiyari	68.9	44.3	24.6	5.5
Lorestan	63.6	41.1	22.5	3.4
Ilam	64.1	40.0	24.1	5.0
Kohgiluyeh & Boir Ahmad	66.0	39.9	26.1	7.0
Bushehr	71.2	50.6	20.6	1.5
Zanjan	68.6	46.4	22.2	3.1
Semnan	77.4	63.2	14.2	–4.9
Yazd	77.0	61.6	15.4	–3.7
Hormozgan	61.0	41.7	19.3	0.2
Iran	71.0	51.9	19.1	

Source: Iran Statistical Center, 1990.
* Literacy rate is defined as the percentage of literates in the population six years and older.
** Shows deviation from the national average difference between the male and female literacy rates.

points below the national average, while in Kordestan the gap is 12 percentage points above the national average.

The school enrollment rate reflects the educational status of children. Table 3.3 summarizes the data on school enrollment by gender and place of residence in different census-years. While in both census-years the gap in the school enrollment between female and male children is notable, it has declined between 1976 and 1986. In 1976, the rate of school enrollment of female children was 21 percentage points lower than the rate for male children at the elementary level (grades 1–5). This gap had declined by almost half by 1986.

In urban areas there was only a 6 percentage point difference between male and female children enrolled in elementary school

Table 3.3 School Enrollment Rate of Children in Iran by Age and Sex*

Panel 1: Elementary School (Grades 1–5)

	Total		Urban		Rural	
	1976	**1986**	**1976**	**1986**	**1976**	**1986**
Male	82.3	87.6	92.1	93.5	74.6	82.3
Female	61.0	75.1	85.5	89.7	41.7	61.5
Difference	21.3	12.5	6.6	3.8	32.9	20.8

Panel 2: Middle School (Grades 6–8)

	Total		Urban		Rural	
	1976	**1986**	**1976**	**1986**	**1976**	**1986**
Male	76.0	77.5	90.2	86.5	61.8	68.8
Female	49.4	56.2	77.4	77.0	23.4	35.7
Difference	26.6	21.3	12.8	9.5	38.4	33.1

Panel 3: High School (Grades 9–12)

	Total		Urban		Rural	
	1976	**1986**	**1976**	**1986**	**1976**	**1986**
Male	47.5	40.2	63.6	51.1	25.4	10.3
Female	25.8	24.6	45.0	37.1	6.7	2.7
Difference	21.7	15.6	18.6	14.0	18.7	7.6

Source: Iran Statistical Center, 1980, 1988.
* School enrollment rate is defined as the percentage of children of each age group enrolled in school.

in 1976 and this gap declined to 3 percentage points by 1986. But in rural areas the rate of elementary-school enrollment for female children in 1986 was still about 21 percentage points lower than the rate for male children.

The decline in the gender gap in school enrollment is apparent for the middle school (grades 6–8) too (see panel 2 in Table 3.3). Note that compared to elementary-school enrollment rates, the rates for middle-school enrollment are lower for all places and both sexes, but much lower for female children. The gender gap was 27 percentage points in 1976, declining to 21 percentage points in 1986. In urban areas the gap decreased 3.3 percentage points, from 12.8 per cent in 1976 to 9.5 per cent in 1986. For rural areas the decline was 5 percentage points, from 38 per cent in 1976 to 33 per cent in 1986. Yet, despite this declining trend, only 36 per cent of the eligible rural female children were enrolled at the middle-school level in 1986.

At the high-school level (grades 9–12) the rate of school enrollment of female children is 21.7 percentage points less than the rate for male children in 1976. The rate of high-school enrollment for both male and female children has dropped between 1976 and 1986, but more so for males than females, resulting in a smaller difference between male and female high-school enrollment. Note that the rate for high-school enrollment for women has not changed much between 1976 and 1986, and is over 15 percentage points lower than for men. In the decade covered by the census, it seems marriage was the alternative to school for female children in this age group. According to the Iran Fertility Survey, more than 50 per cent of Iranian women marry before age 17 and the remaining 50 per cent are mostly married by age 20.[4]

Changes in the enrollment rate in urban areas are much bigger than in rural areas. In urban areas the rate of school enrollment for female and male children has declined significantly, from 64 per cent in 1976 to 51 per cent in 1986. For female children the decline was 8 percentage points, from 45 per cent to 37 per cent. The differential decline pattern reduced the gap between male and female children. The situation in rural areas is worse. By 1986 less than only 3 per cent of the rural female children were enrolled in high school, and only 10 per cent of the rural male children. The relatively small gender gap in high-school attendance in rural areas, about 7 percentage points, has to be seen in the context of the alarmingly low high-school attendance in rural areas for both sexes.

Summary: While literacy rates and elementary-school attendance for both males and females were rising between 1976 and 1986, with a narrowing gap between the sexes in urban as well as rural areas, middle-school and high-school attendance rates have been falling, with a slightly narrowing gap between the sexes due to a higher drop in attendance by males. It seems that while literacy is considered worthwhile by the government and the people for both males and females, higher education, especially in rural areas and for women, is not.

Female Status and Access to Economic Resources

Women have always contributed to the economic activity of households, particularly in the rural areas of Iran. A number of household chores within the rural household are essential economic activities. In addition, rural women contribute their labor to agricultural production. Urban women may bring extra income to their households by weaving carpets or participation in home industries and trade. Such economic contributions by women are not reflected in the census data, and the important question of who controls the income generated by these extra activities is not covered in the census either. While there are no quantitative data yet available on these issues, one can infer from descriptions in the literature that economic contributions of women to the household are significant in rural areas and in small cities.[5]

Although we can assume that women's labor input in the informal economic sector has an influence on other aspects of women's status, the census data give information on work only in the context of the formal sector of the economy. Given this limitation, the data from 1976 (see Table 3.4) show a wide gap between the economic activities of men and women in Iran. Note that economic activity here includes both paid employment and unpaid family work. The rate of economic

Table 3.4 Economic Activity Rate of Men and Women in Iran*

	Total		Urban		Rural	
	1976	1986	1976	1986	1976	1986
Male	70.8	68.3	63.9	66.8	77.9	70.3
Female	12.9	8.1	9.0	8.3	16.5	8.0
Difference	57.1	60.2	54.9	58.5	61.4	62.3

Source: Iran Statistical Center, 1990.
*Economic activity rate is defined as the percentage of individuals working or looking for a job in the total population 10 years and older.

participation of women ten years and older is about 58 percentage points lower than for men. It is clear that after more than 15 years of social and legal reforms of the Pahlavi regime designed to improve the position of women, the gap in participation in the labor market between men and women was still very high in 1976.

The 1986 census shows that the economic activity rate of women has declined since 1976. In fact, for all women the rate of economic participation declined by about one-third, from 13 per cent in 1976 to 8 per cent in 1986. Most likely, the high overall unemployment rate during the lengthy Iran–Iraq war pressured women to withdraw from the workforce. However, the decline in the economic activity rate of women is also consistent with the strong emphasis on the priority of familial and household roles for women in the Islamic Republic. In general, both the economic and sociopolitical environments have favored a decline in the economic activity rate of women in the last decade. This is particularly reflected in the data on the rate of paid employment reported in Table 3.5. Note that in this analysis paid employment is a better indicator of the status of women, as it is adjusted for unpaid family workers. The rate of paid employment for women declined from 10 per cent in 1976 to 7 per cent in 1986, and the gap between men and women increased from 80 percentage points to 85 percentage points in favor of men.

The economic and non-economic roles of young women between the ages of 15 and 24 have changed in the decade covered by the 1986 census, as can be seen in Table 3.6: the employment rate declined; the school participation rate declined; and the full-time home-maker rate increased. The same pattern of change is also evident for women 20 to 24 years old. Clearly, the roles of wife and mother have become more important for young women between 1976 and 1986.

Table 3.5 Rate of Paid Employment for Men and Women in Iran*

	Total		Urban		Rural	
	1976	**1986**	**1976**	**1986**	**1976**	**1986**
Male	89.8	92.7	89.8	91.5	91.8	94.3
Female	10.2	7.3	10.2	8.5	8.2	5.7
Difference	79.6	85.4	79.6	83.0	83.6	88.6

Source: Iran Statistical Center, 1990.
*Percentage of gainfully employed males and females ten years and older in the population.

Table 3.6 Economic and Non-economic Activities of Women 15–24 Years Old

	15–19 years old		20–24 years old	
Roles	**1976**	**1986**	**1976**	**1986**
Employed	13.1	5.1	15.3	7.5
Looking for job	2.6	4.4	2.5	4.7
Student	25.1	24.6	5.6	3.8
Home-maker	58.1	63.1	75.4	81.2
Others	1.1	2.8	1.2	2.8
Total	100.0	100.0	100.0	100.0

Source: Iran Statistical Center, 1990.

Female Status, Health, and Access to Nutrition Resources

Food is a scarce resource in many Third World countries. In societies where female status is low, allocation of food resources is biased against female children, which results in female malnutrition. Another indicator for low female status is the disparity in access to health services for prevention and treatment of illness among male and female children. The disparity is seen, for example, in slow medical response to illness among female children and a tendency to provide the cheapest available healthcare for them.[6]

Differential access to health services and food is reflected in differential mortality rates between male and female children. Three types of data from demographic surveys and censuses in Iran show excess female mortality. An indirect measure of excess female mortality is the sex ratio of children from one to four years old. The sex ratio, measured by the number of males per 100 females in humans on the average is 105 at birth. In societies where excess female mortality exists, this ratio will increase for children at ages one to four. Another indirect measure of excess female mortality from demographic sources is life expectancy at birth. Life expectancy at birth is the average number of years someone will live after being born. In societies where women have lower relative access to health and nutrition resources than men, female life expectancy is lower than the life expectancy for males. This is contrary to the regular pattern observed in the majority of human populations, where female life expectancy is higher than male life expectancy.

A third measure of excess female mortality is in the comparison of mortality rates of males and females at different ages.

The data from the 1976 census show excess female child mortality, especially in rural areas. While the sex ratio for children from one to four years old is about 108 for all areas, the figure for rural areas is 110. This high sex ratio suggests that more male children survived their first four years than did female children.

The calculation of life expectancy at birth from the 1976 census reveals a higher life expectancy for men than for women: 55.8 for men and 55.0 for women.[7]

The age-specific mortality data for children, calculated from one of the most reliable demographic surveys in Iran, support the excess female mortality hypothesis. According to the data from this survey (see Table 3.7), infant mortality for females is 110 per 1000 compared to 101 per 1000 for male infants. Excess female infant mortality is about 9 per cent. The situation is worse in rural areas where the figures are 129 for female infants and 118 for male infants.[8] In rural areas excess female infant mortality is about 10 per cent. Excess mortality continues during all childhood ages. As shown in Table 3.7, the age-specific mortality rate is higher for females than for males up to age 14. However, excess mortality is higher among children aged four and younger.

In the decade 1980–90, official surveys and reports suggest that infant and child mortality rates declined significantly.[9] There are as yet no data available regarding differential child and infant mortality by sex. Therefore, we do not know if the rates of decline in child mortality are the same for males and females. However, a 1986 pilot study of women's attitudes toward food needs and food distribution in their families in Iran suggests a difference in the access to food for boys and girls which can be expected to influence mortality rates for both sexes.

The remainder of this chapter will deal with these attitudinal data about food distribution, collected from mothers in the city of Shiraz in 1986 in a pilot study relating female status to food distribution. The results provide topics for future research in this area.

Female Status and Mothers' Attitudes Toward Food Distribution

As discussed in the previous section, one of the mechanisms linking gender to health status is differential food distribution and malnutrition in male and female children.[10] More specifically, excess female child mortality is related to malnutrition resulting from discrimination in food distribution. Female children are fed a lower quantity and quality

Table 3.7 Age-Specific Death Rate for Children in Iran, 1976*

	Total			Urban			Rural		
Age	**Male**	**Female**	**Difference**	**Male**	**Female**	**Difference**	**Male**	**Female**	**Difference**
Infant	101.4	109.9	–8.5	59.8	61.0	–1.2	118.2	129.5	–11.3
1–4 years	14.7	18.9	–4.2	8.9	10.4	–1.5	17.3	22.8	–5.5
5–9 years	2.0	2.5	–0.5	1.2	1.2	0.0	2.4	3.2	–0.8
10–14 years	1.0	1.6	–0.6	0.9	1.6	–0.7	1.2	1.5	–0.3

Source: Iran Statistical Center, 1977.
*Death rate is defined as the number of deaths per 1000 in the age group.
Note: A negative sign shows death rate higher for females than males.

of the food available to the family. This pattern of discrimination is practiced from early childhood on, and the surviving female children are socialized to accept and practice it throughout their lives. Hence, it can be expected that such discriminatory beliefs and practices are reflected in mothers' attitudes toward food distribution.

The data presented here were collected in the city of Shiraz in southern Iran in 1986. Shiraz is a major commercial, educational, and industrial urban center with a population of about 850,000 according to the 1986 census.[11] The population for this study consisted of married women with children. A sample of this population was obtained by using available information about the eight subdivisions of the city as the sampling frame. In each subdivision at least 50 married women were interviewed. These women were selected through systematic random sampling by visiting the housing units. In each house a married woman was interviewed.

During the survey a total of 576 protocols was obtained with the use of a short questionnaire with 18 questions on a series of socioeconomic factors, attitudes, and beliefs regarding male authority, and patterns of food distribution to family members (see Appendix 1).

Mothers' Attitudes Toward Food Distribution

In a society where gender stratification is rigid, female children are discriminated against in access to resources. In the case of Iranian society, this is reflected in the answers of mothers to a series of questions about their food distribution practices. For example, women in the sample believe that it is very important that they serve the men in their house first, as a sign of respect. About 44 per cent of them agreed with the statement, '. . . it is very important that the male head be served first.' Another 44.4 per cent agreed with this statement to some extent. Only 11 per cent disagreed.

Another question asked in this regard was: 'Do you agree with the statement, "to prevent problems with the male head (husband), it is very important to give him the best food in the house"?' About 45 per cent of the women absolutely agreed (and therefore probably give the best food to the male head to avoid complaints); another 11 per cent agreed to some extent (see Table 3.8).

Male superiority in receiving food is further expressed in the response to the following question: 'Some women believe that the male head of the household should receive the most and the best food because he is the breadwinner. Do you agree with this statement?'

Table 3.8 Per Cent Distribution of Responses to Attitudinal Questions About Food Distribution by Women in Shiraz

Attitudinal statement	**Agree**	**Somewhat agree**	**Disagree**	**Total**
Male head of household should be served first	44.0	44.4	11.6	100.0
It is very important to give the best food to the male head of the household	44.8	11.3	43.8	100.0
Male head of the household should be given the best food because he is the breadwinner	63.9	27.6	8.5	100.0
Boys need more food than girls	64.1	29.2	6.7	100.0
Men and boys need more food because they use more energy	19.2	69.1	11.7	100.0

Source: Aghajanian, 1986 survey in Shiraz.

About 64 per cent of the women agreed without reservation; 28 per cent agreed to some extent.

When women were asked if they agreed that boys should get more food because they are more active, 64 per cent agreed absolutely, 28 per cent agreed to some extent. The same attitude is reflected in the responses of women to the following question: 'When you prepare a favorite, delicious food, whom do you serve the largest and the best part?' More than 51 per cent of the women said they serve the largest and best part to their husbands, and the rest said to their sons. Not a single mother mentioned a daughter or herself.

Differential in the Attitudes Toward Food Distribution

While gender stratification is a general characteristic of Iranian society and cuts across classes and social groups, its rigidity is different in different social groups. To examine the variation in this respect, a composite index was constructed from some of the items in the questionnaire and was regressed on social and economic characteristics of women (see Appendix 2). The higher the score on this index, the more egalitarian is the attitude of women toward the distribution of food to male and female members of the household.[12] Results of the regression analysis are shown in Table 3.9.

Table 3.9 Effects of Socioeconomic Variables on the Attitude Index About Food Distribution*

Socioeconomic variable	Number of women	Mean score
Women's working status		
Home-maker	461	6.3
Working	112	7.15
Eta coefficient	.27**	
Women's education		
None	103	5.3
Some elementary	199	6.43
Some high school	221	6.87
Some college	50	7.28
Eta coefficient	.44†	
Husband's education		
None	65	5.21
Some elementary	194	6.25
Some high school	214	6.8
Some college	100	7.2
Eta coefficient	.40†	
Number of living children		
1–3	310	7.3
4	104	6.5
5 and more	157	5.6
Eta coefficient	.38†	
Grand Mean		6.5

Source: Aghajanian, 1986 survey in Shiraz.
*Attitude index is constructed from a number of items reported in Appendix 1. A higher score on this index means a more egalitarian attitude by mothers.
** † Differences in the means are statistically significant at 0.05 and 0.01 respectively.

The first variable in the model is the employment status of mothers. This turns out to be an important factor in explaining a woman's differential attitude toward sons and daughters. If the mother is working outside the home she has some extra income with which she can make more food available to the household members. This decreases the necessity to make choices about who is to get what food, and the mother can be expected to have a less discriminatory attitude toward her daughters regarding food distribution. The finding from our regression analysis supports this hypothesis: women who are working for wages have a higher average score on the composite index.

Mother's education is the second factor considered in explaining the discriminatory attitude. Women who have no education have the lowest score on the discriminatory index, that is, they have the highest level of bias against their daughters. As education increases, the disparity attitude decreases. Women with more than high-school education have the lowest score.

A strong relationship also exists between the husband's education and his wife's attitude toward boys and girls regarding food allocation. Women married to educated men have a much more egalitarian attitude than women married to men with little or no education. One potential reason for this is that the better educated men may be more willing to break with the gender tradition and encourage an egalitarian attitude. Another reason for this finding is that households with better educated men are economically better off, and therefore are less under pressure to establish a rigid stratification in food distribution.

The impact of the number of children on food distribution is also shown in Table 3.9. Women with five or more children have a less egalitarian view of food distribution among their children than women with fewer than five children. As the number of children declines, the mothers show a more egalitarian attitude. This suggests that the more children a mother has to feed the more likely it is that she will tend to allocate scarce food unequally, and therefore the more likely that she will discriminate against her daughters.[13]

Summary

This chapter provides an update on social and economic indicators of the status of women, utilizing the most recent census and my own research data. It focuses on some aspects of education, economic participation, and health of women and female children as indicators of the status of women relative to men. Objective indicators of the status of women are favored over ideological, institutional, and cultural aspects, which are discussed by other authors in this volume and elsewhere.

The available data from the last two censuses of Iran show a marked inequality in access to educational resources between female and male children. This inequality grows with their age. The widest gap is at the high-school level where the school enrollment rate for female children is half the rate for male children. The most recent data show a decline of inequality in access to education at the elementary and middle-school level, and an increase at the high-school level.

Access to paid employment has always been limited for Iranian women, although women always have contributed to the household economy, without any pay. Even during the 1970s, when governmental policies encouraged acceptance of non-familial roles for women, only a small percentage of women were active in the job market. By 1986, the economic situation of women declined not only due to discouraging policies regarding non-familial roles but also because of limited employment opportunities in general. In fact, high unemployment helped to justify pressures on women who were employed outside the home to resign in favor of male job-seekers.

Iran, a rich country with one of the highest oil revenues in the world, in the 1970s not only had a high infant mortality rate but also a higher mortality rate for female infants than for male infants. Such differential infant mortality rate is the reflection of discriminatory practices in nutrition and healthcare favoring male children. According to government reports, there has been a considerable decline in the overall rate of infant mortality by 1990, but no data are available on gender differentials in mortality.[14] The 1986 pilot study of mothers' attitudes toward food distribution reported here suggests that mothers in a large urban center have a discriminatory attitude toward their daughters in terms of food distribution. A multivariate analysis of the data suggests that the educational status of a mother and her husband, and a mother's outside employment correlate negatively with this discriminatory attitude, while the number of children correlates positively with it.

The analysis of data in this paper suggests that a system of gender stratification is deeply rooted in the Iranian culture. Under conditions of economic depression and limited resources, it can be expected that the ingrained gender inequality will become even more rigid and more easily expressed than in times of plenty, and that discriminatory practices against women will reassert themselves, especially in the lower socioeconomic classes and in rural areas.

Appendixes to Chapter 3

Appendix 1

Questionnaire: Food Distribution Attitudes of Mothers in Shiraz
Interviewer: Ask the following questions of the sample women with children:

1. What is your occupation?
2. What is your husband's occupation?
3. What is the highest grade you have finished in school?
4. How many children do you have?
5. How many sons?
6. How many daughters?
7. How many people live in this household?

Interviewer: Record the immediate reaction to the following questions:

8. Some women believe that the male head of the household should get special respect and more importance than other family members. Do you agree with this? (Certainly; To Some Extent; No.)

9. Some women believe that sons are more beneficial to the family when they grow up than daughters. Do you agree with this? (Certainly; To Some Extent; No.)

10. Some women believe that elders should be specially respected and given priority over younger members of the family. Do you agree with this? (Certainly; To Some Extent; No.)

11. Some women believe that boys need more food than girls. Do you agree with this? (Certainly; To Some Extent; No.)

12. Some women believe that children do not need much food. Do you agree with this? (Certainly; To Some Extent; No.)

13. Some women believe that since the male head of the household is the breadwinner, he has to have more and better food than others in the house. Do you agree with this? (Certainly; To Some Extent; No.)

14. Some women believe that the men and boys in the family use more energy and need more food than the women and girls. Do you agree with this? (Certainly; To Some Extent; No.)

15. Some women believe that to avoid problems with the male head of the house, it is better to give him the most and best food in the house. Do you agree with this? (Certainly; To Some Extent; No.)

16. Some women believe that a housewife should only pay attention to her husband's wishes in cooking and serving food. Do you agree with this? (Certainly; To Some Extent; No.)

17. Do you think malnutrition is worse for men or women? (For Men; For Women; There is no difference.)

18. When you cook the best and most favorite food, who gets the largest share?

Appendix 2

The composite index of the 'superiority attitude' in the distribution of food was constructed from the following questions:

1. Some women believe that boys need more food than girls. Do you agree with this? (Certainly; To Some Extent; No.)

2. Some women believe that since the male head of the household is the breadwinner, he has to have more and better food than others in the house. Do you agree with this? (Certainly; To Some Extent; No.)

3. Some women believe that the men and boys in the family use more energy and need more food than the women and girls. Do you agree with this? (Certainly; To Some Extent; No.)

4. Some women believe that to avoid problems with the male head of the house, it is better to give him the most and best food in the house. Do you agree with this? (Certainly; To Some Extent; No.)

5. Some women believe that a housewife should only pay attention to her husband's wishes in cooking and serving food. Do you agree with this? (Certainly; To Some Extent; No.)

Each woman was scored 1 for each answer of 'certainly;' 2 for each answer of 'to some extent;' and 3 for each 'no.' Then the scores on the five items were added to calculate a total score. This total score was used in the regression analysis. The higher the score, the more egalitarian was the woman's attitude in the distribution of food to male and female members of the household.

4· The Majles and Women's Issues in the Islamic Republic of Iran

Haleh Esfandiari

Since the establishment of the Islamic Republic in Iran in February 1979, the government has enacted, by decree or through law, a large body of new regulations and legislation governing and often altering the legal rights, conditions of employment, and social standing of women. This legislation was not enacted in a social vacuum. In the Assembly of Experts, which drafted the new constitution, and in the Majles, or parliament, matters touching on the rights and status of women were widely debated.

These debates tell us a great deal about the attitudes toward women among the clerical hierarchy, government officials, and elected representatives to legislative bodies who since the revolution have dominated Iran. The debates also provide insight into the dilemma facing the few women elected to the Assembly of Experts and to parliament. Inevitably, these women regarded themselves, and were seen, as representatives of and spokespersons for women and their interests. But these women did not have an easy role.

Many of these women were relatives (wives, daughters) of prominent clerics or revolutionary figures and they identified with the new regime. They had to adopt a posture that at once met new standards of propriety for women in a regime determined to 'Islamize' society and that also responded to the concrete needs of women—illiterate and educated ones, members of the working class and middle class, housewives and professionals—in a wide variety of areas. On both minor and major policy issues, they found they needed to articulate a position that would satisfy the requirements of what was deemed 'correct' from an Islamic viewpoint yet also protect the rights and meet the demands of their female constituents.

The revolutionary government in Iran, moreover, devised its policy toward women against the background of more than two decades of considerable gains for women in the area of marriage, divorce, and child custody laws and employment regulations. Women had entered the workforce in large numbers and in a large variety of roles. The number of women in schools and universities had vastly increased. Women's participation in social, economic, and political life had expanded considerably. The realities underlying these changes had become an integral part of Iranian attitudes and thinking—and not only among the educated or upper classes. Women, moreover, were aware of the gains they had made, quickly understood the threat certain forms of 'Islamization' posed to these gains, and were determined not to permit a turning back of the clock.

Dealing with issues pertaining to women thus confronted the revolutionary government with a dilemma. For example, in 1962 Ayatollah Khomeini spoke out against granting women the right to vote. He described the extension of suffrage to women as an instrument for the moral corruption of women and of society in general. But in 1978, when the revolutionary movement against the rule of the Shah was gaining momentum, Khomeini encouraged women to come out into the streets and join the anti-Shah protests. He praised them for doing so and later lauded their role in the overthrow of the monarchy.

In April 1979, in the referendum to determine the form of Iran's post-revolution government, Khomeini urged women to cast their ballots in favor of an Islamic Republic. Women in tens of thousands followed his advice. Having actively sought the support of Iran's women, he could not in 1979 deny them the ballot or the right to be elected to representative bodies, which in 1962 he had condemned as corrupting. Male delegates to the Assembly of Experts and to various parliaments were not always eager to address issues pertaining to women's rights. But, given the extensive changes that had taken place in the status of women in the period preceding the revolution, they discovered that the 'women's question' simply could not be ignored. It remained part of the agenda and indeed has preoccupied Iran's leaders since the 1979 revolution.

This article focuses on the manner in which the 'women's question' was perceived and articulated in the debates in the Assembly of Experts during the writing of the new Constitution and in debates in the first and second parliaments (1980–84, 1984–8) on legislation relating to women.

Since the establishment of the Islamic Republic, regulations and legislation, including issues affecting women, have been enacted by a number of different bodies. From February 1979 until the first Majles convened in June 1980, all laws emanated from the Revolutionary Council, which ruled by decree. The Assembly of Experts sat between August and November 1979 and drafted the new Constitution, which was approved in a national referendum in December. Once the Majles convened, it took over from the Revolutionary Council the task of enacting legislation. At all times, Ayatollah Khomeini, as Iran's supreme leader, was deemed to have the authority to issue religious opinions and decrees which, for all practical purposes, had the effect of law. The reimposition of Islamic dress on women, for example, came as a result of a ruling by Khomeini.

The tide appeared to turn against women within days of the establishment of the new regime. There were no women in the Revolutionary Council or in the government of Mehdi Bazargan, whom Khomeini appointed the first prime minister of the Islamic Republic. Women in the civil service who continued to work in senior decision-making positions across the watershed of the revolution were soon purged or given early retirement. In March 1979, Khomeini reimposed Islamic dress (*hejab*) on women working in government offices. Later this requirement was extended to all women. The Family Protection Law of 1967, which granted women the right to divorce, made polygyny very difficult, gave preference to mothers in child custody cases, and raised the age of marriage for both girls and boys, was suspended on the strength of a decree issued by Ayatollah Khomeini's office.

The Assembly of Experts

The suspension of the Family Protection Law, the reintroduction of Islamic dress for women, the active tolerance of the practice of temporary marriage, the attempt to separate men and women in university classrooms, the exclusion of women from certain fields of study in higher education caused great anxiety, especially among educated and politically aware women. The elections for the Assembly of Experts took place in the summer of 1979 in an atmosphere of uncertainty. A small number of women, along with a large number of men, stood as candidates. Only one woman, Monireh Gorji, was elected to the 73-member body. Ms Gorji was a school teacher and a member of the Islamic Republic Party, the political organization of the clerics associated with Khomeini.

Ms Gorji was the sole voice representing Iranian women in the assembly, but her stand on women's issues often seemed equivocal. She seemed aware of the gains Iranian women had made in the fields of politics, education, and family law under the old regime. She also seemed to feel that she had to speak for women's interests. But she often interpreted these interests in ways not in keeping with the aspiration of a great number of Iranian women to preserve and advance the gains made under the monarchy. She sat in the assembly wrapped in her black *chador*, thus indicating her acceptance of the new Islamic dress code imposed on women. Criticized by women for her appearance and reluctance to speak out on issues, and accused of bringing shame on Iranian women, she responded by lashing out against her accusers: 'I have not brought disrepute on you', she told Iranian women. 'I did not ruin the honor of women. On the contrary, with my *chador*, I have defended the lost honor and reputation of the sisters. That honor was lost fifty years ago [when the veil was abolished in 1936 under Reza Shah].'[1] As to her silence, she remarked: 'I am not a person to jump into the middle of the discussions. I don't see any reason for it.'[2]

Repeatedly, she took the position that mere reversion to 'true' Islam would solve all women's problems. Early in the new session, she emphasized that her guidelines would be Islam and the *shari'a*, or Islamic law, from which she would not deviate. 'I am not the slave of people', she said at another point. 'I am the slave of God. And after being the slave of God, for a short period of time, I put on the garment of service to the people. If what God has said is implemented, there will not be any shortcomings and any deficiencies for any group of people, including women, especially Muslim women.'[3] If she often apologized for her boldness in addressing such a 'learned assembly,' she seemed well versed in Islamic learning herself and had little trouble citing the Traditions, or sayings, of the Prophet, the Quran, or the rulings of the *shari'a* to support her points. She insisted that the solution to all women's problems lay in the Quran. Women, therefore, should sit and discuss the Quran. As a guideline to women, she even quoted a verse of the Quran, in which God addresses the Prophet: 'Tell your wives: if [you] want luxury and a worldly life, come and get your divorce. You are welcome to go. But if you don't want to go, undergo Islamic education and training.'[4]

Ms Gorji asserted she was opposed to polygyny, but blamed women for agreeing to marry men who already had wives and children. She thought the praiseworthy intent of rulings on marriage of the early Islamic period should not be misconstrued. For example, in permitting a man to take a second wife, Islamic law was designed to protect orphans and families lacking a breadwinner and generally to serve principles of justice, she said.

Often, she seemed inclined to go along with the views of the rest of the assembly, irrespective of the manner in which these impinged on women's interests. For example, Ayatollah Sadduqi argued before the assembly that a woman cannot be deemed qualified to become president or prime minister, simply because she can change diapers, wash a baby, or breastfeed: 'Suppose you choose a qualified woman to become president or prime minister,' he said. 'One morning, we see that the prime minister's office is closed. We ask why? We are told, because the lady [prime minister], gave birth the night before. This will only bring shame on us.'[5] Ms Gorji never took issue with Ayatollah Sadduqi.

Again, she went along with the assembly when it voted articles barring women from judgeships or the presidency, the highest position in the executive branch. She was aware that Ayatollah Khomeini interpreted Islamic jurisprudence to mean women could not serve as leaders of the community or sit as judges, and clearly she was not about to challenge his opinion. At times, she seemed ready to concede to the male members of the assembly that women lagged behind men in experience and mental development. Ms Gorgi rarely spoke on issues other than those pertaining to women; by contrast, the male members of the assembly took an active part in all discussions, including those pertaining to family matters and the rights of children and women.

However, Ms Gorji seemed also aware of the travails of what she described as her 'suffering sisters.' Sometimes she did stand up for women's rights, even if in an oblique way. If she repeatedly referred to Islamic law, she appeared at times to interpret it in a manner protective of women's interests. If she too readily conceded that women lagged behind men in development and capability, she blamed this on lack of education and experience rather than on innate deficiencies.

For example, in her first address to the Assembly of Experts, Ms Gorji said she was there because her 'suffering sisters' expected certain things from the body charged with drawing up the Islamic

Republic's Constitution. In an Islamic society, she said, women are human beings too. It was wrong to separate men and women when discussing the rights of the people. And since, 'unfortunately, women's rights were not observed and were even ignored, therefore one finds it sometimes necessary to defend them.'[6] She repeatedly called for the inclusion of an article in the Constitution establishing a special court to hear women's grievances and legal cases relating to the family.

On one occasion, she described a trip she had made to Yazd, a city in southeastern Iran, a year before the revolution. She was very much impressed with the men of Yazd, she said, but described its women as still in a primitive stage of development. And (with due apologies to 'educated women') she described the mental development of women as generally inferior to that of men. But she blamed this on social conditions and lack of education and other opportunities: 'I do not accept that women are lacking in intelligence, lacking in faith, and lacking in reason',[7] she said. She called for special schools and special education to advance the mental and cultural development of women and to allow them to function shoulder-to-shoulder with men.

Even the timid Ms Gorji faced an uphill battle in an assembly dominated by males and by traditional attitudes as to what constituted 'male' and 'female' work. Ayatollah Sadduqi, for example, responded to this interjection by Ms Gorji by caustically remarking that if women wanted equality, they should work shoulder-to-shoulder with men in digging irrigation channels and at construction jobs; it was not enough to sit behind a desk and do secretarial work.

If Ms Gorji imagined her presence in the constituent assembly, or the pleas of women for rights and guarantees, would influence the decisions of the representatives, another cleric, Ayatollah Safi, was quick to disabuse her. On matters relating to marriage, divorce, and polygyny, he said, the jurists and the men in the assembly would base their decisions on the rulings of the Quran. They would do so even if these rulings upset women or were disliked by some men. And since the Constitution would reflect God's commandments, the members would decide these issues in the same way, whether or not there was a single woman in the assembly, and explain their decisions to the people.

The assembly agreed early on that women's rights should be recognized in the Constitution. When the Constitution was completed, however, it turned out that only four of its 175 articles dealt with women's rights and family matters. The adoption of these articles followed the established procedure: drafts of each article were circulated among the deputies; a period was set aside for debate, in which members spoke for or against the draft or proposed amendments; and the proposed article was then put to a vote.

There was strong sentiment in the assembly in favor of emphasizing the importance of the family as one of the fundamental pillars of society; and Article 11 of the Constitution incorporated this idea. Ms Gorji went along with this sentiment, but tried to use the occasion for another oblique plea for a recognition of the special claims of childbearing women. She agreed that the family is a pillar of society. But, she said: 'the role of the family is fundamental and the role of the woman in the foundation of the family is vital. Therefore, the rights of women, especially the rights of mothers during the period when, to form another human being [i.e. during pregnancy], they are truly forced to endure difficulties . . . should be recognized.'[8]

However, the debate on this article indicated that for many members of the assembly the emphasis on the sanctity of the family was motivated by a number of other considerations: keeping women in the home, restricting the participation of women in the workforce and, more generally, maintaining the separation of the sexes in society. For example, Abdol-Karim Musavi-Ardebili, a leading cleric who was later to become Chief Justice, noting that the preservation of the family must be one of the more important principles of the constitution, asserted that luring women away from home to the workplace weakens the family and eventually destroys it. He of course did not object to women working, he said, but only as long as 'it did not do injury to the rights of her children, the duties of motherhood, and [the wife's duty] to care for her husband.'[9]

Ayatollah Mohammad Beheshti, the vice-president of the assembly, was at pains to stress that emphasis on the role of the woman at home, raising children and caring for the husband, did not imply that women's work was 'maid's work.' The value Islam attaches to the woman's (traditional) role, he said, is much greater. Islamic teaching, he pointed out, accords much importance to the relationship between children and their parents and emphasizes the mutual responsibilities of the parents toward one another. But Abol-Hasan Bani-Sadr, who was to become the first president of the Islamic Republic, objected to the vagueness of the discussion, which, he noted, dealt with the family and not specifically with women's rights. He noted that 'for a century, the rights of one half of the population have been ignored. Men beat their wives and call it the strengthening of the family.'[10] His, however, was a lone voice.

Controversy was also generated by Article 20 of the Constitution, which, in its final form, specified that men and women enjoy equal protection under the law, in keeping with Islamic principles. Musavi-Tabrizi considered the article both a concession to women and a response to what he described as the accusation that Islam accords dominance to men, is unjust toward women, and ignores women's rights. The article was drawn up in consultation with Ms Gorji, he said, and 'we caved in to our sister.'[11] He explained that the terminology, 'in keeping with Islamic principles,' was included in Article 20 because Islam bars women from serving as judges and from leadership positions. On the other hand, he noted, women could vote and be elected to the Majles, had the right to work in offices as long as they observed the Islamic dress code, and could hold property.

A major disagreement arose over the phrase, 'equal protection under the law' in the article. The conservative members of the assembly wanted assurances that the word 'equal' did not violate Islamic teaching. For example, Ayatollah Sadduqi suggested that the article should specify that 'women are equal under their own laws and men under their laws.'[12] For the conservatives, 'equal but separate' was the crucial issue. Several members were concerned that a provision regarding military training for women would lead to a mixing of the sexes. Deputies repeatedly asked who would train the women and whether men and women would be trained together. Safi, a cleric, was opposed to giving women military training at all, and reminded the assembly that if military training was suitable to women, the Prophet would have given his daughter military training. Another cleric, Musavi-Tabrizi, reminded the assembly that 15 years earlier Ayatollah Khomeini had spoken against women participating in the armed forces. But both the opponents and the proponents of military service for women, it turned out, could cite Islamic tradition in support of their position. Thus a number of clerics argued that there was nothing wrong in women participating in *jehad* and the defense of their country. 'Did not the Prophet allow [the woman] Nusaybeh Jarraheh to defend him with a sword in the battle of Uhud?' asked the cleric Khazali.[13]

The anxiety the drift of these discussions was causing some women in the country is reflected in a rumor that swept Tehran during the debate on Article 20, namely that the assembly was about to write into the Constitution an article incorporating traditional Islamic rulings on marriage and divorce. Women were about to demonstrate in the streets of the capital to show their anger. The assembly president, Ayatollah Hosayn-Ali Montazeri, had to deny that any such articles were contemplated. The reaction of Ms Gorji reflects, once again, the fine line she felt she had to walk between loyalty to the views of the ruling clerics and the sentiments of the female constituency she felt she must represent. Ms Gorji condemned the women who intended to take part in the demonstrations; they would bring shame only on themselves, she said. At the same time, she asserted that the worries and fears of women in general were justified. Her sisters, she remarked, 'fear that tomorrow their children will be taken away, fear that tomorrow they will have no control over their own lives, fear that . . . in an instant, a man who does not deserve to be called a man, can by an unjust decision [i.e. securing divorce on demand, as a man could do under Islamic law] utterly destroy a life and the efforts of a lifetime.'[14] It was for these reasons, she said, that a special court to hear the grievances of women was needed.

Ms Gorji did not feel she could oppose such a well-established principle under Islamic law as a man's right to secure a divorce on demand. But again, she sought relief for women in a special reading of Islamic law. According to the Quran, she said, divorce should observe the principle of human dignity. If a man divorces his wife after 50 years of marriage, she asked, what becomes of the principle of human dignity?

Article 21 of the Constitution charged the government with responsibility for protecting women's rights 'in conformity with Islamic law,' and for providing the means for women to develop their full personalities. The article also required the government to provide women with support during pregnancy and child-rearing, and with insurance coverage in case of widowhood. It required that the guardianship of children, under certain circumstances, be awarded to the mother. Here, and in other articles dealing with women and the family, the Constitution established general principles. It was left to the Majles and the government to draft, enact, and implement the laws and regulations implied by these general principles.

The Majles and its Enactments

The Constitution articulated a concept of women's rights within an Islamic context, and in adherence to the *shari'a*. Women who had hoped for stronger guarantees under the Constitution had to direct their attention and energies towards parliament and the government. These women also felt it necessary to have women deputies in parliament to speak for their anxieties, voice their demands, and ensure that existing laws pertaining to women's rights were not tampered with.

The Constitution was ratified in the fall of 1980 and elections for the first Majles were held in the same year. The elections took place in two stages. A number of women belonging to various political parties ran for parliament. Four women were elected to the 270-member house. Only some of the laws pertaining to women's rights and the debates surrounding them in the first Majles (1980–84) and the second Majles (1984–8) will be discussed in this article. Rather than a comprehensive survey, my intention is to provide a sense of the nature and flavor of the debates, an insight into the range of views common among Iran's new legislators, and an understanding of the environment in which women's issues were considered and decided in the Islamic Republic. The four women elected to the first Majles were A'zam Taleqani, Gowhar Shari'eh Dastghayb, Mariam Behruzi and Atefeh Raja'i. In the second Majles, Marzieh Dabbagh replaced A'zam Taleqani. The other three women were re-elected.

Ms Taleqani and Ms Dastghayb were high-school teachers. Both were university graduates and both were related to well-known clerics. Ms Raja'i was an elementary-school teacher. Her husband, Mohammad-Ali Raja'i, was the second prime minister and later president of the Islamic Republic. He was killed in a bomb explosion in August 1981. Ms Behruzi was a religious preacher, with high-school education. Ms Dabbagh had a traditional religious education. She had been politically active before the revolution and had spent time in prison under the old regime. Thus the four women who were elected to the first Majles had close affiliations with the new ruling group.

Once parliament met, it became clear that Ms Taleqani was among the more outspoken and active members of parliament. She not only pushed for women's rights but she took part in most of the discussions. One of the first bills considered by the Majles pertaining to women's rights was a bill permitting women in the civil service and in government companies and organizations to work only half-time, with the permission of the senior official at their place of work. This was a bill that had been drawn up under the previous regime and was intended to facilitate female employment.

The debate on the bill showed that while no one dared object to women working outside the home, most deputies would have preferred to see women stay at home. The government presented the bill to the Majles and was supported by the four women deputies and the more liberal-minded male deputies. Along with the government, the bill's supporters argued that by permitting women to work half-time, the proposal was in keeping with the spirit of the Constitution, which emphasized the responsibility of women to look after their families. The bill, they said, recognized the importance of the family and the role of women in the family, but also took cognizance of the great number of women already in the workforce. The government believed that such a piece of legislation would provide women with work and leave them enough time to look after their families.

The more conservative deputies, however, argued hard against the presence of women in the workforce. They supported their position by drawing on Islamic and practical arguments. For example, Deputy Dehqan asserted he was not against women or opposed to their working, but argued that women would perform a better job by staying home and being mothers. This bill, he said, would tempt women to prefer work to their duties as mothers. He also saw a practical reason for women to stay at home: there were many unemployed, educated men, to whom priority in jobs should be given. Ms Behruzi did not agree with him; the country, she said, should make full use of its women, whom she described as a great force in society. Since an Islamic society needs women in occupations such as medicine, education, and law, and since the Constitution calls on the government to facilitate and provide for the development of women, this bill would permit women to work and look after their families at the same time. Mr Foroughi believed that if women wanted fully to accept their responsibilities as described in the Quran, they should not work outside the house. Deputy Akhtari summed up his opposition to the bill by reciting a couplet:

> Don't burden a woman with a man's work
> Intellect [the hat] never resided in a skirt.[15]

Akhtari declared that even if 500,000 women desired the passage of this bill, he would argue with them that the bill was not Islamic. There is no talk in Islam of women working, he said. He also had practical objections to the bill. Women were already benefiting from the right to maternity leave and leave to breastfeed infant children. Now it was proposed to permit women to work half-time: 'If women start working, we will no longer have mothers who will raise a man like the great leader of the revolution [Khomeini], or Beheshti and Motahhari [two other prominent clerical leaders], and other great men in the world.'[16] He went on to argue that if women have the capacity to work they should work full-time. Otherwise, they should not work at all. Deputy Kiavosh agreed with those who believed a woman's duty was to marry and give birth to martyrs. But he explained that women should be helped to fulfill this function as well as to work. He favored the half-time bill.

Two sessions of parliament were devoted to the first reading of this bill. The arguments on both sides were of three kinds: Islamic, practical, and constitutional. The more conservative deputies believed Islam prefers women to stay at home and see to the well-being of the family. They argued that the drafters of the Constitution had emphasized the sanctity and importance of the family. It was the mother who could hold the family together. The practical argument was advanced by deputies who asserted that in a period of high unemployment, priority should be given to men as the principal breadwinners in the family. They also argued that the effect of the bill would be to force the government to hire more women to fill the slots left empty by those women who worked half-time, thus imposing a further strain on the budget. Defenders of the bill referred to the Constitution. The bill, they said, was in accordance with Article 21 of the Constitution which not only did not bar women from work but charged the government with facilitating women's opportunity for growth and development.

The government's representative also argued for the bill on practical grounds. He explained that three groups of women would benefit from the bill: those who wanted to serve their country and also needed the income, needy women, and educated women from whose skills society would benefit. Ms Raja'i argued that approval of the law would prove to the outside world that women's rights are important to parliament. 'Not only are women not dismissed from their jobs,' she said, 'with this bill they are gaining more rights without any harm to women's employment and they are given the possibility to serve their families.'[17] The bill was finally enacted, but not until November 1983, a year after it was introduced.

The next confrontation came when the Ministry of Education presented a bill to parliament proposing up to 12 months of maternity leave for women teachers. Until then, under laws passed under the previous regime, women teachers could take three months' maternity leave. This bill would have granted them an additional six months' leave, for a total of nine months or the full academic year. (Teachers, of course, did not teach during the summer vacations.) The mood in the Majles was against this legislation. Even the women deputies expressed mixed feelings about it. They demanded that such a bill should cover all women. Ms Behruzi went so far as to describe the bill as 'cruel' to other women such as doctors, nurses, and other professionals. She suggested the bill be tabled for the time being.

Opponents of the bill did some calculations for the Majles. If a woman teacher became pregnant every second year over a period of ten years and took a one-year leave of absence each time she was pregnant, one deputy argued, she might as well give up her teaching. Other opponents of the measure noted that if 10 per cent of the 180,000 women teachers became pregnant every year, 18,000 teachers would be on leave yearly; that would create havoc in the school system.

But Deputy Harati, a defender of the bill, disagreed. The work of a teacher, he said, was different from that of someone who does office work. What does it matter, he asked, if, over a 30-year career, a woman took five years of maternity leave? He added: 'One day you say a woman's duty is to be a good mother and if she wants to work she should be in the field of education. The next day you deny her the necessary facilities.'[18] He suggested that women be granted the additional six months' leave and give up part of their salary. Deputy Raja'ian had a better solution—building day-care centers to enable working women to put children under seven years of age into day-care. His main objection to the bill was that the government would have to replace women teachers on such long leaves of absence with male teachers. He found this unacceptable, since men would be teaching young girls.

Another deputy, Dehqani, agreed with the women deputies and other women who did not approve of the bill because it made an unfair distinction between women teachers and women working in other fields. Deputy Rahmani, however, urged his colleagues to pass the bill. It did not discriminate in favor of women teachers, he said. Rather, women teachers should be allowed to take a year off in maternity leave and this provision should gradually be extended to cover other women as well. Deputy Fada'i disagreed with this suggestion: 'This is discrimination. When we have marches all women participate. Why should not [the others] enjoy such benefits? Anyway, the women deputies are against this bill. Why should we have to defend it?'[19]

Despite the Minister of Education's assertion that the proposed legislation was crucial for attracting women to the teaching profession and would not be a burden on the budget, the bill was rejected by a majority of the deputies.

In the second Majles, some of the bills on women's issues pending from the first Majles were taken up. Two of these bills will be examined here: a bill pertaining to the right of the mother to be recognized as guardian to her minor children and a bill concerning sending students abroad for further education.

The bill on the guardianship of minor children had been approved in 1982, on the recommendation of the Majles judicial committee, for implementation on a three-year trial basis. It came up for consideration by the full house, and for permanent enactment, in 1985. According to this bill guardianship of a minor would be given to the mother in the case of the 'martyrdom' of the father, unless the court ruled the mother unqualified for such a responsibility. By then, special civil courts (successors to the Family Protection Courts of the former regime) had been established to rule on family disputes, including matters of divorce, child custody, temporary marriage, and polygyny.

Ms Dastghayb was very critical of these special courts. She explained that she kept receiving letters from women complaining that these courts never ruled in favor of women and did not give women a proper hearing: 'they don't let [women] speak; they just implement the law; they separate the child from the mother . . . and move the child like a stone or a piece of chalk from one place to another.'[20]

Deputy Panahandeh disagreed with granting the guardianship of a minor to the mother. He feared the effects of a 'corrupt' mother on the child. 'If the mother becomes corrupt,' he said, 'the children will become corrupt too.'[21] Therefore, he said, the courts should determine the suitable guardian on a case-by-case basis. Some deputies argued that Islamic law gave the mother custody over a daughter up to the age of seven and over a son up to the age of two. This law, they said, should not be tampered with.

In the second reading of this bill, some deputies argued that during the three years the bill had been implemented on a trial basis, no one had raised any objections to it on the basis of Islamic law; there were thus no grounds for reopening the debate on the bill. Anyway, said Deputy Khalkhali, 'mothers have a softer and kinder heart. Mothers don't remarry. If they do, they look after their children. It is men who, when they remarry, ignore their [former] children and wives.'[22] Another deputy explained that the logic behind this bill was to leave the custody of children whose father had become martyred with the mother and to let her keep the children even if she remarried. Khomeini, he said, had given such a right to the mother. Parliament would not want to act against the rulings of Khomeini, another deputy added.

Other deputies reminded the Majles that Ayatollah Khomeini had encouraged the widows of martyrs to remarry. A deputy who wondered what would happen if the man who married a widow did not want her child was told that the court would decide what to do with the children in such cases.

Some conservative deputies found it difficult to concede that the mother should have sole responsibility for the financial affairs of a minor. According to Islamic law, the financial affairs of a minor must remain in the hands of the Islamic jurist (*vali-ye shar'i*) who is authorized to look after the affairs of minors who lack guardians, and many deputies wished to uphold this practice. But one deputy found this impractical. 'What do you expect?' he asked. 'Should the *vali-ye shar'i* visit [the mother] every day and tell her to buy this kind, rather than that kind, of powdered milk? If this is what you want, just take away the guardianship from the mother altogether.'[23] The argument went back and forth between the more conservative and less conservative members of the Majles. When the bill was finally passed, the mother retained custody of minor children in case of the father's death, even if she remarried, but the *vali-ye shar'i* was put in charge of the financial affairs of the minor. If the minor lacked financial means, the government was to provide the mother with funds for the child's upkeep. Ms Behruzi described the law as one of the major accomplishments of the Islamic government.

Another bill that caused considerable debate provided government funds to send students abroad for study. The bill contained a controversial clause which specified that only married female students could be sent for study abroad and only when accompanied by their husbands. Deputy Zamani, objecting to this clause, accused the Majles of creating obstacles to further education for 50 per cent of the population. Learning does not distinguish between men and women, he said, and people in pursuit of learning do not become corrupt. The Majles, he argued, was forcing women to accept any kind of marriage, voluntarily or involuntarily, in order to study abroad. Deputy Khalkhali was not persuaded: 'Women are not forced to go abroad to study,' he asserted. 'If they want to go, they have to accept the law regarding marriage.'[24]

Ms Behruzi explained that men and women are equal in Islam, and that God had removed all the differences between men and women so that men cannot infringe on women's rights. Approval of the clause, she argued, would discriminate between men and women of the same age and holding the same degrees. Both deserve to go abroad for further study, but the boys are told they can go while girls must enter into forced marriages in order to do so. Deputy Abd-e Khoda'i argued that the issue was not discrimination but the difference between men and women. He believed there was no need for a woman to study, say, agriculture and to sit on a tractor. He pointed out that all the deputies knew how corrupt society was abroad. 'In their universities,' he said, 'girls sunbathe. Their dormitories are without supervisors. They are free to move from city to city.'[25] He was concerned that the more religious the Iranian girls were, the more they would be at risk abroad. Deputy Movahedi-Savuji suggested that foreign female students sunbathed in order to attract the attention of the young Iranian men who went abroad for study. Thus male Iranian students should also be required to get married before they were sent abroad. Ms Dastghayb picked up on this point and suggested that in selecting students for foreign study priority should be given to married students, male and female.

The opponents of the restriction on women going abroad to study argued intensively, but faced a wall of opposition. The bill was passed with the controversial clause intact: women could go abroad for study only if married and accompanied by their husbands.

A Balance Sheet

In addition to remarks made on items of legislation placed on the Majles agenda, women deputies occasionally referred to issues relating to women's rights in pre-agenda speeches, most often on the occasion of the birthday of the Prophet's daughter, Fatemeh, and his granddaughter, Zaynab. They generally spoke of the rights and privileges women have under Islam and the gains women made under the Islamic Republic. They then turned to the problems and grievances of women. They complained about the failure to implement the clauses of the Constitution. For example, very early in the first Majles, Ms Taleqani and Ms Dastghayb had drafted a bill regarding family matters. The bill was held up for several months in the relevant committee. The two women complained about this delay, but their complaint fell on deaf ears.

Women deputies also complained bitterly about the operations of the special civil courts that ruled on family matters. They worried about the frequency with which divorce was granted to men. They asserted that the Islamic judges responded to complaints regarding the ease with which men could obtain divorces by remarking that God's command is such that any time a man wants to divorce his wife, she has to accept his wish and leave. The *hejab* was another recurring topic in parliamentary discussions. Not only women deputies but almost everyone in parliament professed to believe that the majority of Iranian women approved of the *hejab*. Those who did not approve, it was argued, must be educated by the mass media about the significance of the *hejab*. Deputies chastized the government for not enlightening women on this subject or implementing the requirement on Islamic dress more forcefully.

When a rumor spread in Tehran that the Majles was about to pass a bill regarding the *hejab*, the deputies felt obliged to deny it. In a passionate speech, Ms Behruzi compared the women who did not observe the *hejab* to people who trampled on the Quran. For her such women, with their made-up faces, belonged to the swamps of Europe. As far as she was concerned, the *hejab* was God's command and a symbol of the chastity of Iranian women. (Two years later, Ms Behruzi criticized the Turkish government for preventing Turkish women from using Islamic dress, saluted those Turkish men and women who stood up to the Turkish government, and asserted that their resistance was due to the 'light' that shone from Islamic Iran on other nations.) Another woman deputy, Ms Dabbagh, echoed these sentiments and warned the Turkish leaders opposed to Islamic dress not to fight God, the Prophet, and the Quran. She reminded them that the *hejab* is God's command and an unconquerable fortress in which the personality of women is preserved. In Iran, violation of the *hejab*, under the law for Islamic punishments, carried a sentence of 74 lashes.

Aside from Ms Taleqani, who took part in discussions on a wide range of subjects in the Majles, the other women deputies confined their remarks to bills relating to women's issues. The discussions in the Assembly of Experts had established a pattern which was repeated in the Majles. In general, women deputies were consulted before a bill pertaining to women's rights was presented to the plenary session. Laws dealing with women's rights had to be in harmony with Islamic law and the Constitution. But the interpretation of the Constitution insofar as it applied to women varied. The more conservative deputies pressed for total and strict adherence to Islamic law. They cited the Quran, referred to the Traditions of the Prophet, quoted the *shari'a*, and argued that practices not prevalent in the time of the Prophet were not needed now either. Under pressure, they paid lip-service to the idea of equality of men and women under Islam, but urged total separation of men and women.

The less conservative deputies interpreted the same laws and the Constitution differently. They argued that Islam is tolerant and just and that therefore equality between men and women should be promoted. They saw their duty as facilitating the implementation of the true spirit of the Constitution. Like the women deputies, they too were aware of the pressures being exerted by women for more favorable legislation. They knew that it was not possible to ignore the aspirations and desires of one half of the population. Time and again, women deputies referred to hundreds and hundreds of letters they received from women complaining about the mistreatment and discrimination they suffered at the hands of men.

The government appears to have sought to accommodate some of the wishes of women. Thus, while implementing the harsh Islamic penal code, such as lashes and stoning for various violations, the government, as noted, also introduced bills to extend maternity leave and provide for half-time work for women. The government further tried to find ways of preserving parts of the Family Protection Law approved under the former regime by issuing circulars to the civil courts and government departments, thus circumventing the Majles.

The question of how to deal with the active participation of women in the newly established Islamic Republic was from the beginning a dilemma for the leadership in Iran. Ayatollah Khomeini had only objected to women becoming president or judges. The Constitution, in compliance with Islamic law, barred women from the presidency and presiding over the courts, but did not prohibit women from joining the government at any other level or from voting. It was left to the government and to parliament to deal with specific issues such as polygyny, divorce, child custody, half-time work without loss of benefits or pensions, maternity leave, equal right to study abroad on government scholarships, financial support for war widows, elderly women, and children, and similar issues of importance to women.

Women deputies pressed for the relevant legislation. They acted within the guidelines set by the Constitution but tried to give the Constitution and the *shari'a* a broader interpretation.

For example, they did not condone the bodily punishment of 74 lashes for violators of the *hejab* but instead suggested that women should be educated regarding the importance and advantages of the Islamic dress code. The women deputies believed that the resistance of some women to Islamic laws governing the country stemmed from their ignorance of the special position of women in Islam rather than from their opposition to these laws.

The gains that Iranian women had made in the domain of women's rights in the decades before the revolution were so important and tangible that there was no way in which the revolutionary government could prevent women from playing an active role in the affairs of the country in the post-revolution era.

The new ruling class, namely the religious leadership, the drafters of the Constitution, and members of the government and parliament, tried to accommodate the aspirations and desires of Iran's women to a certain degree. For the leadership of the revolutionary government, it was also important to project a positive image of the Islamic Republic as a country in which Islam and women's rights were compatible, women were an integral part of society, and Islamic law did not exclude women from public life. Thus the four women deputies, their male supporters in the parliament, and government officials grappled with the demands and pressures that women were able to bring to bear on the regime and their insistence that the state not renege on previous gains women had made.

The women deputies formulated and developed their position on issues relating to women's rights in reaction to events. They were not always successful in their endeavors and often lacked support in the parliament and in the government. Nor were they always representing the demands of the educated and more progressive women in society. Unlike Ms Gorji, who had told the constitutional assembly that she was not in the assembly as a representative of women, the women deputies in the Majles did view themselves as spokespersons for the majority of Iranian women and defenders of women's rights within the framework of the Islamic law. They identified with the Islamic regime, but found they were required by their position to intervene on behalf of women who no longer had recourse to the old laws, many of which had been abolished, and who understandably remained in the dark about how a new body of legislation would affect their status and their rights.

5· Commoditization of Sexuality and Female Labor Participation in Islam: implications for Iran, 1960–90

Fatemeh E. Moghadam

This chapter is in two parts. The first part is theoretical. It aims to place the legal treatment of female sexuality in Islam in the context of economic theory, and to find the relationship between the treatment of sexuality and women's participation in the job market. Specifically, I will argue that female sexuality is treated as a regulated commodity in Islam. As such an integral part of a woman is subject to sale, a woman is not the full owner of her own self. I will also argue that, with few exceptions, within the original Quranic context women are not explicitly legally discriminated against in the job market. However, Quranic regulations concerning female sexuality lay the grounds for various forms of legal discrimination and occupational segregation of female labor. Thus the treatment of women as quasi-commodity, quasi-human sets limitations on the non-sexual aspects of their lives, including participation in the labor market.

The second part explores the applicability of this framework to the case of contemporary Iran. It compares and contrasts female labor participation there in two periods in recent history. I will argue that the secularization policies in the 1960s and 1970s were conducive to decommoditization, deregulation and the growth of participation of women in the labor market, while the re-emergence of Islamic ideology in the post-revolutionary period created opposite tendencies.

In this chapter, I will use some of the concepts developed in gender models by economists.[1] However, these models were developed in the industrial countries of the West, and do not address the issue of ownership of female sexuality. I will argue therefore that the legal commoditization of female sexuality should be incorporated into our analysis of gender economics in Muslim societies.

Studies of developing countries suggest that economic development and modernization do not always improve the status of women,[2] and contribute to the marginalization of poor women.[3] In many instances these women are forced into unpaid family work and low-wage jobs, and they are overburdened by the combination of reproductive labor, housework, and outside work. Where women continue to perform wage-labor, they are discriminated against in the job market. In nearly all such studies writers argue that sociocultural factors tend to reinforce the patriarchal structures. Therefore, an examination of these factors is likely to improve our understanding of gender relations in Third World countries. As the Islamic tradition has exerted a strong legal and sociocultural impact on Muslim societies, this chapter aims at incorporating this tradition into our analysis of gender economics in these societies.

Studies on women and development make frequent references to the role of women in the family, and the treatment of female sexuality within the legal and traditional frameworks. Two pioneering studies concentrate on the treatment of female sexuality in Islam. Mernissi has argued that in Islam the male–female relationship is assumed to be highly sexual, and that women are considered to have sexual power over men which needs to be controlled by veiling.[4] In a careful examination of the Islamic legal system, Haeri has argued that in Islam permanent marriage is a sale, and temporary marriage a lease of female sexuality.[5] These and other writers have studied the impact of these rules on the personal lives of Muslim women and on male–female relations. No attempt has been made to analyze the implications of the legal commoditization of sexuality on female labor. This chapter incorporates this factor into the analysis of gender and the labor process.

Studies on the female labor process in Iran are scant.[6] Most gender studies have used a broad perspective and addressed a host of issues besides employment and education.[7] This chapter, however, is narrowly focused on the implications of the Islamic tradition on female employment.

Commoditization and Regulation of Sexuality

Gender and the Labor Process

The economic literature on gender focuses on women's participation in the job market. Among the major nineteenth-century writers only

J.S. Mill and F. Engels addressed the issue. Both writers related the subjugation of women to their lack of access to job markets, and shared the belief in the emancipating effects of employment outside the home.[8]

More recent studies have focused on the consequences of the division of female labor into non-market time, production for household consumption, and market time.[9] It is generally argued that the traditional division of labor between the sexes has led to a specialization of household work by women. This division of labor has created conditions of economic dependency of married women on husbands, thus reducing the bargaining position of women in family decision-making, and increasing the losses for women in a marital break-up. As childbearing and -raising are time-consuming for women, studies find a negative relationship between fertility and labor market participation. As female participation in wage-labor is expected to be disrupted by childbearing and -raising, smaller investments are made by women in market-oriented human capital, that is, education and skills. Thus, women receive lower wages than men.[10] Differences in the relative investments in human capital also contribute to occupational segregation. Gender issues are also examined in models of discrimination. The sociopsychological origin of discrimination may be a taste or a personal prejudice. In the case of women, discrimination stems from the notion of socially appropriate roles. Discrimination has been considered as yet another factor leading to occupational segregation and to gender-related wage differentials between equally productive workers.[11] On the basis of these studies, I assume that the participation of women in wage-labor will ultimately have an emancipating impact and that the division of labor between household and market-related activities, fertility, human capital, discrimination, and occupational segregation are important variables in the emancipation process. The overburdening and marginalization of some wage-earning women in Third World countries[12] can be viewed as transitional. It can be argued that in the long run an increase in women's participation in the job market, as well as an increase in control over economic resources, is likely to improve the bargaining position of women in the family and in society.

Islam and Female Sexuality

In order to examine the impact of the Islamic legal system on commoditization and regulation of female sexuality, these concepts need to be clarified. An object that is voluntarily bought and sold at an agreed price is a commodity. Once the sale transaction is completed, the original owner loses ownership, and the buyer becomes owner of the commodity. The most popular definition of regulation consists of governmental actions to control price, sale, and production decisions of firms in a presumed effort to prevent private decision-making that would take inadequate account of the 'public interest.'[13] As the government is empowered to grant or condition the right of a company to provide service, regulatory agencies have been established for certification and licencing.

With few modifications, the concepts of commodity and regulation can be used for the discussion of female sexuality in Islam: sexuality is an integral part of a human being and not a lifeless object; the private decisions in question are not those of firms, but of individual women; regulation as defined above is a twentieth-century phenomenon, while most Islamic rules concerning sexuality have their roots in early and medieval Muslim societies; the clergy, ulema, the group in charge of making and interpreting religious rules, historically have been an integral part of the ruling elite in Muslim countries, but they have not always been synonymous with government. Thus, the regulators may not always be government agencies. Finally, 'public interest' in the case of female sexuality assumes a broad spectrum of social and religious mores. For our case, the relevant areas of regulation are: the sale or lease of female sexuality; marketing procedures; conditions of maintenance; procedures for the return of the commodity should it be deemed undesirable; and rules concerning control and maintenance of the product of sexuality, that is, children.

Islam originated in the mercantile and exchange economy of Mecca, and Muslim legal theory was strongly influenced by this mercantile tradition. The city of Mecca, however, had grown out of—and coexisted with—a nomadic tribal rural economy. Thus, legal theory was also influenced by tribal tradition.[14] Military conquests transformed the Muslim state into an empire, and legal theory thus was influenced by the non-Islamic traditions in the empire and the interests of central administration. Medieval Islamic society became subject to nomadic conquests and rules, and the interpretations of the jurists were influenced by these conquests. In summary, Muslim legal theory was a by-product of different socioeconomic systems, but the mercantile tradition left a strong impact on it.

Muslim social rules are affected by the mercantile influence. Rules concerning transactions and contracts, *aqd*, are an important part of the teachings of Islam and the tradition of Islamic jurisprudence, *fiqh*. The various passages in the Quran that deal with marriage in essence treat female sexuality as a tradeable object. In a Muslim marriage the buyer (the man) and the seller (the woman or her guardian) should agree voluntarily on the terms of the contract and on the price for female sexuality, *mehr*.[15] Although in some Muslim countries—notably Iran—the common practice has been for the man to pay the *mehr* at divorce, legally *mehr* is a price for female sexuality, and is due as soon as the marriage is consummated. Where *mehr* is not paid to the woman, it is considered to be something that is owed to her, and she has the legal right to claim it. At the death of the husband, *mehr* is treated as one of his liabilities. It has to be paid before the dead man's assets are divided among the heirs. In Shii Iran, half of the *mehr* is due if the marriage contract is signed, but the marriage is not consummated. In a marriage contract, the buyer is also responsible for the expenses related to the upkeep of the commodity in question, *nafaqeh*.[16] Once the transaction is completed, the owner has complete and monogamous right to the object. At least in a Shii marriage, the wife should always consent to her husband's demand for intercourse, *tamkin*. *Tamkin* is generally viewed to be the counterpart of *nafaqeh*. Because the man pays for the upkeep of the woman, he is entitled to her sexual services. In the Quran an analogy is drawn between wives and landholdings in terms of ownership rights: just as an owner has unlimited rights to his landholding, a man has unlimited rights over his wives.[17] Just as it is in the interest of the owner to look after his land, women should be treated well by their husbands. In the Quran, there are some injunctions that advise men to refrain from unjust and harsh treatment of their wives, to treat them with justice, *adl*.[18] Should the buyer find the commodity unsatisfactory, he can dispose of it—he can divorce the woman.[19] In this case, if the commodity has already been consumed and if no proof of a violation of the monogamous sale of the sexuality is available, the man has to pay the agreed price, *mehr*.[20] The products of a marriage (children) belong to the man. At a divorce, or at the death of the husband, the wife has no right to the children.

A man—but not a woman—may undertake sexual transactions with more than one partner simultaneously.[21] In the Quran, no explicit limitations are placed on the number of female sexualities a man may consume.[22] While the Sunni sects do not recognize the validity of temporary marriage but limit the number of women a man may marry simultaneously to a maximum of four permanent wives, in Shii Iran temporary marriage, *sigheh*, is legal. Thus, the two categories of permanent and temporary marriage can be viewed as sale and lease options for the consumption of female sexuality. There are no legal limitations on the number of *sigheh*s a man may marry. Thus, in contrast to the commoditized treatment of female sexuality, men are viewed as consumers. Parallels can be drawn to the perception of unlimited human wants and needs for material resources in economic theory. As consumers of female sexuality, men make decisions to get the best utility—satisfaction derived from consumption—from sexual transactions, subject to budget constraints. As is customary for other commodities, willingness and ability to pay are the basis for purchase decisions.

Note that in a Muslim marriage only sexuality is subject to sale. The woman is not subject to total sale. Her position is not reduced to that of a slave. At least in theory, she maintains many independent personal rights, though with an explicit assumption of inferiority to men.[23] For example, women have the right to own property, but are discriminated against in inheritance. Their share is about one-half of that of their male co-heirs. Women also maintain the right to enter contractual agreements on non-sexual matters. With the possible exception of the legal profession,[24] there are no explicit Quranic rules prohibiting women from participating in the labor market. Indeed, the Quran is explicit on the entitlement of women workers to fair wages. Nevertheless, in a Muslim marriage female sexuality including reproductive labor is sold. As sexuality is an integral part of women, married women lose full ownership and control of their own selves. Although not prohibited from selling her labor in the job market, the sale of her sexuality limits the freedom of a married woman to do so. For example, the Quran explicitly states that because men pay their wives' living expenses, they are superior to women, and as husbands are entitled to demand obedience from wives.[25] This can be interpreted to mean that a woman should seek the approval of her husband on non-sexual matters including employment, or that a woman's most important duty is inside the home. Thus a woman's choice of occupation is severely limited. Finally, because the husband has full rights over a wife's reproductive labor, the woman may have no control over the time spent on childbearing and -raising. Her ability to allocate time for market activities becomes subject to limitations that are controlled by the husband.[26] Ahmed has demonstrated that in the early Islamic society women enjoyed more rights than in the subsequent Abbasid (750–1258) period. At times they stipulated favorable conditions in their marriage contracts, and to a limited extent participated in sociopolitical and economic activities. This is attributed to the pre-Islamic tradition of *jahiliya* in Arabia in which women enjoyed more sexual autonomy than they did in Islam.[27] I suggest that another source of this relative autonomy was the mercantile spirit of the early Islamic society which promoted voluntary contracts. In essence, a marriage contract was viewed as voluntary, and women could negotiate favorable terms, including the condition of monogamy for the husband, and the right to divorce for the wife. During the Abbasid period, the political system was characterized by absolute rule and central administration, and women became subject to greater oppression. Although the jurists had to work within the mercantile and contractual context of Islamic law, interpretations were designed to accommodate the absolutist patriarchal state, and oppressive rules were included. In this period, three of the major orthodox Islamic schools, Shaf'i, Hanbali, and Maliki, considered a man's unilateral right to divorce and his right to marry four wives simultaneously to be essential marital rights that could not be altered contractually.[28] Muslim conquests, and the fact that the wives and children of those who fought the Muslim armies were treated as booty and sold as slaves, created a very flourishing female slave market. Many elite Muslim men preferred concubinage to marriage,[29] because a concubine was almost completely commoditized and had hardly any legal rights. The status of many women was thus reduced to that of slaves, and the limited rights of free women were considerably curtailed.[30] By contrast, in the twentieth century many women stipulate monogamy, the right to divorce, and other egalitarian conditions in their marriage contracts. As a gesture of protest to the notion of the sale of female sexuality, some emancipated women in Iran refuse to accept more than a nominal price, *mehr*, at marriage. Thus the commoditization of their sexuality is considerably modified.

In summary, the extent of the commoditization of female sexuality depends on the socioeconomic, historic, and political characteristics of a Muslim society, and on the socioeconomic conditions of the individual woman who enters a contractual agreement with a male partner. However, in essence, the contract is based on the sale of female sexuality for a set and agreed price, *mehr*.

The commoditization of female sexuality in Islam is subject to regulations. Licensing and contract are required for male–female sexual relations. The monogamous aspect of the sale of female sexuality for the duration of the contract is non-negotiable. Childbearing is subject to regulations. There is a compulsory waiting period for women between two successive marriages in order to identify the father of a potential child. After a divorce, a childbearing or a breastfeeding woman is entitled to payments for these labors by the child's father.[31] However, she is not required to breastfeed the child, and if she refuses, the father has to find a substitute. A divorced woman has neither a right nor a responsibility toward the children she has borne; they belong to the father. The woman, thus, does not have a right to her reproductive labor.

Another important regulation is the requirement of veiling for women.[32] The male–female relationship is assumed to be highly sexual, and male sexual desire is considered to be undeniable, eruptive, and potentially disruptive. The religion provides rules that are aimed at promoting social order by preventing men from being aroused. One such preventive rule is that women have to be covered. A woman can be seen unveiled only by other women, by the legitimate owner of her sexuality, or by those men with whom she can only have a sex-neutral relationship.

Veiling has implications on the marketing of female sexuality. It prohibits the direct and visual advertising of female sexuality. Thus, marketing and advertising require the involvement of intermediaries such as family or matchmakers. If a woman assumes autonomy in advertising her sexuality by a full or partial removal of her veil, she is considered to be shameless and morally decadent.

Except for the wives of the Prophet Mohammad,[33] there is no direct reference to segregation in the Quran. However, the requirement of veiling, and the sociohistorical and political conditions of the classical and medieval Islamic societies have given rise to the ideology of segregation. This ideology can be used to reinforce occupational segregation and other forms of discrimination against women in the job market.

In summary, the Quran does not contain many explicit and clear discriminatory rules concerning the participation of women in the job market. However, the status of women as quasi-commodity, quasi-human, with accompanying regulations, has created considerable ambiguity in the non-sexual rights of women. As this position lends itself to the reinforcement of male authority, the interpretations of the ambiguities are likely to be discriminatory against women. Thus, emancipation of female labor in Muslim societies requires liberation from commoditization and regulation of sexuality in the family, as well as women's equal and non-discriminatory access to the job market and to education.

Gender and the Labor Process in Iran, 1960–90

Background

In Iran, state and religion have never been fully separated. Most laws concerning family and other gender-related issues are Islamic. However, under Pahlavi rule (1925–79) the state pursued secularization policies, whereas the integration of state and religion has intensified after the Islamic revolution in 1979. For example, in 1936, Reza Shah (1925–41) forced women to unveil. After his abdication in 1941, unveiling was no longer forced, but a large number of women continued to appear unveiled in public. By contrast, in 1980, the Islamic regime forced these women to re-veil. The moderate changes in favor of women in marriage, divorce, and child custody in the Family Protection Law of 1967 were also reversed by the Islamic government. The Islamic government, however, did not reverse the enfranchisement of women that was introduced in 1963. Participation of women in the electoral process was not considered contradictory to Islamic regulations concerning women.

A discussion of the factors that contributed to the Islamic revolution is beyond the scope of this study.[34] However, a few remarks are relevant to gender issues. In general, the forced unveiling of women was viewed by many—including non-traditionalists—as a symbol of Pahlavi absolutism, and was thus resented. More importantly, however, the clergy and many other traditionally-inclined people considered unveiling as contrary to Islamic regulations, and viewed the unveiled and made-up women as shameless. Unveiled women were criticized for excessive preoccupation with make-up and fashion, and many argued that the presence of these women in government and private agencies threatened to undermine the stability of the institution of the family. Although the secular leftist opposition as well as many secular intellectuals did not directly question the morality of unveiling, they considered unveiling a transformation of women into sexual commodities, *kala-ye jensi*. We may note that this view overlooks the long history of commoditization of female sexuality. Unveiling did not commoditize female sexuality but created the possibility for visual advertisement, and a potential for women to assume relative autonomy in marketing their sexuality. The negative implications of the term *kala-ye jensi*, however, signal the disapproval of the changes by these secular groups.

The economic expansion of the 1960s and 1970s had accelerated rural–urban migration. A large segment of the urban population had rural backgrounds. These people very likely had traditional and religious outlooks which led them to consider the unveiled and made-up women as shameless. Due to recent demographic changes, young people now comprised a larger percentage of the population; the average age for marriage had gone up; many young male rural permanent or seasonal migrants were unmarried or had left their families in rural areas. The disproportionate number of young unmarried men in urban areas is likely to have contributed to gender-related social tensions. Thus, the clergy's allegations of women being prostituted by the Pahlavi government found popular support.

In summary, just before the revolution there existed, to varying degreees, the popular perception in Iran of the illegitimacy and immorality of women who appeared unveiled in public and who tried to be visually attractive. The roots of this perception originated in Iran's Islamic cultural heritage.

The social upheavals of the 1970s that led to the Islamic revolution in 1979 had strong anti-western and anti-imperialist overtones. Many female participants used the veil as a symbol of the return to traditional non-western values. Under the Shah, on the average, the unveiled women were economically and socially better off than the veiled women. The revolution gave a considerable psychological boost to the generally less privileged veiled women by encouraging them to participate actively in social change, and by proclaiming them as morally superior to the hitherto more privileged women. The veil, thus, assumed new meanings and symbolized class consciousness and anti-imperialism. Today, policies of veiling continue to be highly controversial. 'Improperly veiled' women are in danger of being assaulted and humiliated, and forced veiling is seen by many as a symbol of the oppressive attitude of the Islamic regime toward women. Veiling, thus, is symptomatic of both governments' gender philosophies.

In the following sections I will focus on the impact of these gender philosophies on the labor process.

Gender and Labor Process in Iran

I will use the conceptual frame developed earlier to explore changes in the extent of the commoditization and regulation of female sexuality, legal discrimination, and legal segregation of female labor. I assume thereby that the participation of women in wage-labor will ultimately have an emancipating impact, and that the division of labor between household and market-related activities, fertility, human capital, and occupational segregation are variables relevant to the discussion of gender inequality in the labor process in Iran.

It can be argued that the unveiling of women was an important step toward the deregulation of female sexuality, and that it had positive indirect long-term implications for female employment. To a degree, unveiling shifted control of women's sexuality from fathers, brothers, and husbands to the women themselves. It was thus a positive step in the direction of women's autonomy over their sexuality. Unveiling also broke with a long tradition of the seclusion of women. The impact of unveiling on employment was indirect. By promoting desegregation, unveiling contributed to the removal of many legal discriminations against women in the job market and in education. Under the Pahlavis, most white-collar female workers were unveiled. However, desegregation and the removal of legal discrimination at work also facilitated market participation of many blue-collar urban and rural women workers who continued to wear the veil. Initially the participation of women in the job market and in education was slow. However, stimulated by a rapidly growing economy, it accelerated during the second half of the twentieth century (see Table 5.1). Nevertheless, many critics considered the increase inadequate and insufficient.[35]

By 1976, the relative share of women active in the job market continued to be small: 13 per cent of women ten years and older were reported active, in contrast to 71 per cent of men (see Table 5.1). Occupational segregation and differences in investment in human capital between male and female workers existed at all levels, but was less pronounced at the university-trained professional than at lower levels of skills. About one-third of all students in the universities were female, but in science and engineering their share was smaller, ranging from a quarter to one-twelfth, respectively. The majority of working women had educational skills. Most blue-collar workers were employed in traditional industries such as textiles and carpet-weaving. There was a very noticeable absence of women in modern industrial

Table 5.1. The Employment and Education of the Population of Ten Years and Older

	1956	1966	1976	1986
Total population (1000 persons)	12,785	17,000	23,002	32,874
Male	6542	8794	11,796	16,841
Female	6242	8206	11,206	16,033
% in total male				
Active	83.93	77.41	70.76	68.35
Employed	81.53	70.18	64.32	59.53
Student	7.63	15.13	23.55	22.98
% in total female				
Active	9.18	12.59	12.93	8.16
Employed	9.18	11.5	10.81	6.08
Housewife	79.50	73.32	68.78	68.68
Student	2.98	7.43	14.85	16.58
% in total urban male				
Active	78.54	69.24	63.91	66.78
Employed	74.63	65.11	60.70	57.67
Student	16.11	23.69	29.63	24.52
% in total urban female				
Active	9.28	9.94	9.04	8.35
Employed	9.23	9.57	8.50	5.10
Housewife	77.01	68.09	64.19	66.48
Student	8.39	16.39	23.75	20.50
% in total rural male				
Active	86.61	82.91	77.88	70.26
Employed	84.97	73.60	68.09	61.77
Student	3.41	9.38	17.22	21.17
% in total rural female				
Active	9.18	14.29	16.56	7.93
Employed	9.15	12.73	12.97	6.29
Housewife	80.77	76.69	73.03	71.82
Student	0.40	1.68	6.54	11.82

Source: *Salnameh-e Amari-ye Keshvar: 1369* (1990) (Tehran: Markaz-e Amar-e Iran, 1990), pp 62–3.

and entrepreneurial activities. Participation of women in vocational schools conforms to this trend: except in sewing, secretarial, and clerical programs, female students were clearly absent. Some 8000 women annually participated in training programs for rural education, some 7200 in programs for health extension services, and only some 200 in agricultural extension services.

A 1976 report by the Plan and Budget Organization was highly critical of the low level of female employment and of occupational segregation. The gap was attributed to the discrimination of women in the family and by employers. The report called for the provision of facilities such as credit to women for entrepreneurial activities, dormitories for women students in vocational schools, part-time jobs for women, as well as day-care and household-related services for working women. The report emphasized equal potential abilities for women and men, and called the existing conditions an underutilization of human resources.[36] Of course, the existence of such internal government reports and recommendations does not prove that the state's gender philosophy in regard to women's labor was completely non-discriminatory. However, the government aspired to modernize along the lines of western industrialized countries, and thus was willing to promote the emancipation of women. The state also intended to generate economic growth, and thus was interested in utilizing the relatively untapped female labor resource. It favored female participation in wage-labor, and intended to lower occupational segregation and discrimination against women.

In 1980, through forced veiling, the state reimposed the Islamic regulation on female sexuality. However, veiling was reintroduced into a society that was structurally different from that of the early twentieth century when it had been a common practice. The society now was semi-industrialized and more urbanized than earlier. Many women had become accustomed to participating in socioeconomic and political activities. Many young women had working mothers or mothers who encouraged their professional aspirations. Women had actively participated in the revolution, too. The reintroduction of the veil did not result in the seclusion of women, but it did reintroduce the ideology of segregation. As will be demonstrated, it provided grounds for legal occupational segregation, and for legal discrimination of women in higher education and in the job market.

In contrast to its secular predecessor, the Islamic regime uses biological differences between men and women as a basis for legal discrimination against women. The proper role of women is perceived to be in the family. This implies that a woman's time should be spent primarily on reproductive labor and on other non-market labor at home. Thus, the gender ideology encourages economic dependency of women on their sexuality—childbearing and -raising, making and keeping a man interested in marriage. This gender policy has already left an impact on fertility: a 3.95 per cent average annual population growth is reported for 1976–86 in contrast to 2.7 per cent for the earlier period.[37]

The current regime considers certain services such as basic education and healthcare necessary for a Muslim society. The ideology of segregation requires female employment in these areas to cater to women clients. Thus segregation generates limited—and occupationally segregated—employment possibilities. As mentioned earlier, employment and other non-sexual rules in Islam are open to interpretations, and this makes it difficult to prevent women from working altogether. The net effect of the government's policies, however, is an increased commoditization and regulation of sexuality, with negative implications on the labor participation of women.

A comparison of the statistics for the two periods illustrates the impact of ideology on female employment. During the period 1956–76, on the average the number of women active in the job market grew by 3.8 per cent per annum,[38] faster than the population growth of 2.7 per cent. The relative share of the active population rose from about 9 per cent to nearly 13 per cent of the total female population of ten years and older. The relative share of housewives declined from nearly 80 per cent in 1956, to 69 per cent in 1976. The share of female students rose from nearly 3 to 14 per cent. The employment gains were more apparent for the women, whose share in the active population rose from about 9 to nearly 17 per cent. The relative share of rural housewives declined from nearly 81 to 73 per cent; and education rose from less than 1 to nearly 7 per cent. The share of active urban women remained fairly steady at 9 per cent. We may note, however, that the urban population growth accounted for about 4.6 per cent average annual for this period, and was much higher than the national average.[39] Another explanation for the appearance of stagnation in urban employment may be the increase in years of schooling, including higher education, for women, which kept them out of the labor market. The share of students in the urban female population of ten years and older rose from about 8 to 24 per cent.

The decline in the relative share of urban housewives from about 77 to 64 per cent also supports the hypothesis of no stagnation (see Table 5.1).

During 1976–86, the number women active in the job market declined on the average by about 2 per cent each year. The largest declines were observed in the blue-collar urban and in the rural population, an average negative of 10 and 5 per cent per annum, respectively. It appears that in rural areas women have been pushed into unpaid family labor. Urban female unemployment was 6 and 30 per cent for 1976 and 1986, respectively. The decline in active female labor, and the rise in unemployment—especially in urban areas—was in part due to the generally depressed state of the economy. However, for the same period male employment rose by 2.8 per cent per annum.[40] This suggests that the decline was to a large part due to increased discrimination against women. As rural and poor urban women are likely to have been more subject to discrimination in the family and in the workplace than well-to-do urban women, they carried the main burden.

By contrast, employment figures for white-collar female workers rose during this period. This category accounted for 60 per cent of the total female urban employment in 1986, in contrast to about 35 per cent in 1976.[41] This apparent gain is due in large part to the ideology of segregation accompanied by a strong, and successful, effort to enhance basic elementary and high-school education (see Table 5.1), which increases the need for female teachers. In 1985 and 1986, 92 per cent of all women hired by the public sector were teachers.[42] Another likely contributor to the gain is a relatively large pool of female professionals. At the time of the revolution, about one-third of all university students were female. These have graduated and joined the labor-force after the revolution. It is also likely that many middle-class urban women have resisted discrimination with relative success and have thus been able to continue to participate in the job market.

A closer assessment of white-collar female occupations is less optimistic. There are indications of discrimination against women in universities. Women are barred from entry in some fields, and are faced with quotas in several others.[43] Most recent employments are in teaching that requires only one year of training after high school. Although women are still present in many occupations, the bitter complaints of many professional women about the limitations in the choice of professions indicate that the pressure of legal occupational segregation is acutely felt.[44]

There are other differences in the treatment of gender by the state during the two periods. In 1967, the Family Protection Law made the approval of a first wife a necessary precondition for a man's second marriage, thus limiting the practice of polygyny. The law also took away from men the unilateral and unconditional right to divorce, and allowed more flexibility for women who wanted a divorce. According to the law, divorce now had to be settled in civil courts. The law also recognized some rights for divorced and widowed women over their children. Thus, by recognizing moderate rights for women over their sexuality and reproductive labor, these laws modified the extent of the commoditization of female sexuality.

The Islamic government has repealed the Family Protection Law. It argues that marriage is a contractual agreement between two individuals, on which the state cannot impose new rules. Instead, women are advised to stipulate favorable conditions in their marriage contracts. Indeed, the inclusion of such conditions is very popular, at least among urban middle- and upper-class women, but statistical information on the women who make use of this possibility is not available. However, the practice is sufficiently popular for the notary public offices, *mahzars*, to have different printed types of contracts at hand. Usually such contracts include the condition of monogamy, the right of the woman to divorce, and the equitable division of the wealth accumulated during the marriage. In general these conditions are more favorable to women than was the old Family Protection Law. However, the acceptance of these conditions is voluntary by the husband. There is no legal requirement compelling him to accept the conditions. In the absence of empirical data, it is difficult to identify the losers and the winners. However, women who are socioeconomically well off are more likely than poor and uneducated women to demand the inclusion of egalitarian conditions in marriage contracts. In any case, the fact that a man is free to accept or refuse limitations on the extent of the commoditization of the sexuality of his wife demonstrates that in essence female sexuality is a commodity.

Conclusions

In this chapter, I have used economic concepts to examine the legal treatment of female sexuality in Islam. I have argued that female sexuality in Islam is treated as a regulated commodity, and have examined the impact of the commoditization of sexuality on the female labor process. I have demonstrated that in a Muslim marriage female sexuality, including reproductive labor, is sold to the husband. As sexuality is an inseparable part of a woman, a married woman loses full self-ownership. Although Islam does not contain many explicit legal barriers to the participation of women in the labor market, the sale of female sexuality in marriage reduces the autonomy of women to make labor-related decisions. I have also argued that the commoditization of reproductive labor reduces the autonomy of women in decisions to allocate labor time between the job market and childbearing and -raising. The regulations concerning female sexuality, especially veiling, also reduce the autonomy of women, and are highly conducive to the creation of occupational segregation and to discrimination against women in the job market.

Intentionally, I have kept the conceptual and the empirical parts of this chapter separate in order to develop a general conceptual framework for the impact of Islamic legal theory on gender. This framework is especially relevant to the case of contemporary Iran, as nearly fifty years of secularization policies were followed by more than a decade of strong emphasis on Islamic values. I have not rigorously examined the gender philosophy of the Pahlavis in this study, but have examined specific policies regarding women enacted by these rulers, and the impact which the state's efforts in modernization, westernization, and economic growth have had on gender issues. I have demonstrated that the impact on decommoditization and deregulation of female sexuality and participation of women in the job market was significant and positive. By contrast, the recent emphasis on Islamic philosophy has accentuated gender inequality in the family, and has had negative implications for the participation of women in the job market. This negative impact is more apparent among blue-collar rural and urban female workers than among white-collar urban women, and is likely to have a greater impact on the position of poor women in the family than that of the more affluent. Although the ideology of segregation has created some job opportunities for women, it has also induced occupational segregation. Where positive tendencies in the participation of women in the job market are observed, they can be attributed to factors other than Islamic ideology.

In Iran, women have not been full owners of their own selves because of a long history of commoditization and regulation of female sexuality. Female labor has never enjoyed full legal freedom. The recent emphasis on Islamic ideology and law in Iran has increased occupational segregation and discrimination against women, commoditization and regulation of female sexuality, and coercion of female labor.

Our conceptual framework is designed as a methodological tool for studying gender economics, especially women and development, in Muslim societies. However, this approach may have useful applications in the study of gender economics in other, non-Muslim, societies as well.

6· Temporary Marriage: an Islamic discourse on female sexuality in Iran

Shahla Haeri

On a cold November day in 1990 the Iranian President, Mr Hashemi Rafsanjani, stunned his huge audience by a speech he delivered as his Friday sermon. Perhaps for the first time in the history of Islam, in clear, deliberate, and unambiguous terms, a political/religious leader formally acknowledged female sexuality, and suggested that women should feel secure enough to initiate a relationship when they felt the need. From the public pulpit of Friday Prayers, by far the most influential public forum in post-revolutionary Iran, where some of the most crucial policies are announced, President Rafsanjani reviewed the suppression of female sexuality by placing it within an Islamic framework. He said: 'Take, for example, the sexual instinct that God has given us. Some think that if we abstain from satisfying our needs and deprive ourselves from sexual gratification, then this is very good. Well, this is not so. It is wrong. It is anti-Islamic.' Elaborating on this, he said: 'If we had a healthy society, then the situation of all these widows we now have [that is, the women widowed in the Iran–Iraq war] would be very different. Then, when they [widows] felt the [sexual] need, *niaz*, they could approach one of their friends or relatives from a position of confidence and invite him to marry them temporarily, *ezdevaj-e movaqqat*. This they could do without fear of being shamed or ostracized by others.'[1] Having first invoked the divine blessing, Mr Rafsanjani then appealed to nature for further legitimacy: 'Going against nature [one's nature],' he said, 'is absolutely wrong.'[2]

Mr Rafsanjani underscored these themes when he turned his attention to youth and argued:

> Nowadays, in our [modern] society young people mature at the age of 15, and sexual needs are awakened in them . . . Our

> college students are constantly exposed to the opposite sex in the schools, universities, parks, buses, bazaars and the workplace. They are continuously stimulated [by proximity], but have no recourse. Who says this is right? Presently, in our society for our youth to remain pure and honorable, and to respect the societal norms [of chastity and virginity] implies remaining unsatisfied until they are 25 or 30 years old [before they can marry permanently]. They will have to deprive themselves of their natural desires. Deprivation is harmful. Who says this [deprivation] is correct? Well, God didn't say that this need should not be satisfied. The Prophet didn't say so. The Quran doesn't say so. The whole world doesn't say so either. Besides, if one is deprived, then harmful psychological and physical consequences will follow. Science has proven this. To fight nature is wrong.[3]

Admonishing some unnamed self-righteous zealots, who make it their business to set people on the right path, he went on: 'We ourselves create wrong cultural perceptions in our heads and think that this is the right way. The whole thing is in our heads. And we assume [wrongly] that this [sexual relation] is shameful for all.'[4]

Mr Rafsanjani then proposed a solution that apparently left many people confused and at odds with their long-held moral values and cultural expectations. He suggested that the young men and women who might feel shy about going to a mulla[5] to register their temporary marriage need not do so. They can agree among themselves—that is, in a private contract—'to be together for a month or two.' If the performance of the marriage ceremony in Arabic is difficult, he suggested, 'the young couple can recite the formula in Persian and in the absence of a mulla or other witnesses.'[6] By upholding the efficacy of private and verbal contracts at this level, Mr Rafsanjani effectively, but indirectly, challenged issues of parental authority and virginity, thus transgressing sanctioned cultural boundaries.

Mr Rafsanjani's provocative public speech made news headlines in Iran and abroad. It set off a lively debate in the local press, and heated arguments in public and private gatherings both inside and outside of the country. It resulted in an outpouring of printed texts and public discussions that expressed contested views on the institution of temporary marriage, female sexuality, marital fidelity and stability, and the sexuality of youth, subjects that have never before been so publicly, intensely, and persistently debated in the Iranian press. Prominent men and women were interviewed and their opinions solicited. It took an event of the magnitude of the Persian Gulf war to overshadow the growing public discussion of sexuality in Iran.

What are the issues involved here? Is Mr Rafsanjani more 'progressive', or 'modern' than the Shah? How is it that the political/religious leaders in Shii Iran seem to champion the right of women to sexual satisfaction, and attempt to revolutionize the relationship between young men and women? How does the issue of women's virginity, one of the most sacred cultural values, figure in this new formulation of gender relations? Are Rafsanjani's comments inconsistent with Islamic tradition in general and that of the Shiis in particular? Is he giving a new interpretation to the institution of temporary marriage, or is he simply following a well-established but little understood Shii Islamic tradition?

My objective in this chapter is to render Mr Rafsanjani's apparently surprising comments culturally meaningful. I will do so by referring to the historical interaction between the competing discourses of 'modernity' and 'Islam' under the Pahlavis (1925–79) and the Islamic regime in Iran respectively. Focusing on the state's rejection of, or support for, the institutions of temporary marriage and veiling, I will draw attention to the different ideologically supported interpretations of veiling and female sexuality each regime advanced. In the process I will attempt to dispell the monolithic perception of female passivity and of uniformity of sexual ethics in Iran. I will argue that although Mr Rafsanjani's statements may sound surprising, given the projected puritanical image of the state, they are not a radical departure from the Shii Islamic tradition.

Contested Sexuality: State vs the Public

The range of reactions to Rafsanjani's proclamations clustered, for the most part, around two diametrically opposed poles: those who supported temporary marriage and the president's interpretation of it, and those who objected to both.

The leading Iranian 'feminist' magazine, *Zan-e Ruz (Modern Woman)*, took the lead in opposing Mr Rafsanjani's recommendations. In an editorial, *Zan-e Ruz* vehemently objected to the president's comments, arguing: 'One cannot of course deny human drives. But if men and women agree to get together for one, two, or three months, then what is the difference between this and male–female relationships in the West? Besides, what kind of human beings will they turn out to be, those men and women who keep making contracts of temporary marriage?'[7] *Zan-e Ruz* further criticized the president for ignoring the role of 'love', *'eshq*, in marriage. 'Should repressed needs in our society be considered only in their sexual dimension?' they queried. 'What will happen to children born of such marriages? How are we to respond to the psychological, moral, and hygienic problems associated with this form of marriage?'[8] *Zan-e Ruz* was deluged by mail and telephone calls from its readers who expressed support for, or opposition to, the institution of temporary marriage and the president's comments.

On the opposite side, the editorials of the daily newspaper *Kayhan* welcomed Mr Rafsanjani's proposals and argued:

> If, on the one hand, we accept the fact that we cannot and must not leave sexual desire unfulfilled, and if, on the other hand, we accept the fact that we must fight hard against all the corruption and decadence that lead a society into disaster, then we have no choice but to propose correct ways for the gratification of unavoidable sexual needs. Blocking such solutions will mean leading our society toward decadence.[9]

This newspaper also provided a public forum for debating the subject, and carried a series of articles and letters sent in by readers.

One correspondent wrote:

> We regret that this solution has been suggested for college students. How can an educated youth who has understood the real meaning of marriage agree to make a contract of temporary marriage merely to satisfy his[10] sexual desire—and only for a short period of time? Wouldn't it have been better [for Rafsanjani] to have referred to the Prophet Mohammad who has said: 'O youth, whichever of you can marry should do so, and he who does not have the means should fast, and fight his concupiscence.' Before [the publicity granted to temporary marriage], if we were suspicious of illegitimate relations between a couple we could conduct an investigation to discover the truth. But now all options are blocked, and merely by saying that

'we now have [permitted] temporary marriage' the problem is perceived to be resolved.'

Identifying temporary marriage as promiscuity, he went on: 'Has promiscuity reached such a level in this Islamic society as to necessitate a discussion of temporary marriage? If this is so, then what is the difference between our Islamic society and the West?'[11]

Readers not only reacted to the president's comments, but also challenged each other's positions. They argued against long-held 'wrong' assumptions and misunderstandings. In a rebuttal to a letter entitled: 'Temporary Marriage: the Problem or the Solution', a reader made the following statement in support of temporary marriage. 'First of all,' he wrote, 'a young couple who have become intimate with each other can use their mutual knowledge and understanding, something lacking in permanent marriage, to change their temporary marriage into a permanent one.' Challenging the view that maintains temporary marriage is a cloak for illicit male–female relations, he continued: 'Even if we assume that this [temporary marriage] is a form of corruption, *fesad*, with all those rules and regulations it is much more restricted and reasonable [than prostitution].' Appealing to human nature, he further argued, 'Which law or what religion has the right to prevent or suppress this very basic human right and human instinct (to fulfillment of sexuality)?'[12]

The significance of this ongoing debate on temporary marriage, *mut'a* (*sigheh* in colloquial Persian), should be understood within the context of the history of westernization and modernization in Iran. The modern Iranian nation-state gradually emerged as a result of European imperial penetration, interaction with the West, internal intellectual developments and sociopolitical changes that culminated in the Constitutional Revolution of 1905–6. In the process, the intimate relationship that traditionally existed between the state and religion—imaginatively conceptualized as 'ventriloquial' by Tavakoli-Targhi[13]—was fundamentally restructured. Since the mid-nineteenth century the two discourses of modernity and Islam have existed in dialectical tension in Iran. They have concurrently acted and reacted against strategies adopted, and policies formulated and implemented by the other. Through their respective religious, political, and intellectual rhetoric they have defined and redefined themselves vis-à-vis the other, formulating meanings and constraints within which they operate. In the course of the twentieth century the discourse of modernity gradually became hegemonic, forcing the Islamic discourse to 'lie low' and become, eventually, a 'counter-discourse.' After the revolution of 1979, however, the Islamic discourse regained its long-standing earlier hegemony, but with a difference. Responding to a new configuration of relations of power (and knowledge), this new Islamic discourse has passed through the prism of modernity and has emerged, like everything else in the society, transformed, restructured, and reconstructed.

The pace of modernization was accelerated by the Pahlavi regimes (1925–79) which tried to westernize the society, to secularize its legal and educational institutions, and to unveil its women. From 1936, when the state mandated removal of the veil, until the revolution of 1979, when the state required them to put the veil back on again, many Iranian women took advantage of the relaxation in the veiling law and began to appear unveiled in public.

The growing numbers of unveiled women in public and the increasing visual representations of them in the media generated hardly any well coordinated and recognizable public debate or discourse on female sexuality or on gender relations. Issues of women's welfare and changes in family law gradually began to be discussed in parliament and a few select magazines, but there was an overall silence—even discouragement—on the subject of sexual needs. There was little discussion and suggestion for ways to meet these needs, which in the case of men were used as justification for polygyny. Increasingly, young men and women were participating in coeducational colleges and schools, had greater opportunities to socialize in public, and were frequenting the same social space. In a society in which 'proper' social contact between men and women—outside of the limited boundaries of blood or marital relations—is religiously problematic, urban men and women were left without culturally legitimate role-models. The issue of female virginity was (and is) so important that women who took the risk of becoming intimate with a male friend would seriously compromise their chances of marriage—particularly with the same man. Consequently, despite the apparent public tolerance of the association between the sexes, an undercurrent of resentment and disapproval persisted, particularly among a segment of the clerics and their followers.

Since the Islamic revolution of 1979, the new religious/political elite has redefined the male–female relationship in ways that made reveiling mandatory and the institution of temporary marriage proper and desirable. This has become a subject of intense and open discussion, often shocking the sensibilities of middle-class urban men and women who had grown accustomed to the 'desexualized language'[14] (but not the 'sexualized' image) of modernity.

Temporary Marriage: The Erotic Discourse

Before describing the boundaries of the institution of temporary marriage it is instructive to note the Islamic attitude toward marriage and sexuality. The Shii Islamic discourse celebrates marriage and sexuality as positive and self-affirming.[15] Marriage is maintained to be an act of piety, while celibacy is considered evil and unnatural. Islam, according to the majority of Shii—and Sunni—jurisconsults, is a divine religion anchored in human nature, *fetrat*. Its objective is to minimize human suffering and to provide legitimate means to satisfy various human desires. Of particular importance, in their view, is the fulfillment of sexual desire. Both Sunni and Shii jurisprudence, however, share a textual inattentiveness to female sexuality as such. Although Shii legal texts devote extensive attention to such matters as marriage, divorce, custody of children, and the reciprocal obligations of husband and wife, they have remained virtually silent on issues of female sexuality.[16] Male sexuality, on the other hand, is accommodated by polygyny, slave concubinage, and, for Shiis, temporary marriage.

Legally unique to Shiis, temporary marriage is perceived to be a legitimate alternative to that of permanent marriage. The objective of temporary marriage, from a Shii point of view, is sexual enjoyment, *estemta'*, whereas that of permanent marriage is procreation, *towlid-e nasl*.

Underscoring the futility of fighting the sexual instinct, *gharizeh*, Shii legal scholars attempt to contain and control it by situating it in a morally acceptable structure, namely temporary marriage. Until very recently, however, the sexual discourse centered on male sexuality, and could be characterized as a male erotic discourse. With the increasing pace of modernization and borrowing of ideas and technology from the West, and the rise in public consciousness regarding women's issues, Shii clerics, ulema, were obliged to rethink Islamic personal law and its underlying assumptions. They were challenged to offer new, and more 'modern,' or contemporary, interpretations of these laws. Among those, temporary marriage has been singled out for special attention. The contemporary Shii ulema uphold temporary marriage as an institution that is not only compatible with its western counterpart of 'free' gender relations, but that is more progressive and morally superior to it. While allowing a degree of autonomy and free choice to a couple, temporary marriage presumably contains sexual relations within a legal framework.

Temporary marriage, *mut'a*, was apparently a matrilineal form of marriage, and one among several forms of marriage, practiced in pre-Islamic Arabia.[17] It has been legally permitted and religiously sanctioned among the Twelver Shiis, most of whom live in Iran. Etymologically, *mut'a* means enjoyment or pleasure. The custom of '*mut'a* of women,' as it has been called, was outlawed in the seventh century by the second caliph, Umar, who equated it with fornication. Among the Sunnis, therefore, temporary marriage is forbidden, and in theory they do not practice it, although in reality some do.[18] The Shiis, however, continue to consider Umar's command as legally and religiously invalid. They argue that temporary marriage is legitimated in the Quran 4:24, and that it was not specifically banned by the Prophet Mohammad himself.[19] Temporary marriage has remained a point of chronic disagreement, passionate dispute, and at times animosity between Sunnis and Shiis.[20] My discussion here concerns only the beliefs and practices of Twelver Shii Muslims.

In its present form, temporary marriage is a form of contract in which a man (married or unmarried) and an unmarried woman (virgin, divorced, or widowed) agree, often privately and verbally, to marry each other for a limited period of time, varying anywhere from one hour to 99 years. The couple also agree on a specific amount of brideprice, to be given to the woman.[21] Unlike permanent marriage, temporary marriage does not oblige a husband to provide financial support for his temporary wife. A Shii Muslim man is allowed to make several contracts of temporary marriage at the same time, in addition to the four permanent wives legally allowed all Muslim men. Women, however, may not marry either temporarily or permanently more than one man at a time.

At the end of the mutually agreed period the couple part company without a divorce ceremony. After the dissolution of the marriage, no matter how short, the temporary wife must observe a period of sexual abstinence[22] in order to prevent problems in identifying a potential child's legitimate father. The children of such unions are accorded full legitimacy, and, theoretically, have equal status to their half-siblings born of a permanent marriage.[23] Although children inherit from their parents, temporary spouses do not inherit from each other. Moreover, a contract of temporary marriage is renewable for as many times as the partners wish, in contrast to only three times in the case of a permanent marriage.[24]

The Shii ulema perceive temporary marriage as distinct from prostitution, despite structural similarities. For them, temporary marriage is legally sanctioned and religiously blessed, while prostitution is legally forbidden, religiously reprehensible, and therefore challenges the social order and the sanctioned rules for the association of the sexes. Prostitution is viewed as detrimental to the society's general health and welfare by violating its ethics and ethos. On the contrary, the ulema argue that temporary marriage, while performing a similar sexual function, indicates obedience to the law and social order. Those who resort to it, therefore, are perceived to follow a divinely recommended way to satisfy 'natural' urges. Not only is temporary marriage not considered immoral from a religious and legal perspective, it is actually considered to prevent corruption and prostitution.

Although the details of the social history of temporary marriage are obscure, it is probable that the custom has existed in Iran for centuries and has thrived in some social circles (for example, the Qajar royal family). Identifying temporary marriage as an archaic aspect of religion, however, the Pahlavi regime discreetly attempted to push the practice to the margins of society. Fear of a religious backlash prevented the government from banning the custom outright. The Family Protection Law of 1967 made no reference whatsoever to temporary marriage. By remaining silent on the issue, the state effectively diffused a concerted religious objection to the law and was able to move the family reforms through the parliament. It also led the public to believe that temporary marriage had been banned. As a result, the institution of temporary marriage under the Pahlavi regime lost much of the little respectability it had enjoyed previously. The state's disapproval of temporary marriage led to the custom being cloaked in a veil of secrecy. Consequently, many who contracted a temporary marriage often hid it from their friends and family. This kept the specifics of temporary marriage unclear and enigmatic to many Iranians, including some of the men and women who actually made use of the custom.

Despite attempts to revive temporary marriage in present-day Iran, it is still a marginal and stigmatized institution, associated with many conflicting moral values. Its practice has put religion and popular culture at odds. Whereas there is no religious restriction preventing virgin women from contracting a temporary marriage (and Mr Rafsanjani's comments are in accord with the theological tradition here), popular culture demands that a woman be a virgin at the time of her first permanent marriage. While the more westernized and educated urban Iranian middle-class women, and some men too, perceive temporary marriage as legalized prostitution, the more religiously inclined Iranians, particularly the clerics,[25] view it as a divinely sanctioned and 'rewarded' activity, preferable to the 'decadent' western-style promiscuity and 'free love.'[26]

Recent ethnographic research on the institution of temporary marriage suggests that not only are rumors of the demise of the institution grossly exaggerated, but that the institution is alive and well among the lower socioeconomic strata in the society. Women who contract temporary marriages tend to be primarily young divorced women from lower-class backgrounds, but middle-class women occasionally do so as well.[27] Contrary to the popular image of prudish Muslim Iranian women, research reveals that temporarily married women are not only aware of their own needs and their sexual appeal to men (which they enjoy) but that they also often initiate a relationship.[28] By specifically acknowledging female sexuality independently, and proposing temporary marriage as an alternative to marriage and to living together, the Islamic regime has rendered the Shii erotic discourse 'androgynous.' Women of various classes and backgrounds are becoming increasingly aware of it, and publicly or secretively take part in it. At least theoretically it is no longer primarily a male erotic discourse or a male prerogative (and, indeed, may never have been just that).

Unveiled Women, Veiled Sexuality: Discourse of Modernity

The pace of modernization and the adoption of western customs and manners gained momentum with Reza Khan's military coup in 1921 and his eventual ascent to the throne in 1925. Following the lead of Ataturk in Turkey, Reza Shah set out to modernize the country by westernizing it. He issued an imperial order in 1936 that made veiling unlawful for women in Iran.[29] The law posed considerable difficulties for those women who did not wish to leave their homes unveiled, and for men who could not bear to allow their women to appear unveiled in public[30] because to them the forced unveiling of women implied dishonoring men. The unveiling was not only uncomfortable, but was unprecedented and incomprehensible to the majority of Iranians. Until then, it had been forbidden, even sinful, for unrelated men to occupy the same space with women who were unprotected by the prophylactic shield of a veil. Unveiling exposed women to the male gaze, and rendered both men and women insecure and uncertain in each other's company.[31]

The unveiling law was not relaxed until after Reza Shah's removal by the Allied Forces in 1941. His son, Mohammad Reza Shah, who ascended the throne in the same year, granted women freedom to choose whether or not to wear a veil. Many of the women in the slowly growing urban middle class continued to appear bare-headed in public, but rather self-consciously so. Women of the bazaar, merchant and lower classes, however, resumed veiling, though perhaps not as strictly as before.

In 1963, the state granted women the right to vote and to be elected to parliament.[32] The Family Protection Law was passed in 1967,[33] and although polygyny was not categorically outlawed, Iranian women were given the right to sue for divorce in the event their husbands took a second wife. In 1976, the first woman minister for women's affairs, Mahnaz Afkhami, was appointed to join the cabinet,[34] and by 1979, the year of the Islamic revolution, women occupied several seats in the parliament and the senate.

It might be assumed that the secularization of the judicial system, the westernization of the political structure, and the unveiling of women, would be accompanied by parallel development to accommodate this new configuration of male–female positioning in social space, and hence to effect a change in the public perception of sexuality. But this did not happen much, at least not overtly and consciously, and where it did it seems to have taken a negative form. Precisely because of the appearance of unveiled women in public, a compensatory tendency developed to repress any public discourse on sexuality, including that of temporary marriage.

Elsewhere I have argued that within the contractual structure of marital exchange, women are symbolically conflated with sexuality, and are thus perceived to be its very embodiment.[35] A veil covers not only the object of desire, but protects men by blocking from their view that very object.[36] By the same logic, the mere presence of an unveiled woman communicates a sexual message that is culturally inappropriate and morally confusing. The challenge for the policy-makers in the Pahlavi regime was thus to keep a balance between the requirements of modernity (for example, unveiling women), and respect for the public's religious beliefs and sentiments. Changing the public perception of women as sex objects involved a de-emphasis—or silence—on sexuality itself. The state-directed silence thus functioned as a veil to protect unveiled women. Such a policy could also be interpreted as a reaction on the part of the state and of women to the negative attitude expressed by the religious establishment toward unveiling. To counter any hint or accusation of 'prostitution' by some members of the religious establishment, unveiled middle-class Iranian women adopted prudishness, placing great emphasis on chastity and decorous comportment in public.

Within this changing configuration of gender relations and the emerging new consciousness, contradictions and tensions began to manifest themselves in complex forms and on several levels. Under the spotlight of Iranian National Television, for example, male and female singers exhibited the tensions in gender relations in modernized urban Iranian society. While performing duets, male and female singers assiduously refrained from looking each other directly in the eyes, even if the song was about love, lust, and desire, as most popular Persian songs are. Female singers would be particularly evasive. They seemed to wish to communicate 'proper' images of uninterested and chaste women, lest viewers assumed the love song was an expression of a 'real' relationship.[37]

With the removal of the tangible barrier of the veil that ostensibly protected both men and women from temptation, other means of protection had to be devised, means that would be nationally perceived as more compatible with the requirements of the modern age. Respectability and chastity were no longer automatically associated with the veil, nor was the veil universally accorded the high moral value it had previously enjoyed. Morality and respectability were reorganized, and had to be internalized and maintained in the absence of the veil. Female chastity, *effat*, *nejabat*, now was held to be a woman's invisible shield. As the signifiers of sexuality, unveiled women had to be taught to behave appropriately in public, and the public had to be silenced on the topic of sexuality. Secular mass education, as distinct from traditional education at religious centers, was an effective means by which both boys and girls could be socialized to exercise self-control and restraint,[38] requirements of the new era in Iran. Against this background, temporary marriage with its explicit objective of sexual enjoyment was not a topic for discussion. It was not included in educational textbooks (unlike now in the Islamic state), and was excluded from debates and discussion in schools, universities, and other institutions run by the state.

The silence of the state on the subject of female sexuality was reinforced by a negative attitude toward sexuality fostered by some of the clergy who consistently opposed what they labeled as an 'imported' or 'West-toxicated' model of women's emancipation.

Iranian urban middle-class women, including those who were struggling to further women's rights, made a concerted effort to underscore the distinction between veiling and chastity. They also used this distinction as a way to neutralize the negative publicity given to unveiled women within religious circles.[39] Thus, for example, when in the late 1960s the Family Protection Law was debated in parliament, some women, including one of the leading women senators, Mehrangiz Manuchehrian, objected to a clause in the civil law that required married women to obtain their husband's written permission to travel abroad. According to Mahnaz Afkhami, 'Professional women who demanded the removal of this clause were faced with such vehement opposition from the clerics that they had to withdraw their demands. The clerics' reasoning was that such women wanted to go to Europe without their husband's permission only to prostitute themselves.'[40]

Perceiving temporary marriage as a backward male prerogative to exploit women, Senator Manuchehrian and other women objected to its legal existence. Women's magazines, such as *Zan-e Ruz*,[41] equated temporary marriage with legalized prostitution and carried several articles in which they enumerated the actual and potential abuses inherent in this form of marriage. When they called for its abolition, however, the response of the religious leaders in Qom and Tehran was swift and sharp. The late Ayatollah Motahhari (d. 1979) accused those who opposed temporary marriage of being mindlessly westernized and hopelessly unaware of the progressive nature of this Islamic law.[42]

Most middle-class Iranian women perceived temporary marriage as degrading and a threat to the security and stability of the family. Many divorced lower-class women, however, perceived it, though not without ambivalence, as a way to escape their marginal, restrictive, and unfavorable status as either divorced or widowed women. Given the stigma attached to divorce, many of these women are not welcome back in their own natal families and often have nowhere to go. They are vulnerable and marginalized. Temporary marriage, therefore, provides them with some relief, with an 'escape,' as an informant put it. The motivation of many divorced women for engaging in this form of marriage is not so exclusively to find a source of economic support, as has been maintained by Shii juridical texts and in orthodox Shii circles, but a desire for love and affection, for human companionship which was lacking in their broken permanent marriages.

In 1978 many middle-class Iranians in Tehran assumed that temporary marriage was an obsolete institution, that it was no longer relevant in the modern age, that it was no longer being practiced, and that even if it existed, it was primarily contracted by lower-class women. These assumptions proved to be wrong, for since the establishment of the Islamic state, temporary marriage has re-emerged in full force, with the blessing of the state. The temporary hegemony of the discourse of modernity during the Pahlavi regimes, therefore, was not uniform and all-inclusive. In the realm of family relations the Islamic discourse had maintained its vitality among the lower classes, the merchants and the more religiously-inclined groups; this vitality eventually reasserted itself in the revolution of 1979.

Veiled Women, Unveiled Sexuality: Islamic Discourse

With women required to veil again, the Islamic regime has attempted to revive the institution of temporary marriage, to remove its negative connotations, and to reintroduce it from a new perspective. The topic is extensively discussed in an educational religious textbook (1980/81).[43] Initially, the state's concerted effort to revitalize temporary marriage had to do with the plan to reassert indigenous Islamic institutions. It also supported the attempt of Ayatollah Motahhari and his followers to show Islamic institutions to be inherently progressive and advanced. Following the same tradition, Rafsanjani has reaffirmed the hegemony of Islamic discourse, a discourse that, although momentarily repressed, was articulated in response to challenges of modernism while opposing the Pahlavi regime's efforts to westernize the country. By drawing on a distinctly Shii discourse to periodically discuss the institution of temporary marriage, Rafsanjani brings to the public's attention the moral 'superiority' of this form of sexual relation over its 'chaotic' and 'decadent' western counterparts.

Is President Rafsanjani thereby merely following a trend? I argue that he is saying something new, and that he is providing a re-reading of an ancient tradition within a modern social context. This particular interpretation, however, is not without its history. Ayatollah Motahhari is to be credited with first conceptualizing the institution in its modern form. In his book, *The Legal Rights of Women in Islam*,[44] he shifted the long-standing Shii strategy from defending the legitimacy of temporary marriage against Sunni opposition to that of upholding it as a socially relevant and psychologically functional modern institution. He referred to it as 'one of the brilliant laws of Islam', timeless and universal, devised for the welfare of humankind.[45] Specifically, he proposed that young adults, as opposed to married men and divorced women, ought to benefit from the advantages of this uniquely Islamic (read Shii) institution. The argument he made in his book has since become a popular refrain:

> The characteristic feature of our modern age is the lengthening of the span of time between natural puberty and social maturity, when one becomes capable of establishing a family . . . Are the young ready to undergo a period of temporary asceticism and put themselves under the strain of rigid austerity till such time as there may arise an occasion for permanent marriage? Suppose a young person is prepared to undergo temporary asceticism; will nature be ready to forgo the formation of the dreadful and dangerous psychological penalties which are found in the wake of abstaining from instinctive sexual activity and which psychiatrists are now discovering? [Trans from the source.][46]

His reformulation of the philosophy of temporary marriage, echoed repeatedly in the conversations I had with mullahs in Iran in 1978 and 1981, is that the concept of temporary marriage is one of the most advanced and far-sighted aspects of Islamic thought; it indicates Islam's relevance to human society (modern or ancient) and Islam's understanding of the nature of human sexuality.[47] Following the same line of reasoning, however, Rafsanjani brought up a point that was not given much attention by Ayatollah Motahhari in his scheme of sexuality, namely that of female desire. Although Ayatollah Motahhari uses the generic term 'youth' to refer to a young person, male or female, in the Persian language the term for youth, *javan*, has been associated primarily with males. By specifically acknowledging female sexuality, and publicizing it during his Friday sermon, Mr Rafsanjani pushed his mentor's argument to its logical conclusion.[48]

It was this public recognition of an autonomous female sexual desire, independent of its male counterpart, and the recommendation of an active female role in initiating marriage by the Republic's president, that seems to have set off the controversy. The most vociferous opposition to Rafsanjani has come from urban middle-class women, who maintain that such official approval of temporary marriage threatens the stability of their marriages.[49] They have been categorical in their condemnation of the institution, and suspicious of the state's support for it.[50] Indeed, beyond promoting the advantages of temporary marriage, the state does not have any well coordinated plans to minimize the loopholes in the law and to educate the public, particularly women.

For that matter, most middle-class women conceive of the institution of temporary marriage in its traditional configuration as a male prerogative. This certainly has been the case in the past, but with the changes spearheaded by the Islamic regime it may not remain so. However, a majority of middle-class Iranian women seem to be hesitant to seize the moment and actually rethink issues of virginity, gender relations, and sexuality, and to offer fresh interpretations of these institutions and relations. A vast majority of middle-class women, as represented in *Zan-e Ruz*, have been thus less open to consider other possibilities than their lower-class sisters, who have resorted to temporary marriage for a variety of reasons, though not always to their advantage. Given that permanent marriages are arranged and one's choice of a life partner is limited, one could imagine, as indeed some lower-class women do, that prior to their actual permanent marriage, women might demand a short-term temporary marriage in order to get to know their future spouse—however minimally. Presently, however, women who resort to temporary marriages reduce their chances of a permanent one. A contract of temporary marriage, with its specific objective of exchange of money for sexual pleasure, offends the sensibility of modernized urban Iranian middle-class women—and some men—who have gradually adopted the idea of 'love' marriages. Indeed, under the Pahlavi regime representatives of women in the parliament as well as the media (such as *Zan-e Ruz* and *Ettela'at-e Banovan*) objected to the payment of brideprice, *mehr*, in a permanent marriage. They perceived such payment as degrading to women. The middle-class opposition to valorizing temporary marriage seems to be inspired by the pre-revolutionary discourse of modernity as westernization. Despite their increasingly sophisticated dialogue with the regime, Iranian middle-class women have refused, or been reluctant, to look at male–female relationships within the new configuration of temporary marriage suggested by Rafsanjani.

Once again we encounter the clash of modern and Islamic discourses. The irony of it is, however, that Mr Rafsanjani, though a cleric and a political leader, is talking about sex in the name of modernity, not so much in its 'western' form, but within an Islamic framework. Although in line with Shii tradition, Mr Rafsanjani seems to be operating within the parameters of a new discourse, one we may call 'Islamic modernity.'

7· Images of Women in Classical Persian Literature and the Contemporary Iranian Novel

Azar Naficy

Shahrnush Parsipur's novel, *Tuba va Ma'na-ye Shab* (*Tuba and the Meaning of the Night*, Tehran, 1989) begins with a series of interesting images. It opens at the end of the Qajar dynasty, at a time when western thought and new ways of living directly begin to influence and change the traditional closed society of Iran. The heroine's father is an *adib,* a poet-scholar, and yet a simple man who is preoccupied with philosophy and poetry. One day as he walks the streets immersed in his thoughts, a foreigner on horseback runs him down. The insolent foreigner whips the *adib* across the face. Later he is forced to go to the *adib*'s house to apologize. This incident is the *adib*'s first and last direct encounter with the western world. The most important result of the encounter is his startling discovery that the earth is round. Before, he had been vaguely aware of the earth's roundness, but he had preferred to ignore it.

For several days the *adib* contemplates what the roundness of the earth means for him. He instinctively realizes the connection between the foreigner's presence, the roundness of the earth, and all the changes and upheavals yet to come. After several days he announces his conclusion: 'Yes, the earth is round; the women will start to think; and as soon as they begin to think they will become shameless.'

The most important point in these scenes is that women play a central role in any form of change in the society. Indeed, in most Iranian narratives women are central to the plot and given much space. My main goal in this chapter is to analyze various images of women in the contemporary Iranian novel by looking at their antecedents in classical Persian literature. In fact, I would like to construct a literary history for the recurring images of women in the contemporary Iranian novel, reviewing them through the shine and shimmer of their enigmatic past.

The first known Iranian counterpart of *Romeo and Juliet* is a beautiful narrative poem, *Vis va Ramin (Vis and Ramin).* Written in the tenth century by Fakhr al-Din Gorgani, it is probably the oldest as well as the most important Persian narrative of its kind. In one scene in the poem Ramin, who has not seen Vis since they were children, watches Vis's litter go by. 'A sharp spring wind' lifts ('steals') the litter's curtain, revealing Vis. Ramin's first glance at Vis is 'disastrous'; he swoons, and is thrown off his horse. *Vis va Ramin* is followed by a long series of similar love stories, most notably *Khosrow va Shirin*, *Shirin va Farhad*, *Layla va Majnun*, and *Bijan va Manijeh.* Like Vis, the women in these stories are equal in love and courage to their men. They are brave and independent, and have a loyalty most of their men lack. Most important of all are the dialogues they create. They create a negative dialogue with the outside world, which is insensitive to their love, and a positive dialogue with their lovers, through which they defy the rules of tradition. In fact, the structure of the narratives is built around these two parallel dialogues.

An archetypal image for transcending a particular confine of Persian culture is the softly radiant image of Shahrzad, in *Hezar va Yek Shab* (*One Thousand and One Nights* or *Arabian Nights*). The king in the frame story represents ultimate masculine power. Because of a woman's 'deceit', he severs all positive relations with women and in fact with the whole world. The king is powerful enough to revenge his wife's betrayal through first marrying and then killing a virgin every night. This power masks an inherent weakness: without a healthy relationship with a woman, without trust in the possibility of such a relationship, the king is gripped by a disease which is literally destroying his whole kingdom.

Shahrzad, a victim of the king's tyranny, is a symbol of courage, rationality and wisdom. She must use what is called 'woman's guile'[1] in order to save the kingdom and restore peace to the king. The way she uses this 'guile' gives her the power and confidence to direct and stage the drama which step by step brings the king back to sanity. The fact that she successfully uses the tale, the narrative, as the king's medicine points to the healing power of fantasy over 'reality.'[2] Shahrzad uses her wisdom and skills—and uses them consciously—not only to change but also to heal her man.

In all the above-mentioned narratives the relationship between the male and the female characters is the center round which all other relations revolve. Essential to all these relationships is what I would like to call 'creative subversion.' This term needs further elaboration.

All these narratives are created within a highly hierarchical and masculine society. All are supposed to revolve round the male hero. But it is the active presence of the women that changes events, that diverts the men's life from its traditional course, that shocks the men into changing their very mode of existence. In the classical Iranian narrative active women dominate the scene; they make things happen. Like the wind in *Vis va Ramin* they open their lovers' eyes to new insights and discoveries which determine the course of the men's future actions.

This subversive relationship redirects the traditional course of male–female relationships. The hero's submission to love in one way or another softens and 'civilizes' him, making his familiar world intolerable. This change is brought about less by the heroes' own will than by the active pressure of the women in their lives. The king in *One Thousand and One Nights* is healed; Farhad loses Shirin and dies; Bijan's life is saved by Manijeh; Khosrow, whose masculine identity is reinforced by his sexual conquests—even as he pines for his beloved—repents, and is united with Shirin, only to be killed while sleeping by her side; and Ramin is finally rewarded with Vis, with whom he lives for 81 happy years of married life.

Majnun's case demands closer attention. After his beloved Layla's forced marriage, Majnun becomes a mad mystic and spends the rest of his days in the wilderness. Majnun's love for Layla has been interpreted, according to the mystical tradition, as a stage toward higher 'reality.' But looking at it from the lovers' point of view it makes more sense to say that Layla's love transforms Majnun to such a degree that the world with its rules and conventions is no longer tolerable to him. In the same manner Layla also negates the traditional role assigned to her. She dies rather than submit to a forced marriage.

My last example from the classical tradition is the heroine in 'The Black Dome,' a story in Nezami's *Haft Paykar* (*Seven Beauties*). The story is about a king who arrives in a town where all the inhabitants are in mourning. Demanding to know why, he is made to go through the same process. He is taken outside the town and put in a large basket. A huge bird carries him high up in the air and drops him in a heavenly pasture where he meets a most beautiful lady served by lesser beauties. Every night the lady invites him to a feast and frolics with him until he desires to make love to her. At that crucial moment, she asks for patience and refers him to one of her beautiful servants. He calls her 'fancy.' In order to get her, he must show patience, but patient is the one thing he cannot be. He fails the test and loses her forever. Like the town's inhabitants, he too wears black for the rest of his life, mourning his loss.

The beautiful lady in Nezami's tale makes an important point about all the other images: they all are part of the poet's vision, a vision which in essence negates and defies external 'reality.' These images feel real to us not because they are portrayed realistically, but because their texture fits well the fictional reality created through the narrative. This fictional reality is created only as a backdrop to their mystical and transcendental identity; in a sense it is an extension of that identity. Within the context of a transcendent world, the women in the classical Iranian narrative either create love and peace in their men or taunt and tempt their men. Either way they disturb the present state of affairs, opening a path to a different world.

The images of women characteristic of the classical Iranian narratives have persisted down to the period when Iranian society as well as its literature were changed fundamentally. Of the few long narratives in Persian written after the introduction of the novel form in Iran in early 1900s, the one in which the women are most central is Mohammad-Baqer Mirza Khosravi's three-volume romance-novel, *Shams va Toghra* (*Shams and Toghra*, Tehran, 1910).

In one scene the hero, Shams, relates to his mistress, Queen Abesh, his feelings about the three women in his life. Toghra, his first love and wife, is his favorite, if for no other reason than that of seniority. Mary the 'Venetian,' a foreigner who acts like a typically shy and submissive Iranian girl, is so good and correct that he cannot help but love her. The Queen herself is irresistible because she is so skillful in the carnal arts. The serene and integrated image of the women in the classical tales is now divided into three. The hero's love does not make him concentrate on one woman; rather, it directs him toward different women. *Shams va Toghra* thus shows the Iranian narrative at a transition point. The story, with its tedious digressions, vacillates between a novel and a romance.[3] As such, it makes a number of interesting cultural points. It is again a variation on the

Romeo and Juliet theme. But Shams is luckier than Romeo; he marries his Juliet halfway through the second volume and continues to marry other women with the consent and blessing, nay, the insistence of his beloved.

The world of *Shams va Toghra* is still a masculine world, but it has lost its previous cohesion, and the men have lost their self-assurance. The women in classical Iranian literature were a part—a very central part—of the narrator's world view, which in essence moved against the dictates of its world. In *Shams va Toghra* the narrator no longer has a coherent world view; nor does he have a sense of himself, his world, or the new fictional form he is working with. In other words, he is constantly vacillating between the old and the new ways of appraising 'reality' as well as fictional reality.

The women in *Shams va Toghra* have kept the guile of the women in earlier tales, but do not use it to subvert the hero's attitudes, or to defy the conventions of their world; guile is used as a means of survival in a world where submission has more worth than imagination, where no man would listen for one out of a thousand nights to the tales of a woman. The women in earlier tales used guile in order to survive as well as to subvert and change their men. In *Shams va Toghra* the women no longer subvert; they only submit.

Like the female images in the classical tales, the women in *Shams va Toghra* are idealizations. But unlike the earlier images, Khosravi's women characters are empty of connotations and meaning. They lack the luminosity and circularity of the women in the classical Iranian narratives, who feel more real to us even though their creators paid no homage to 'reality' or to what we call realism. Toghra and her female companions are mere figments of the narrator's imagination, products of a divided mind which is constantly confused by the new order of social and personal relations imposed upon it.

As the images of women within the Iranian narrative change from vision to daydream, their active and subversive function is turned into a passive and submissive one. The divided mind of the male narrator no longer can create a whole vision: it divides the whole image into fragments. None of the women in *Shams va Toghra* is rounded and complete; each of them represents a part of the complete woman; body, mind, and soul are disconnected. As Shams explains to the Queen, he needs three different women to satisfy his different needs.

As the mind discovers the roundness of the earth, as it begins to lose its own identity without gaining a new sense of wholeness (or roundness) of the self, it begins a process of disintegration in which it can no longer handle and control the 'reality' around it. This is the reason why these fictional women are not complete in themselves. They have moved away from the transcendental and unreal world of the earlier narratives to the concrete and 'earthy' world of the novel without gaining the individuality and particularity needed to illuminate and activate their presence. Without a private, individual self, without some 'interiority,' these images become orphans left in someone else's story. The women ruling with wit and majesty over the fertile land of classical Iranian literature are stripped and divided in the later romance-novels, and mutilated and murdered as in Hedayat's *Buf-e Kur* (*The Blind Owl*, Bombay, 1936). From then on, they wander around in the deserts of contemporary Iranian fiction, homeless, shadowy, and weightless.

The introduction of the novel in Iran coincides with many profound social changes which Tuba's father had the foresight to predict. One of the most important of these changes is the creation of new images for women, especially during Reza Shah's reign. The unveiling of women decreed by Reza Shah, like the veiling several decades later, caused an upheaval, and symbolically expressed conflicts and contradictions that ironically made women, without any major action or decision on their part, the center of hot and violent controversy.

During this period, almost simultaneously both 'realistic' and 'psychological' fiction started to be written. In both of these genres the role of women and women's relationships or lack of relationships with men are central. The images of women in these novels almost always become identical with, or symbolic of, the novel's central 'message.'

Sadeq Hedayat's short novel, *Buf-e Kur*, is divided into two parts, each a central metaphor for the other. Near the end of each part the narrator kills a woman—in essence the two aspects of the same woman. It seems as if in these two (symbolic) scenes the narrator mourns the breakdown of the idealized and sun-speckled relationships of men and women in classical fiction.

In a sense *Buf-e Kur* creates a distorted version of the typical classical Iranian tale. In this story all the elements of the previous narratives exist, only in reverse form. The narrator in *Buf-e Kur* too uses external 'reality' only to express his inner 'reality.' The women and men in his narration are mainly symbolic rather than real. In fact, the women in *Buf-e Kur* symbolize the two polarized images of the classical Iranian narrative: the inaccessible ethereal (*athiri*) woman and the all too accessible temptress (*lakkateh*). To the narrator in *Buf-e Kur*, however, both these women are inaccessible.

In this narration, Hedayat portrays not a vision, not a figment of the imagination, but an obsession which, as expressed in the famous opening lines, eats away all the narrator's moments and leads to his complete destruction. The reader is confronted with three different archetypal images of woman the mother, the beloved, and the whore. All carry seeds of destruction, all are madly desired, and two are destroyed by the narrator who never recovers.

Like the frame story of *One Thousand and One Nights*, *Buf-e Kur* demonstrates that the male character is not necessarily a victim of female guile, but rather a victim of his own obsessions. In both these stories the close and paradoxical interrelationship between the oppressed and the oppressor and the role the victim plays in her own oppression or liberation are demonstrated. But the female characters in *Buf-e Kur* are much more passive than the female characters in the classical Iranian narratives. There the women use their powers of imagination to save themselves and to create a new world; in *Buf-e Kur* the exact opposite happens. The attempt to communicate between the two sexes leads to the narrator's frustrating discovery of his own impotence—an impotence which is obviously symbolic of a helpless and disintegrating psyche. The only time he succeeds in making love to a woman is when he enters his wife's (*lakkateh*) bed, disguised as one of her many lovers; and the sexual act itself is so violent that in order to release himself from her grasp he 'inadvertently' kills her with a knife he has brought to bed with him. Sexual fulfillment and death become synonymous.

Buf-e Kur offers many interesting insights into the cultural assumptions underlying male–female relations in Iran. It also illustrates a breakdown of dialogue between men and women. In the novels which follow in the wake of *Buf-e Kur,* we observe a lack of dialogue (a sign of the disintegration of the psyche), and a lack of structural cohesion.

In *Buf-e Kur* the process of the self's disintegration leads to a replacement of dialogue with monologue, and to an urge toward destruction arising out of impotent desire. The male character in *Buf-e Kur* becomes the first in a series of impotent and obsessive characters who crowd contemporary Iranian fiction. The inability of writers to create active female characters and a dialogue between them and the male characters becomes a major obstacle to the development of the Iranian novel.

The disintegration of fictional characters in the Iranian novel may also point to a fundamental cultural problem, namely, the disintegration of the male Iranian psyche under the pressures and demands of two diametrically opposed cultures: one, the vanishing culture of the past with its unified and hierarchical view of women; the other, the modern western-imported culture of the present with its doubting, ironic view of the world and its fast-changing view of women.

The images of women in *Buf-e Kur* are said to be based upon the narrator's obsessions and his negation of 'reality,' but they are still more real and have more fictional life than the images which later appear in the so-called realistic novels. In these novels the preoccupation with women becomes so obsessive that unlike in *Buf-e Kur* it reveals the writer's own obsession. In these works the aesthetic distance between the writer and the work breaks down; there exists no cohesive structure which can place the images in creative relationship to one another. These narratives become veiled and insincere autobiographies; they also become loose and chaotic, not individualized and concrete—mere slogans, demonstrations of condescending goodwill toward women and unfulfilled, unnamed desires about them.

The main character's lament in Hushang Golshiri's *Barreh-ye Gomshodeh-ye Ra'i* (*Ra'i's Lost Lamb*, Tehran, 1977) is one of the best examples of what happens to the displaced male psyche, to a man's desire and longing for the security of his mother's closed and circular world that, like a womb, created space, blood, and nourishment for him. Ra'i decides to leave his beloved because she cuts her hair short, flings her bag over her shoulder, and might commit the ultimate blasphemy of dyeing her hair blonde. An unstated question hangs over the whole novel, creating an atmosphere almost of bewilderment: what happened to that tamely secure image of the raven-haired beauty who spent all her moments at the service of her man?

The secure male-dominated world of the past has broken down. What remains is the residue of the past in the writer's unconscious with no direct relationship to the new world. The mind is in constant struggle with this world. On the one hand, it desires to come to terms with the new reality; on the other hand, it has no firm grasp of it, no real understanding. A vague hostility and mistrust toward the new reality called the western world seeps into the Iranian novel, and colors the images of its women more than any other image.

The author becomes afraid of the suddenly real woman. In the past, the woman was a part of his vision; later she became a figment of his imagination, a tame if coyly evasive object of his desires—a presence which could be made to evaporate in the twinkling of an eye. To re-create fictionally a creature that he is wary of in reality becomes an almost impossible task.

Thus, something interesting happens in these novels: a movement away from the symbolic images of the classical tales, which somehow feel very real, to the 'real' images of 'realistic' fiction, which feel symbolic. The writer chooses a fixed pattern of thought, an ideology to define and capture this new 'reality,' stripping it of its threats, bringing it under control.

This process can be best observed in the 'realistic' tradition in Iranian literature. These 'realistic' novels were influenced mainly by the now archaic and anachronistic school of social realism. In structure, they followed the rigid and linear form of the nineteenth-century novel. The characters in these novels are supposed to be 'real,' from the working class or the peasantry.

The women in these works are usually patient and strong; their contradictions are mainly external, reflecting the class conflict within the society. They lack what I call 'interiority': the individuality, the inner conflicts and contradictions which give western realistic novels such amazing lights and shades. For example, Mahmud Dowlatabadi's *Ja-ye Khali-ye Soluch* (*Soluch's Empty Place*, Tehran, 1979) begins with Mergan, the heroine, waking up one morning to find that her husband has left her and their three children. From the very first page the narrator turns a theme which has many dimensions into a purely social issue. When describing Mergan and Soluch, he informs us in the tritest terms of how love becomes meaningless between people without money. At every crucial stage of the novel the narrator upstages his characters with tedious moralizations and unnecessary elaborations. The dialogues are constantly interrupted by the narrator addressing the reader.

Even novelists with no particular ideology share this attitude with the narrator in *Ja-ye Khali-ye Soluch*: they feel more committed to ideas than to the story or the characters in the story. Women as the most obvious victims of social injustice become the center of these novelists' moralizations and simplifications, and woman the victim becomes a popular theme in this literature.

The motif of women as victims dates back to Moshfeq Kazemi's *Tehran-e Makhowf* (*Tehran, the Fearsome*, Tehran, 1925). In Kazemi's novel all the prototypes of the socially victimized woman exist, from the beautiful young girl in love with a noble and penniless young man, harassed by greedy, insensitive parents, to the duped and penitent 'fallen woman.' From then on we encounter images of women as social victims in a number of novels which could be categorized under the dubious title of 'popular novel.' These women are either love-stricken, like the suffering young heroine in *Tehran-e Makhowf*, or, like Ahu in Ali-Mohammad Afghani's *Showhar-e Ahu Khanom* (*Ahu Khanom's Husband*, Tehran, 1961), are cheated by another favorite figure of popular novelists, the 'vamp' who steals the heroine's husband.

The popular novel develops into at least two different branches: the first is open and explicit about its form; it makes no pretensions at being literary art and exploits the theme of 'victimized woman' versus 'vamp' or 'greedy parents' to create tension and capture the reader's attention. Most outstanding in this group are the novels of Hosayn-Qoli Mosta'an. The second group shuns the first and claims to have 'serious' intentions. It uses images of women mainly as vehicles of social protest. Some of these writers, like Kazemi, are genuinely interested in the fate of women and their emancipation. But whatever these authors' intentions, their works combine two 'spicy' elements to appeal to their readers' self-righteousness and taste for 'action': women and social protest.[4]

The Iranian art novel was deeply influenced by the popular novel, especially in its use of male–female relationships as a vehicle to introduce action and justify moralizations, rather than as a theme worthy of exploration of its complexity and problems. If a popular novelist like Mosta'an used moralizing to justify risqué action, a more 'serious' novelist like Afghani used action to make ideological and social criticism palatable to the readers. Even a highly serious novelist like Sadeq Chubak in many short stories and in the well-known psychological novel *Sang-e Sabur* (*The Patient Stone*, Tehran, 1960) makes the fallen woman his central character. In Hedayat's *Buf-e Kur*, the 'lakkateh' is a powerful figure representing the narrator's obsessive personality as well as his moral and sexual impotence. In Chubak's novel the 'lakkateh' is transformed into a good-hearted prostitute, a caricature of the already caricature-like prostitutes in Dostoevsky's novel's.

In novel after novel, Iranian writers create and re-create two extreme and worn images of women, that of victims and that of bitches. In both cases the possibility of a meaningful male–female relationship becomes a mere mirage. With the exception of two novels written by women, no real attempt is made to untie the ropes of social protest from the captured images of women, to let the women lead us to whatever buried treasure they have hidden in the depths of their shadowy existence. But even the two well-known women writers, Daneshvar and Parsipur, are unable to represent the rich contradictions and inner complexities of their fictive characters.

In Simin Daneshvar's *Suvashun* (Tehran, 1969), the author tries to explore the sensibilities of a happily married woman, who nonetheless suffers from the uncompromising and heroic stance her husband takes against the corrupt Iranian regime and its foreign masters. Daneshvar's presentation of Zari creates some uneasiness in the reader; it seems as if beneath the straightforward and explicit descriptions of Zari's innermost feelings there exists some deep emotion which has found no expression, as if some deep resentment wishes to surface and mock Zari's most sacred loyalties. But Daneshvar never dwells on this hidden and disturbing aspect of Zari. At the end when her husband is killed, Zari takes up his political cause loyally and with conviction. Daneshvar, like her equally famous late husband, Jalal Al-e Ahmad, makes social statements through her characters. She, like him and a whole host of other writers, denounced ideology but followed Sartre's then popular dictum on the necessity of 'committed prose.' She simplified her heroine's real suffering, Zari's agony over having to choose between a husband she loves and an independence of mind she so desperately needs.

Shahrnush Parsipur's first long novel, *Sag va Zemestan-e Boland* (*The Dog and the Long Winter*, Tehran, 1976) is a first-person narration about the trials and tribulations of a young middle-class Iranian girl. In the first part she creates the illusory relations the girl is caught in. But in the second part suddenly the narrative breaks down, it switches from realistic presentation and description to a stream of associations involving the girl's dead brother, his imprisonment and sufferings. As in her later novel, *Tuba va Ma'na-ye Shab*, Parsipur begins with concrete images of a woman's life and then trails off into vague musings.

After the Islamic revolution, the formerly veiled and symbolic allusions to the political system and the government turned into overt and explicit criticisms of the Pahlavi era. In Reza Barahani's voluminous novel, *Razha-ye Sarzamin-e Man* (*Secrets of My Native Land*, Tehran, 1989), naive Armenian servant-girls and fully experienced wives of high Iranian officials are seduced by unfeeling and overpowering American soldiers. To compensate for this symbolic seduction of Iranian women and equally symbolic cuckolding of the Iranian men by the exploiting Americans, we have brave and heroic women such as Tahmineh, whose name is a reminder of the wife/mistress of Rustam, the unflinching Iranian legendary hero. She becomes the symbol of uncorrupted Iran.

In Barahani's *Avaz-e Koshtegan* (*Song of the Murdered*, Tehran, 1983), we have a rare attempt to portray a modern woman. But alas, she is the wife of the hero, a writer and university professor who is constantly harassed and tortured by the Savak. In response to his regrets over the insecure life he has made for his wife and daughter, the woman gives him, and the reader, a full lecture over three pages, in which she lauds him for exposing the Shah's regime to the whole world, while 'all were silent.' Unlike most men, she says, who 'used their beautiful wives' to gain wealth and power, he has taught her to assist him in his perilous work. She continues to eulogize him. Quoting from the great Iranian poet, Sa'di, she calls him the 'voice of the murdered.' She thanks him for 'granting' her the 'possibility' to 'wipe torture from the Iranian jails.' Thus, a very complex social and political issue is turned into a lusterless version of 'Mission Impossible,' and a many-levelled, multi-dialogued relationship is turned into a banal monologue echoing itself, the wife doing what the husband cannot do directly: use their relationship to create him as a hero.

Little wonder that the reader of these novels has an eerie feeling, as if the images avenging their mistreatment refused to come to life and refused to support their authors' claim that serious human issues are at stake. Generally in novels several layers of relationships are created in the interactions among individuals. The private world of these individuals becomes the flesh, the inner layer that gives substance to the other layers of social, moral, and philosophical matters. The images in most of the Iranian novels lack flesh. Their inability to have relationships turns the characters into mere echoes of one another and ultimately of their creator.

Esma'il Fasih's *Soraya dar Eghma* (*Soraya in Coma*, Tehran, 1983) is one of the few Iranian novels that attempt, in the best tradition of popular fiction, to create the image of a modern independent woman. It follows—in fact downright copies—Hemingway's *The Sun Also Rises* in terms of plot, theme, characters, and events. The romantically cynical hero leaves war-torn Iran for Paris to visit his niece, Soraya, who is hospitalized and in coma. There he meets several, mostly unsavory, Iranian exiles among whom he finds a very attractive, equally cynical, intellectual lady. She is so overpowering that the man becomes metaphorically impotent. All the other characters in the novel are like vague recollections of characters in Hemingway's novel. Neither the woman's showy and frustrated cynicism nor the hero's frustrated feelings for her create any deep or lasting impressions upon the reader.

In most of the novels written after the Islamic revolution, the images of women are continuations of the images in pre-revolutionary literature. These novels lack active interaction between male and female characters. Some, like Ahmad Mahmud's 'war novels,' have no main female character. In many of the others, dialogue between men and women is avoided by the absence of the men or by their psychological, if not physical, impotence. The young and controversial Muslim novelist and film-maker, Mohsen Makhmalbaf, dedicated his novel, *Bagh-e Bolur* (*The Crystal Garden*, Tehran, 1989) to 'the women, the oppressed women of this land.' This novel is crowded with women whose men have either been killed in the war or will be killed by the end of the novel. The novel ends with a strangely peaceful procession of widows and children with the only man left in the novel, one who has been castrated in the war.

Amir-Hosayn Cheheltan's *Talar-e Ayneh* (*The Hall of Mirrors*, Tehran, 1991), set around the time of Iran's Constitutional Revolution (1906), is again filled with women. The novel's main point seems to be the relationship or, better, the non-relationship between Mirza, a 'revolutionary' from an upper-class family, and his sick and dying wife. Their beautiful daughter is apparently an exact replica of her mother. Mirza is vaguely blamed, perhaps, for neglecting his loved and loving wife. This feeling, like all others, is never expressed concretely. The novel ends with the death of the wife. The grief-stricken husband is struck by the shadowy image of his daughter whom he mistakes for his dead wife. Seldom has a writer offered the readers so many dangling, and at times dazzling, images without life or substance.

Thus, throughout the 1980s the Iranian novel vacillates between the ideological commitment and the obsessional male projections, leaving women characters shallow and intangible. It is surprising and regrettable that such a sweeping generalization safely can be made about a major part of contemporary Iranian literature.

Over the past five or six years a new trend can be seen in the work of a younger generation of Iranian writers. Iranian fiction has entered a new era whose most distinctive feature is its transitory nature. The Islamic revolution, like any great upheaval, has shaken all values and norms within the society. Some norms have persisted or reappeared in different forms. But this era, in Iran as well as in the world itself, is generally an era of doubt and uncertainty. Now, the images of women have to be rethought and redefined. Under extreme pressure, women must look at themselves not only as members of their society or their country, but as individuals whose very private lives and liberties are being redefined.

In this state of flux, when everything is questioned, when the present feels more unreal than the past, the earlier seemingly tangible and real images of women can no longer function. In the most recent novels, the images seem to have gone on strike altogether, as if they refuse to work under the present conditions. In the new novels, especially those of younger writers (two of whom are women), the narrative voice either breaks down or becomes one long toneless monologue, and the characters are even more shadowy and unreal than in earlier novels. The novels express a tendency to preach, and doubt and uncertainty about what is being preached.

In *Tuba va Ma'na-ye Shab,* we see this process. The anecdote I quoted at the beginning of this chapter shows that Parsipur is aware of the Iranian male intellectuals' instinctive fear of the social issues directly related to women. In this sense, her novel, like Moniru Ravanipur's latest novel *Del-e Fulad* (*Heart of Steel*, Tehran, 1991), provides interesting insights. Both novels are about a woman's search for her place in the world. But this search never comes into focus, never becomes concrete, internalized or fictionally real. The heroine in Ravanipur's novel, a contemporary woman writer, is less tangible than a shadowy ghost in the mind of a delirious patient. Ravanipur skillfully generalizes her character out of existence.

Tuba va Ma'na-ye Shab also becomes one long narrative in the mind of its narrator/author. It begins with concrete images, but ends as a pseudo-philosophical treatise. Rather than creating interrelated images and voices, the novel presents a series of voices that are not differentiated, and which do not create dialogue. In essence, *Tuba va Ma'na-ye Shab* is just one voice, monotonous, at times hysterical, pouring out what has been stored up for many long years. The book's structure is based upon commentary and not image, monologue, not dialogue; and thus does not fit the form of the novel which is supposed to be multi-voiced, concrete, and individualized.[5] *Tuba va Ma'na-ye Shab* is almost frightening; it seems like an endless cry in the void. The Iranian novel for the past few years seems to have either created voices without images, as in *Tuba va Ma'na-ye Shab,* or images without voices, as in *Talar-e Ayneh.*

The importance of this stage in the history of the Iranian novel is its transitory nature and the doubt it has cast upon all previous fixed images. The tension between the novelist's tendency to preach and moralize and the uncertainty which runs counter to any form of preaching is an expression of this doubt. The contradictory quality of these novels makes them interesting; but it also makes the reader feel as if s/he was reading about images created in a void.

One further point needs to be mentioned, although its elaboration is beyond the scope of the present chapter. The literary problem in Iran is not only to create fictionally real and creatively subversive images of women, but also to create a proper framework that could embody such images. Also, unlike the claims made by some feminist critics about western women, the problem in Iran is not that Iranian women, as opposed to Iranian men, have not yet developed their own narratives, but that both women and men have as yet to create their own contemporary form of narrative, their own form of the novel.

Dialogue is by nature subversive; it simultaneously asserts one's own argument and undermines it by destabilizing it, turning it into a question through the other side's argument. Since its beginning, the Iranian novel has been only superficially subversive because its writers concentrated on social or political statements. There is a need for creating subversive literary images as well as dialogues among these images.

The images in the void teach us that without tracing the complexities and ambiguities which surround the modern woman, without understanding her private world, no coherent image of women can be created. In fact, a truly subversive novel would present the image of woman as a private self, and within that context would create many levels of reality surrounding and emanating from the self, including the social, historical, and philosophical levels of experience.

But writing in the void is better than writing according to fixed formulas. Courageously accepting the existence of this void perhaps will lead us to a creative reappraisal of where we stand in relation to our literary past and future.

Going back to the first example in this chapter, I agree with the *adib* that once women become aware of themselves, once they begin to think independently, they create a great upheaval. In the Iranian novel this upheaval has not yet happened; it has not as yet created the 'real' woman, the full woman, body, soul, and mind. Without her, men in the Iranian novel will continue to be either absent or impotent. The Iranian novel awaits that great moment, when those wise, strong, and gracious women of the classical Iranian narrative will find their worthy peers within contemporary Iranian fiction.

8· Veiled Vision/Powerful Presences: Women in Post-revolutionary Iranian Cinema

Hamid Naficy

In post-revolutionary Iran cinema is flourishing and women have begun to play a major role both behind and in front of the camera. This chapter will provide a brief historical account of women's involvement in film-making, and, more importantly, an investigation of fundamental principles which drive the representation of women on the screen. Specifically, the aims of this chapter are: first, to trace briefly the emergence of women directors of feature films in post-revolutionary Iran; second, to theorize on the manner in which the principles of modesty and sex segregation extend to relations of power and to the development of an aesthetics of veiling and unveiling and a system of looking—all of which are uniquely encoded in cinema; and third, to examine briefly the nascent theme of love in post-revolutionary cinema in the light of the evolving principles of modesty.

Women Directors

In the post-revolutionary Iranian cinema more women directors of feature films have emerged in a single decade than in all the decades of film-making preceding the revolution. This achievement was made possible partly by the incorporation of a complex system of modesty (*hejab* in its widest sense) at all levels of the motion picture industry and in the cinematic texts.[1] A major goal of this system was to disrupt the direct discursive link between the representation of women and the promotion of corruption, amorality, and pornography which the Pahlavi cinema is said to have established. To that end it became necessary for the post-revolutionary government to strengthen two existing discourses: the 'injection' theory of cinematic power and the 'realist illusionist' theory of cinematic representation. The injection theory posits that the mere exposure to unveiled or immodest women would turn autonomous, centered, and moral male individuals into dependent, deceived, and corrupted subjects. This is evident in the pronouncements of leading clerics, among them Ayatollah Khomeini, who made the following comment soon after coming to power:

> By means of the eyes they [the Shah's government] corrupted our youths. They showed such and such women on television and thereby corrupted our youth. Their whole objective was to make sure that no active force would remain in the country that could withstand the enemies of Islam so they could do with impunity whatever they wanted.[2]

The realist illusionist theory claims a direct and unmediated correspondence between 'reality' and its representation (illusion) on the screen. For the illusion to be Islamically modest, reality had to become (or be made to appear) modest. This necessitated a 'purification' process for women on and off the screen. The film industry now is open to women as never before as long as women abide by very specific and binding 'Islamic' codes of modesty involving dressing, looking, behaving, acting, and filming. These codes, first instituted in 1982, have evolved gradually and steadily toward liberal interpretations. The evolution of the codes and the use of women both behind and in front of the cameras have occurred in three overlapping phases: absence, pale presence, and powerful presence of women.[3]

During the first phase, immediately after the revolution (early 1980s), the images of unveiled women were cut from existing Iranian and imported films. When cutting caused unacceptable narrative confusion, the offending parts were blacked out directly in the frames with markers. In local productions, women were excised from the screens through self-censorship by a frightened industry unsure of official attitudes and regulations regarding cinema.

In the second phase (mid-1980s), women appeared on the screen as ghostly presences in the background or 'domesticated' in the home environment. Women rarely were the bearers of the story or the plot. An aesthetics and grammar of vision and veiling based on gender segregation developed, which governed the characters' dress (long, loose-fitting), behavior and acting (dignified, no body contact between men and women), and gaze (averted look, no direct gaze). The evolving grammar of filming discouraged close-up photography of women's faces or of exchanges of desirous looks between men and women. In addition, women were often filmed in long shot and in inactive roles so as to prevent the contours of their bodies from showing. Both women and men were desexualized and cinematic texts became androgynous. Love and the physical expression of love (even between intimates) were absent.

The third phase has appeared gradually (since the late 1980s) and is marked by a more dramatic presence of women both on the screen in strong leading roles and behind the camera as directors. *Beh Khater-e Hameh Chiz* (*For Everything*, 1991), directed by Rajab Mohammadin, is an example of the changed portrayal of women on the screen. All the actors are women in this film, which examines the difficult lives of garment workers with moving realism. Mohammadin's own comments about his film express the perception of the changes: 'Previously, Iranian women were being portrayed as miserable, ignorant and superficial creatures being used by men as objects or for decorative purposes. I wanted to tell a story in which women were virtuous, active, and socially constructive.'[4] The strong presence of women behind the camera was officially recognized in 1990, when the 9th Fajr Film Festival—the foremost national film festival in Iran—devoted an entire series of programs to 'women's cinema.'[5] Of particular significance in this cinema is the emergence of a new cadre of women directors of feature films trained after the revolution (see Table 8.1). Prior to the revolution, only one woman, Shahla Riahi, had directed a feature film (*Marjan*, 1956).[6] Today, there are at least seven women directors active.

In the last decade, Iran's women directors have been prolific. Several women have directed one or more films a year. Increase in quantity, however, has not been matched by a corresponding improvement in quality, which remains uneven. It would be inaccurate to assume or to expect that women directors working in the Islamic Republic necessarily present a better rounded or a more radically feminist perspective in their films than do male directors. This is particularly true for the years immediately after the revolution, but since then the situation has gradually and steadily improved. Looking at the film career of one of the most active and accomplished women

Table 8.1. Women Directors of Feature Films in Post-revolutionary Iran

Director's name	Films directed	Production year
Tahmineh Ardekani	*Golbahar*	1365/1986
Feryal Behzad	*Kakoli*	1369/1990
	Darreh-ye Shaparakha (*Valley of the Moths*)	
Rakhshan Bani-E'temad	*Kharej az Mahdudeh* (*Off the Limit*)	1366/1987
	Zard-e Qanari (*Canary Yellow*)	1368/1989
	Pul-e Khareji (*Foreign Currency*)	1369/1990
	Narges	1371/1992
Marziyeh Borumand	*Shahr-e Mushha* (*City of Mice*)	1364/1985
Puran Derakhshandeh	*Rabeteh* (*Mute Contact*)	1365/1986
	Parandeh-ye Kuchak-e Khoshbakhti (*Little Bird of Happiness*)	1368/1990
	Zaman-e az Dast Rafteh (*Lost Time*)	1369/1990
	Obur az Ghobar (*Passing Through the Dust*)	1369/1990
Tahmineh Milani	*Bachehha-ye Talaq* (*Children of Divorce*)	1369/1990
	Afsaneh-ye Ah (*Legend of the Sigh*)	1370/1991
	Tazeh Cheh Khabar? (*What's New?*)	1371/1992
Kobra Sa'idi	*Maryam va Mani* (*Maryam and Mani*)	1359/1980

directors, Rakhshan Bani-E'temad, it becomes clear that her artistic development parallels the transformations from the first to the third phase of Iranian cinema itself. In her first feature film, *Off the Limit*, Bani-E'temad uncritically shows a wife so confined to the home that her husband must do the shopping for daily necessities. American and Iranian audiences abroad have consistently expressed surprise that a director of such a traditional representation of women is a woman herself. In her next film, *Canary Yellow*, however, the director depicts the women of a family, particularly the mother, to be strong, mature, and level-headed and the men of the family as either naive, unscrupulous, or silent. Finally, in her last film, *Narges*, she not only continues to focus on the lives of ordinary—even marginal—people, but also transgresses the limits on the depiction of love in the cinema by examining a love triangle involving two women and a man. Bani-E'temad won the first prize in the 1992 Fajr Film Festival for directing *Narges*, the first woman in the Iranian cinema to garner such an award for a feature film. This is a recognition by the film industry and the public alike not only of Bani-E'temad's own development and maturity as a director but also of the contribution of women to cinema.

Whereas Bani-E'temad's style may be labeled as social realism, Puran Derakhshandeh's style may be designated psychological realism. Bani-E'temad's cinema is largely satirical, whereas Derakhshandeh's works are chiefly somber. Derakhshandeh's films examine the theme of lack of communication, often by focusing on handicapped people (usually women), whom she takes as symbols of 'all those who are internally handicapped in our society.'[7] Whether it is a deaf boy in *Mute Contact*, a deaf and mute girl in *Little Bird of Happiness*, or an infertile gynecologist in *Lost Time*, the 'affliction' is handled with a kind of humanism characteristic of the post-revolutionary ethical cinema. In the first two films, the handicapped children are helped by women who make the effort to establish contact with them, and in the latter film the infertile gynecologist realizes that her individuality, professionalism, and marital happiness depend less on her as a mother than on her as a human being.

In her second film, *Legend of the Sigh*, Tahmineh Milani deals with a subject rare in Iranian cinema: women intellectuals. A frustrated female writer in a creative crisis sighs deeply, only to have the sigh materialize as a kind character who enables her to become five different people. The possibility of having multiple identities and the freedom to choose one or several of them, however, seems to have been thwarted for at least one reviewer who noted that 'in the end she [the writer] finds out that under any circumstance she is a helpless, humiliated, and dependent person, that because of her physical and psychological makeup, she is a captive of ruthless and selfish men.'[8] On the other hand, the High Council of the Ministry of Islamic Guidance, perhaps sensing the subversive potential of multiple identities and the individual's right to choose one or another identity, declared that 'the characters of this film do not provide appropriate role models for our youth.' For at least six months the council refused to grant the film an exhibition permit.[9]

While women's presence as directors is impressive, women are underrepresented in many technical areas of the film industry such as production, distribution, and exhibition.[10] Generally, the strong presence of women in the post-revolutionary cinema has been achieved through persistent negotiation between film-makers, spectators, and government bureaucrats charged with regulating and promoting cinema.

The Constitution of the Self and of Vision

In many non-western societies with strong hierarchical and group contextual relationships, including Iran, the self is not fully individuated or unified as it is purported to be in the West, but is thought to be familial and communal, that is, defining itself foremost as part of one's family and community. This produces a contradiction between an inner 'core' or private self and an outer 'shell' or public self—both of which are integral to the overall sense of the self. Psychologically, the core is supposed to be private, stable, intimate, and reliable while the exterior is construed to be unstable and unreliable, the domain of surfaces, corruption, and worldly influences.[11] The self's duality necessitates a boundary zone—however amorphous and porous—which can be thought of as a veil or a screen. This veil or screen protects the core from contamination from the outside and, acting similarly to 'screen memory,'[12] prevents the core from leaking to the outside. It accomplishes this by triggering various defensive strategies of camouflage, dissimulation, disavowal, aversion, indirection, evasiveness, cleverness, self-presentation, and ritual courtesy. These strategies are used in Iran to hide what is most pure and valued—the inner self. Veiling thus is operative within the self and is pervasive within the culture.[13] In traditional architecture the hidden core is expressed by the inner quarters of the house, occupied by women and the family, while the outer sphere is embodied in the outer quarters, occupied by men and visitors. The gendered spatial configuration informs strategies of veiling and unveiling in both social and discursive practices.[14] Instances of veiling abound in Iranian culture: the inner rooms of a house protect/hide the family; the veil hides women, decorum and status hide men; high walls separate and conceal private space from public space; the exoteric meanings of religious texts hide the esoteric meanings; and the perspective-less miniature paintings convey their messages in layers instead of organizing a unified vision for a centered viewer.[15]

The practice of veiling motivates people to search for hidden, inner meanings in all they see, hear, receive in daily interaction with others; to interpret constantly all products of social interactions, while trying to conceal their own intentions at the same time. Iranian hermeneutics is based on the primacy of hiding the core values (that is, of veiling) and of distrusting manifest meanings (that is, vision).[16] Since women are a constitutive part of the male core self, they must be protected from the vision of unrelated males by following a set of rules of modesty which apply to dress, behavior, eye contact, and relations with men. These include veiling: with the onset of menses, women must cover their hair, body parts, and body shape by wearing either a veil (a head-to-toe cloth) or some other modest garb, including head scarf, loose tunic, and long pants. Further, the related/unrelated rules (*mahram/namahram*) govern the segregation and association of men and women: a woman need not wear a veil in front of male members of her immediate family (her husband, sons, brothers, father, and uncles). All other men are considered unrelated and women must veil themselves in their presence and men must avert their eyes from them. In the aesthetics of veiling, the voice has a complementary role: before entering a house, men are required to make their presence known by voice in order to give the women inside a chance to cover themselves or to organize the scene for the male gaze.

It must be emphasized that veiling as a social practice is not fixed or unidirectional; instead, it is a dynamic practice in which both men and women are implicated. In addition, there is a dialectical relationship between veiling and unveiling: that which covers is capable also of uncovering. In practice, women have a great deal of latitude in how they present themselves to the gaze of the male onlookers, involving body language, eye contact, types of veil worn, clothing worn underneath the veil, and the manner in which the veil itself is fanned open or closed at strategic moments to lure or to mask, to reveal or to conceal the face, the body, or the clothing underneath.[17] Shahla Haeri aptly notes the dynamic relationship that exists between the veil and vision:

> [N]ot only does the veil deny the penetrating male gaze, it enables women to use their own judiciously. Because men and women are forbidden to socialize with each other, or to come into contact, their gazes find new dimensions in Muslim Iran. Not easily controllable, or subject to religious curfew, glances become one of the most intricate and locally meaningful means of communication between the genders.[18]

This 'communication' involves not only voyeurism and exhibitionism but also a system of surveillance, of controlling the look and of being controlled by the look. Veiling-unveiling, therefore, is not a panoptic process in the manner Foucault[19] describes because in this system vision is not unidirectional or in the possession of only one side. Both women and men see and organize the field of vision of the other.[20]

The social principles of modesty and veiled vision govern male–female social interactions in daily life as well as in the movies. In post-revolutionary cinema, however, they are more pronounced than they were before. In the remainder of this chapter I will focus on a discussion of modesty, veiling, and unveiling as inscribed chiefly in filmic texts.

Veiling and Unveiling in the Cinema

In Iran, modesty in its most general sense was encoded in the regulations put into effect in 1982 which govern the film industry. According to these regulations, Muslim women must be shown to be chaste and to have an important role in society as well as in raising God-fearing and responsible children.[21] Women, further, must not be treated like a commodity or used to arouse sexual desires.[22] These general and ambiguous guidelines have had profound effects on the use and portrayal of women in cinema. The most significant, in the period immediately after the revolution (phase 1), is self-censorship of film-makers or avoidance altogether of stories involving women in order to evade entanglement with the censors.[23] Women rarely were the bearers of the story or the plot. Statistics compiled by Purmohammad show a very low presence of women heroes in films made as late as 1987: of 37 films he reviewed, the chief protagonist in 25 films was a man, in three a woman, and in seven men and women shared equal billing.[24]

Until recently (phase 3), if women were cast at all, they were given small parts as housewives or as mothers, reflecting the roles for women stipulated in the regulations. Further, various forms of modesty imposed on women in the movies have tended to distort the portrayal of family life and love relationships because women are shown covering themselves even in front of close relatives. Modesty also has necessitated so-called Islamic behavior on screen: women must be dignified and avoid activities and movements that show even as little as the contours of their bodies through their modest attire. As a result of this demand, women actors usually were given static parts or were filmed in such a way as to avoid showing their bodies.[25] In addition, this code of behavior forbids physical contact between men and women (even if they are related by marriage or by birth). Like the dress code, the code of behavior undermines the veracity of relationships and the expression of feelings on the screen. In the first six years after the revolution, principles of modesty encoded in these regulations made it structurally impossible to produce a 'realistic' representation of women.

In addition, these principles tended to undermine the art of acting and to create problems for the female actors who had to try to express their feelings to their screen fathers, brothers, sons, and uncles in psychologically unrealistic ways, without touching them.[26] Principles of modesty have also affected the manner in which actors look at one another and the way the camera films them. These will be explored in the next section. Moreover, these principles have forced film-makers to avoid certain historical periods (such as the late Pahlavi era) which were declared incompatible with principles of modesty. Such constraints—which have gradually lessened—have affected the relationships among men on the screen as well, resulting in fascinating gender reconfiguration and reinscription. For example, in *Noqteh-e Za'f* (*The Weak Point*, 1983) directed by Mohammad Reza A'lami, the relationship between a political activist and the security agent who captures him displays strong but deeply ambiguous and incommensurate sexual undercurrents in an Islamic society which severely punishes homosexuality or gender crossovers. In the film, the two men are interacting as though one of them (the captive) was a woman. The two engage in activities that are shown typically in boy-meets-girl-falls-in-love formula films. Playing soccer in the park, they pass the ball back and forth to each other like two lovers, and at the beach, seated side by side, they gaze at the horizon while a wild horse gallops by and an extradiegetic (outside the filmed world) romantic music seals the moment.[27]

The aesthetic of veiling which governs the actors' behavior, dress, emotional expression, and the narrative structure of a film also affects the mise-en-scène and the filming style. Nowhere is this more clearly visible than in the film *Off the Limit*, directed by the woman director, Bani-E'temad. The film is about a young couple who discover that their newly acquired home is located in a district that has been omitted accidentally from city zoning maps, and for all intents and purposes does not exist and is not subject to the jurisdiction and protection of any legal or police authority. As a result, thieves and robbers have a field day in this no-man's-land, which ironically is called 'Chaos City' (*Hertabad*). The residents are placed off limit, out of bounds, and therefore made invisible (veiled). However, in a move toward self-determination (visibility), they begin to enforce the laws themselves, capturing the thieves, and reforming them. The name of the city is changed to 'New City' (*Nowabad*). In a society racked by revolutionary chaos, where all previous boundaries have become problematized, the film seems to urge a positivist, can-do attitude to create new boundaries and to restore order. This order, however, is potentially no less problematic than the chaos which it replaces.

Boundaries not only regulate the society within the diegesis (the world of the film) but also the visual style and the mise-en-scène of the film. Vision is constantly obstructed by objects and boundary-marking features such as fences, walls, and columns. Long tracking shots with these obstacles in the foreground highlight them as visual barriers. These can be taken as metaphors for modesty (*hejab*) which sets women apart from men and purportedly protects them from the male gaze. The reciprocity of veiling and unveiling necessitates that the obstructions which seem to conceal certain things from view also serve to reveal something, namely, the intention of the director. Indeed, in one of the early shots of the film, before the residents of Chaos City have realized their zoning problem, the camera looks down from above the walls of a house into the adjacent street. In the background we see the male protagonist walking down the street, parallel to a wall. In the foreground, a fence made of barbed wire and dry bushes on top of the wall is partially obstructing the view of the street below. Toward the end of the film, after the community has become energized and has taken up the enforcement of the laws, we see a similarly composed shot, but with a major difference. The foreground is no longer a decrepit fence but a row of beautiful flowers in full bloom. Clearly, the director's activist vision that beauty and prosperity require political will and independent action is inscribed in the visual style of veiling and unveiling the film.

Modesty and the System of Looking

The constitution of the self as dual means that a series of distances are posited—between inside and outside, self and other, and women and men. Additionally, since the constitution of the self as familial and communal is not total or hermetic, distance is always created between individual sovereignty and group membership. These and other forms of dualities, splitting, and separations create ambivalences and a desire for unity through reunion of subject and object, with profound repercussions for vision and hearing.

Distance is a constitutive component of pleasure derived from looking. Freud posited scopophilia (pleasure in looking at another as an object of sexual stimulation) as a libidinal drive that works through pleasure and unpleasure. In its pleasurable aspect, scopophilia demands a distance between subject and object because 'it is in the play of absence and distance that desire is activated.'[28] Veiling and the system of looking which has developed to deal with it hide aspects of women (and to some extent of men) and thereby create the necessary distance that motivates and promotes pleasurable looking as well as listening. They also tend to turn the object of the look into an erotic object. Veiled women thus may become highly charged with sexuality, which ironically subverts the purpose of the religious principles of veiling and the 'commandments of looking' (see below), namely to protect women from becoming sexual objects. A person draws pleasure from listening to or viewing a scene that he/she is not supposed to be privy to. To be sure, walls and veils segregate people but they do not isolate them completely. Indeed, they tend to invite curiosity and afford pleasure through voyeurism and eavesdropping. Overtly repressive, veiling promotes not only voyeurism and its obverse, exhibitionism (unveiling), but also a culture of surveillance. These effects of veiling are inflected in Iranian miniature paintings in the figures shown inside homes, palaces, and gardens who are peering or listening from behind windows, curtains, doors, and bushes.

The Islamic system of looking and the semiotic of veiling and unveiling as developed in Iran seem to be based on at least four suppositions. First, the eyes are not passive organs like ears which merely gather information from the outside world and transmit it to the brain for processing. Eyes are active, even invasive organs, whose gaze is also construed to be inherently aggressive.[29] This notion is condensed in the following quote by Ayatollah Ali Meshkini: 'Looking is rape by means of the eyes . . . whether the vulva admits or rejects it, that is, whether actual sexual intercourse takes place or not.'[30] Second, women's sexuality is so 'excessive' and powerful that if it is uncontained or if men are allowed unhampered (unveiled) visual access through the gaze, it is supposed to lead inevitably to the wholesale moral corruption of men and of society as a whole. Third, men are utterly weak vis-à-vis women's sexual powers. A woman's look at a man or a man's look at a woman is expected to set in motion a progression of events which inevitably culminate in improper sexual relations.[31] Fourth, women are inherently exhibitionistic, as Ayatollah Motahhari has stated: '[t]he desire to show off and display one's self is a particular trait of women.'[32] Therefore, the Islamic edict to cover is addressed only to women.

The Gaze and Spectator Positioning

These suppositions carry important theoretical implications for cinematic spectatorship. In western film theory the male gaze is construed as an aggressive, controlling, sadistic agent that supports phallocentric power relations.[33] Traditionally, two chief types of looks have been identified in cinema: one based on scopophilia and the other based on identification of the looker with the object of the look. The first type of look, based on Freud's theories, is voyeuristic. The second, based on Lacan's theories, is narcissistic. In both types of looks, the aggressive male gaze is said to turn the woman into an object for men's pleasure, to be looked at, to be controlled, to be possessed. There is, however, a third type of look, based on the concept of masochism.[34] This type, derived from Deleuze's theories,[35] is very relevant to the type of look necessitated by modesty because masochistic identification seems to account for ascribing 'excessive' power to women over men by pointing to the aberrant pleasure the men draw from being subjected to this female power.

The Islamist reading of the gaze seems to correspond to the masochistic interpretation because it posits that the owner of the look is more affected by his/her own look at another than is the target of the look. Men's postulated weakness in sexual temptation by women is the source of men's pleasure. Although men try to control women through their gaze, they are lured and captured by the sight of women and, in the words of one writer, are thereby 'humiliated' and made 'abject' by them—a situation from which men draw pleasure.[36] Likewise, as spectators, women obtain masochistic pleasure from being 'controlled' by looks from men, and from watching women being looked at, controlled, and possessed by men. While both men and women draw masochistic pleasure as spectators, the source of pleasure is different: men draw pleasure from being 'humiliated' by women while women obtain pleasure by being 'controlled' by men.

If the masochistic effect of the gaze on its male owner is not only based on the overcathexis of sexuality in women but also on the pleasure men draw from their own 'abjection,' it is germane to examine the sources of this abject pleasure. In the moral discourse, film's putative power to introduce corruption and perversion in its audience stems from the film's direct relationship with pornography. About the effects of pornography in films on spectators, Zizek has noted:

> Contrary to the commonplace according to which, in pornography, the other [the person shown on the screen] is degraded to an object of our voyeuristic pleasure, we must stress that it is the spectator him- or herself who effectively occupies the position of the object. The real subjects are the actors on the screen trying to rouse us sexually, while we, the spectators, are reduced to a paralyzed object-gaze.[37]

The look that places the spectator in such an awkward, perverse position is the one exchanged between the actors on the screen engaged in pornographic acts. It is also the 'look' of the projected film at the spectators, causing them to sense that they have been caught in the act of viewing voyeuristically a socially perverse act. This realization of the returned look of the screen turns the pleasure of voyeurism to unpleasure, inducing in the audience a feeling of shame and discomfort.[38] Since in the Islamist discourse the sight of unveiled, unrelated women represents pornography, this formulation explains why men of necessity must feel humiliation and shame when exposed to such views: the owners of the look (spectators) as well as the subjects of the look (actors) are thereby debased and humiliated.

The Averted Look

Modesty and the psychology and the ideology of the dual self tend to produce a unique system of looking which prevents or, alternatively, encourages, the masochistic pleasure of humiliation and abjection. In Iran, major religious leaders (*mojtaheds*), such as the Ayatollahs Khomeini and Sayyed Abolqasem Musavi Kho'i,[39] in their books have developed or affirmed 'commandments for looking' (*ahkam-e negah kardan*). These commandments, for example, forbid males or females to look, with or without lust, at bare bodies or body parts of the people of the opposite sex to whom they are unrelated. Males are forbidden to look at women's hair and women are obliged to cover it. Looking at sexual organs of others is forbidden whether it is done directly, through a glass, in a mirror or reflected in water (or, by extension, in the movies).[40]

In reality, of course, men and women do look at each other even with desire and lust, but to satisfy the rules of modesty, a situationist grammar of looking has evolved that ranges from direct gaze to what I have called the averted look. In this case people avoid looking at others directly. People of lower status avoid looking directly at people of higher status and traditionalists in particular avoid direct eye contact with unrelated men and women. When meeting each other, they tend to look down or to look at the other's face in an unfocused way so as to avoid definitive eye contact.[41] On the other hand, someone who is not looking, or a stranger (an unrelated person), is scrutinized with a direct gaze. This play between the averted and the direct gaze is partially responsible for the contradictory impression by outsiders that Iranians are both evasive (shifty) and aggressive (pushy).

At first glance, the averted look appears to be the opposite of Zizek's 'looking awry,' an anamorphic look that, according to him, makes things clearer than does the direct gaze because it is charged (and is distorted) with the desires and anxieties of the looker, thereby producing an object that is clear and distinctive.[42] On closer examination, however, the averted look proves to be anamorphic like the awry look because, on the one hand, it is charged with voyeuristic and masochistic desires of the looker and, on the other hand, it inscribes the codes of modesty, thus producing understandings that are clearer than those obtainable through the unveiled direct gaze.

The play of the gaze between direct and averted was inscribed in Iranian cinema during the pre-revolutionary Pahlavi era. However, because the direct gaze of desire was prohibited after the 1979 revolution, the averted, unfocused look has been predominant in film ever since. A prominent contemporary film actress told me in an interview in 1988 that actors and actresses have been discouraged from establishing direct or desirous eye contact in cinema.[43] My own review of over fifty films made since the revolution confirms the existence of these aesthetic and moral proscriptions in the acting style and in cinematography. With few recent exceptions, men and women on the screen do not look at each other with desire; in fact, the look, which in the pre-revolutionary era was often direct and highly cathexted with sexuality, has been desexualized. As a prominent director, Dariush Mehrju'i, told me: 'In post-revolutionary cinema the religiously unlawful (*haram*) look does not exist. Women must be treated like one's own sister.'[44] The desexualized look is the cinematic equivalent of the averted or the unfocused face-to-face look. Among the consequences of the cinematic neutralization of the look are the avoidance of close-ups of women and also of shots showing men and women looking at each other directly. In addition, for quite some time after the revolution, women were usually filmed only in long and medium shots. All of these factors tend to subvert the system of 'suture' (symbolic insertion of spectators into the film's story) based on point-of-view shots and on the direct (unveiled) relay of the gazes between characters in shot reverse-shot situations. The unfocused look, the averted look, the fleeting glance, the desexualized look, and the long-shot—all instances of inscription of modesty in cinema—problematize the western cinematic theories which rely on audience implication through suturing because they impede audience identification with characters on the screen.

Absent also is the kind of glamorous close-up photography resulting from direct gaze that highlights the physical beauty of the woman, which tends to transform her image into something satisfying in itself, promoting fetishistic scopophilia. If the figure of the female is a threat to the male, as some feminist theorists posit, in post-revolutionary Iranian cinema it is not disavowed or coopted by fetishism, but by voyeurism.

Inscribing the Spectator in the Text

In the classic Hollywood cinema style, the spectator is made 'invisible' through various strategies of mise-en-scène, shot composition, and editing which do not acknowledge the presence of the spectators—thus turning them into voyeurs.[45] Spectators, however, are not just subjects of the film texts but subjects also in history, and their relationship to the film is not merely textual or psychological but also social. As social rules, the rules of modesty in Iran implicate the spectators. In post-revolutionary Iran, spectators are considered to be unrelated (*namahram*) to the persons projected on the screen and thus must be treated as if they were present at the time of filming. This necessitates that women and men within the diegesis observe the rules of modesty and the codes of dress, gaze, and behavior not only in relationship to each other but also vis-à-vis the spectators. As unrelated spectators, film audiences cannot be privy to intimate moments between related males and females, such as exchange of amorous gazes and body contact (touching, hugging, or kissing). This forces the actors playing the parts of husband and wife, for example, in the privacy of their bedroom to behave as though they were not alone. It makes the private space public and renders modesty triumphant. Thus, in post-revolutionary Iranian cinema, the spectator is not only encoded in the film text through strategies of editing and suture but also is inscribed in the profilmic situation itself. This creates a real dilemma for directors as well as for actors, male and female. Mohsen Makhmalbaf, an Islamist film-maker and the most well-known and promising film director to emerge since the revolution, explained the dilemma:

> Suppose in your screenplay you are showing the private life of a husband and wife. If the woman covers her face really well because of the presence of spectators, this action would indicate either a lack of intimacy or the existence of a dispute [between the husband and the wife] and naturally in real life something like this [veiling of intimates] would not occur. If we want to show them walking around in such a manner as though they are husband and wife (even if they are so in real life), then it becomes un-Islamic because spectators are unrelated to that woman.[46]

The central message here is this: when in doubt, err on the side of veiling, that is, inscribe the spectators as structurally unrelated to the screen.

Love Enters

Recently, however, tentative steps have been taken by film-makers to question, and even subvert, the averted gaze and the inscription of modesty and asexual behavior, producing a fluid cinematic atmosphere and a number of transgressive filmic texts. For example, the theme of love, which was almost absent from films in phases 1 and 2 because of restrictions on dress, looking, touching, acting, mise-en-scène, and cinematography, has begun to be explored in a few recent, phase 3, films. As expected, however, this has proven to be a very sensitive subject, fraught with contentiousness and uncertainty. Fakhreddin Anvar, a deputy director of the Ministry of Islamic Guidance, noted this situation when he said:

> In poetry we have had a tremendous amount of experience with this matter [love] but in cinema we have no expertise. Should we close this area off and say that no one at all can enter it and no one at all may consider it? . . . We cannot shut the door on this matter, which has a range beginning with love for humankind and for society and extends to love for God almighty. In this arena, the distance between health and salvation and deviation and perversion is as thin as a hair's width.[47]

This sensitivity toward the hitherto taboo subject of love has resulted in conflicting reactions to film-makers who have dared to approach the subject openly. Until recently, films such as Bahram Beiza'i's *Bashu, Gharibeh-ye Kuchak* (*Bashu, the Little Stranger*, 1985) dealt with heterosexual love in an indirect and oblique manner, sometimes by using children as substitutes for adults, particularly for women. This multidimensional film deals with issues of ethnic diversity, nationalism, war, dislocation, and exile deftly and dramatically. The narrative fabric is interwoven with the textured relationship of Na'i, a single mother in rural northern Iran, and Bashu, a boy from Khuzestan escaping the Iraqi attacks. Women have always played a central role as narrative agents in Beiza'i's films and, in *Bashu, the Little Stranger*, Na'i occupies such a position: she works her fields, takes care of her children and, in accepting the dislocated boy, defies tradition and the authority of her family and village elders. What adds to the enrichment of this relationship is the ambiguous position of Bashu both as a boy Na'i takes care of and protects and as a man she nurtures and loves and on whom she depends. When her children warn her of the presence of Bashu the stranger among the bushes, Na'i is off camera and the film cuts to a shot showing empty space. Suddenly, Na'i rises into the frame in a surprising close-up, her hair and chin covered with a white scarf, emphasizing her dramatic and intense eyes. With this one shot, which draws attention to the alluring possibilities of unveiled vision, direct gaze, and scopophilia, Beiza'i breaks years of entrapment of films by rules of modesty. Defying those rules, Na'i gazes directly into the camera in close-up—something that she does several time henceforward. Visually addressing both the spectators sitting in their seats and Bashu hidden in the bushes, this shot conflates their points of view with the result that from then on both the spectators and Bashu can be said to be subjects of Na'i's gaze just as Na'i is the subject of theirs. In this way, Bashu becomes a substitute for the spectators: men identify with him vis-à-vis Na'i as a man, and women see him as a surrogate son or brother. This ambiguity turns him into a dual vehicle, sending and receiving both love and compassion. Finally, the direct relay of looks between the characters in *Bashu, the Little Stranger* positions the spectators as related to the characters, thereby ensuring their suture into the diegesis. Unlike Makhmalbaf, here Beiza'i clearly favors unveiling, but working within the confines of a modesty-driven society, love enters his film only indirectly, intricately, and ambiguously. That the film's release was delayed for quite some time may have less to do with its implicit anti-war message (which is the usual reason given) than with its bold transgression of codes of modesty and spectator positioning.

In the 1991 Fajr Film Festival, for the first time since the revolution, four feature films dealing directly with the theme of heterosexual love were screened: *Shabha-ye Zayandehrud* (*Zayandehrud Nights*) and *Nowbat-e Asheqi* (*A Time to Love*) both directed by Mohsen Makhmalbaf, *Naqsh-e Eshq* (*Image of Love*) directed by Shahriar Parsipur, and *Sayeh-ye Khial* (*Shadow of the Imagination*) directed by Hosayn Dalir (all the directors are male). While the latter two were considered by some film reviewers[48] to have exhibited attributes of 'spiritual and mystical' love and thus were accepted, Makhmalbaf's films were rejected on the grounds that, among others, they encouraged 'carnal and earthly' love, especially *A Time to Love* which explored the possibility of a ménage à trois. It seems that the director, who had begun as an 'Islamically committed' film-maker, had finally crossed the 'hair's width' of the line noted earlier that separated the acceptable from the unacceptable treatment of love. He was also accused of overtly supporting the revolution and its ideals while maintaining a hidden link to its enemies.[49] Even though he defended himself publicly against a critical campaign launched in opposition to him and his films[50] both films were shelved after their festival premières and have not been screened publicly. That only a year later Bani-E'temad received the best director award for her film *Narges*, involving a love triangle theme, a narrative emphasizing the psychology of male–female relationships, and a filming style highlighting the direct gaze, demonstrates the shifting and multilayered contexts within which the post-revolutionary cinema works.

The shift toward a bolder treatment of love and transgressive looking, however, seems to be taking root. Several recent films questioned the semiotics of the gaze and the aesthetics of vision and veiling—so far with positive results. For instance, the film *Arus* (*Bride*, 1991), directed by Mehrdad Fakhimi, centered on the love relationship between a newly-wed couple. It utilized close-up photography of the bride's face and the direct gaze in ways that border on fetishistic scopophilia, but the film was widely exhibited, became the talk of the town, and garnered the highest box office record in the history of Iranian cinema. The switch in this film from the averted glance to the direct gaze might be one significant reason for its popularity with audiences and the popular press. In *Bride*, *Narges*, and other recent films heterosexual love is expressed more directly than in films of half a decade ago, such as *Bashu, the Little Stranger*, and it is accomplished without children as substitutes for adults.

The institutionalization of modesty in post-revolutionary cinema which discouraged the expression of emotions and intimacy between men and women has interesting consequences for the interpretation of scenes shot in the somewhat relaxed new style. For example, mere close-ups of women or two-shots showing a man and woman alone together engaged in simple conversation may be coded by the director and decoded by spectators as intimate love scenes even though the contents of the shot itself do not show such intimacy in any obvious way. In this manner, an 'innocent' shot becomes charged with intimacy and sexuality. This example and others throughout this chapter suggest that in order to understand the evolution of the representation of women in Iranian cinema, codes and texts as well as meanings and contexts must be examined.

The restrictions placed on women in the post-revolutionary cinemas of phases 1 and 2, such as relegation to minor parts and domestic space and observance of strict codes of modesty, served to create a representation of women as 'modest' and 'chaste' and prevented them from becoming sexual fetishes. However, such a representation also replicated the dominant/subordinate relations of power that exist between men and women in the society at large.[51] '[T]he unconscious (formed by the dominant order) structures ways of seeing and structures of looking.'[52] As I have noted, however, the ways of seeing which the dominant patriarchal and Islamic ethos engenders is very complex and contradictory: at the same time that it oppresses women, it empowers them. A positive effect of the incorporation of modesty at all levels of the motion picture industry and in the cinematic texts themselves has been to decouple the direct discursive links previously established between cinema, women, corruption, and pornography. Thus 'purified', the film industry in recent years has become open to women as a proper profession so long as the 'Islamic' codes of behavior are observed, and so long as women directors adopt a male point of view. Thus, although the social roles of professional women in the film industry have become clearer, the image of women on the screen continues to be fraught with ideological, theoretical, and psychological ambiguities and tensions as it is overcharged and encoded with both desire and aversion.

9· Sources of Female Power in Iran

Erika Friedl

Reports of the position of women in Iran and in other Middle Eastern countries contain a seeming paradox: women are said to be subordinate to men, second-class citizens, oppressed, veiled, and confined, unequal to men legally and in access to resources. This gender inequity further is said to be validated, supported, and mystified by local gender ideologies and a superstructure formed by the teachings of the Quran and other religious scriptures, by Islamic law, and by folk notions about male–female differences.[1] Yet, on the level of everyday life and popular culture, Iranian women, especially mature matrons, are widely perceived as 'powerful.' They are described as running the political affairs of their sons and husbands,[2] as controlling the lives of everyone in the household—omniscient, beloved, respected, and feared matrons much like the stereotypical Jewish mother of western folk culture.

No matter how contradictory the concept of the oppressed-yet-powerful woman might seem, the contradiction is contrived.[3] Indeed, I will even argue that subordinated people, women in this case, not only can be both oppressed and powerful simultaneously, but that they can derive power to effect changes in their own and in others' affairs from the very relations of inequality that define their position: from concrete, adversarial circumstances in their lives, from the existential conditions to which they are confined, unfavorable as they might be.[4]

Women arrive at their position of power vis-à-vis the power elite through dynamic processes, each with its own dialectic logic. In this chapter I will trace a few of these processes. I will focus on some examples of the power that women in Iran are said to have: on how they access it, how they use it, and where it takes them. In so doing, I will try to show the connection between women's oppression and women's power and will attempt to put the discussion of this seeming paradox into the context of an analytic-methodological frame. However, as the chapter is based on qualitative research and poses qualitative questions, I will refrain from supporting my statements with quantitative data and empirical analyses. Such data and analyses are provided in other contributions to this volume.

Specifically, I have selected four topics that illustrate the power-potential of women. The first topic, resistance, is an abstract concept, manifested through a bundle of tactics used to counter hegemonic domination.[5] These tactics can be used in all life situations, and create specific power dynamics. The other three topics are concrete and specific: women's work and employment, religion, and political conditions. These three pertain to everyday circumstances of life and are examined for their potential power-content through the use of several brief, illustrative examples.[6]

Resistance as Power

Resistance can take women in three different directions.

1. Power differences between dominants and subordinates—any dominants and their subordinates—inevitably lead to resistance against demands, controls, and restrictions of superiors.[7] Dominants in turn perceive the resistance as attempts to challenge, even usurp, their power (in a Zero-Sum game) and thus label resisters as 'bad.' In our case, women do resist domination; their resistance is anticipated, and hence women are said to be by nature obstinate, shameful, foolish, sinful, or childish. As such, it is argued, they must be carefully watched and treated with commensurate firmness if need be ('need' being determined by those in authority), with yet another commensurate backlash of more resistance to be expected. Resistance therefore can, and often does, lead to more suppression: to punishment, discreditation, loss of honor, and confinement rather than freedom, choice, or autonomy.

For example, in Iran (as elsewhere) women's compliance with the dress code is taken as a measure of both state control on the national level, and of men's control over their families on the individual level. One of the duties of male and female Revolutionary Guards is to publicly enforce the dress code (including the men's dress code, which is much less restrictive and much less focused on than the women's). If a woman's hair shows from under her headscarf the transgression not only is proclaimed a private sin but is also taken as a political statement of resistance to the nation's moral code and to women's place in the social hierarchy of the Islamic Republic, and thus may be punished. By resisting the dress code, individual women do make a statement of protest, but unless they can turn their individual resistance into a mass protest, they cannot use their gesture as a source of power to effect a desired change in the dress code or in their personal position. Their lonely protest is easily quelched.

2. Suicide is one of the most dramatic gestures of resistance. Suicide as a strategy of resistance to demands or to mistreatment by figures of authority (usually within the woman's family) is ineffective for the woman who dies, but the suicide death of one woman can give weight to the resistance efforts of another woman who can use the threat of suicide as a source of power to get her will.

For example, in the early 1970s, a young bride in a village in southwest Iran, apparently traumatized by her husband's sexual demands, killed herself shortly after her wedding. Several years later, her younger sister successfully resisted her parents' plan for her marriage by threatening to kill herself like her elder sister. Thus, she turned her sister's death into a source of efficacy for her own resistance. However, she had to pay a price for her success: her behavior was labeled 'obstinacy,' and thus supported the local view that women who threaten or commit suicide are foolish and unable to withstand the devil's temptations. The young woman's resistance was taken as further proof of the alleged emotional and rational weakness and vulnerability of women.

3. The third extreme direction resistance can take is women's own acceptance of the dominants' view of female resistance to hegemonic authority.[8] Women in Iran who accept this view—and there seem to be many—believe that women are inherently weak in body, intellect, and emotional resilience. In extreme but by no means isolated cases, they maintain that all women are inherently 'bad,' probably even hell-bound, and that women's only hope for salvation lies in proper guidance which will save them from themselves, as it were. Accepting the male paradigm, women paradoxically can turn the male view into a source of power for themselves in relation to others in low positions: women can use the paradigm to control, 'guide,' and subordinate other women.[9] For example, female Revolutionary Guards patrolling the streets to watch over the propriety of other women, mothers-in-law critically watching their daughters-in-law, or *hezbollah* (Party-of-God) women in offices and schools controlling the dress and behavior

of officemates or students are enforcing conformity and quelching resistance to male authority. By taking up the cause of male/state authorities, including the expectation of resistance to domination and the perceived need to nip it in the bud, these women can achieve a substantial measure of power over other women. But this support undermines the position of women in general, including their own vis-à-vis their husbands or brothers. Not even the collaborators can easily convert this male-derived power over other subordinates into autonomy in their private lives.

Only on rare occasions can women use the acceptance of male/state expectation of women's resistance successfully to control men. One such instance is the popular tactic of manipulating the notion of women's, especially older women's, alleged ignorance as an unassailable excuse for acts of insolence.[10] Women may claim illiteracy when transgressing a written order; they can feign ignorance and act disingenuously when caught violating a rule or when aggressively pushing their cause; or, presenting themselves as insignificant underdogs with little to lose they can—and do—argue and plead for others in dangerous situations.

For example, in 1989 in a small city in southwest Iran I met a mother lobbying for days with security authorities (all men) on behalf of her arrested son. Lobbying did not hurt her, an old woman of no account, but would have put the young man's male relatives into serious difficulties had they tried it. Victories gained this way are usually small, however, and each attempt is taken as further proof of women's general moral and intellectual inferiority.

In very rare cases, women manage to turn restrictive orders against the authorities themselves. For example, a woman principal of an all girls' school I know was ordered by her male supervisor not to let any man enter the school premises. When the supervisor appeared a few days later to check on administrative matters, the principal refused him entry on grounds of his own order. Tongue-in-cheek (as in this case) or seriously, women can claim the fool's freedom more easily than men. Although resistance based on the acceptance of male rule in government or in the family may lead to small personal victories for individual women, it cannot be expected to alter the skewed power balance between dominants and subordinates in general. Such resistance is a tactic for getting by and getting even, not for redress.

Resistance can take a great many forms, each with different consequences for the generation of power. I will briefly discuss four such forms which I have found to be used frequently: disobedience, subversion, refusal, and crying for help.

1. Open disobedience of male orders leads to conflict, hidden disobedience to distrust. Both conflict and distrust lead to greater oppression and tighter control, thus creating a vicious circle of tyranny and rebellion.

For example, a young woman in a small town in southern Iran who disobeyed her husband frequently and for good reasons, as she and many others thought, was often beaten by him in the course of the resulting fights. On one such occasion she fled to her brother, who ordered her to stop arguing and to do her husband's bidding. When she now refused to obey her brother, he beat her, and her relatives and neighbors called her 'crazy' for being disobedient in such a foolishly demonstrative way. Another young woman I know had for years refused all orders by her relatives to marry one of her suitors, on pain of severe punishment at each refusal and near ostracism by her family. Although successful in her resistance, she paid a high price in comfort and reputation. Moreover, when her eventual later marriage to a man of her choosing turned out disastrous, villagers characteristically saw a direct connection between her earlier disobedience and her eventual calamity.

In the setting of contemporary post-war Iran, social workers and healthcare professionals in Shiraz reported in 1989 a sharp rise in cases and severity of domestic violence. These observers explained that as the economic base for the domestic superiority of men in the family was eroding, women were criticizing, disobeying, and challenging their husbands more openly than before, and men felt they had 'no other choice' than to put their wives in their places violently.[11]

An example of hidden disobedience leading to distrust is the common case of the husband who forbids his wife to visit her parents and bitterly complains that he expects her to visit them anyway, behind his back. Such distrust leads to accusations of disobedience even if there was none. The wife will feel wronged if she is falsely accused, or will find it necessary to lie to her husband if she has indeed visited her parents, thus sowing more distrust between herself and her spouse.

Disobedience as a tool of power for women works best if it is supported by dominants against other dominants: a father supporting his daughter against her husband; a son backing his mother against a half-brother. It can also be successful if one woman's disobedience is backed by other women in an act of solidarity that the men find hard to break. But because solidarity requires more organizational structure than women in Iran, especially rural women, usually have, it is relatively rare outside of the family. Within the family, solidarity is easiest to achieve between mothers and daughters and among sisters, whereas between mothers-in-law and daughters-in-law, and among sisters-in-law, relationships are potentially so fraught with tensions that solidarity seems to be hard to attain.

2. Subversion, in the form of minimal compliance with controversial rules or the outright subversion of such rules is at once a form of testing the limits of the rules and the tolerance of the rule-makers and thus is an expression of one's dissatisfaction with them. This form of resistance can very easily be interpreted as disobedience requiring respective reprisals.

In Iran, for example, the rule for women to cover their hair in front of unrelated men is subverted when a woman drapes a big scarf loosely over her head, holding it in place not by a tight knot or a safety-pin under her chin but by slinging one end of the scarf over the opposite shoulder. The headdress which is meant to conceal has become an ornament; the intent is subverted and the woman who wears it makes a political statement by turning an object of control into one of protest. Usually, women get away with this gesture, but whenever increased attention is paid to women's compliance with the dress code, these women are the first ones who get reprimanded in one form or another. Another example of this form of resistance is the aforementioned episode of the principal who subverts the intent of her supervisor's letter.[12]

3. A woman's refusal to obey her husband's (or father's) orders or to perform expected services challenges the man and inconveniences him. A woman who refuses a demand hopes that her husband will try to prevent the inconvenience and remedy the contested situation before precipitating a showdown. However, any kind of refusal by a woman in everyday situations, from refusing to cook or to fetch a glass of water for her son, to denying sex to her husband, is sanctioned negatively in the Islamic moral code. For a woman, refusing obedience or services to her husband (or, in varying degrees, to other men in positions of authority over her), no matter how extreme the demand, is a sin, and a very 'female' sin at that. It is a sin said to be typical of women, and this notion in turn is part of the script by which

women are socialized. Women who resort to refusal as a tool of power are told they are courting punishment in the afterlife as well as in this life.

In the most extreme and most effective case of refusal, a woman leaves her husband to live with her father, brother, or grown son. Her husband then must cope with women's chores, including the care of young children, and is greatly inconvenienced. His difficulty can be compounded if his own mother and other female relatives, in tacit solidarity with his wife, refuse to help him. Sooner or later, out of necessity, he will decide to negotiate for his wife's return, presumably agreeing to measures that will redress his wife's complaints and will improve her situation. Wright reports a case from the Doshman Ziari in which two sisters even left their husbands in order to force them to make a political move the women favored.[13]

This strategy too requires the support of another man (a woman's father, brother, or son) who can be mobilized by the woman against the man she refuses to obey. In order to be successful, this strategy furthermore can only be used infrequently by any particular woman; if she leaves once too often, her husband might divorce her. This power game is further played at the cost of both the man's honor and the woman's reputation and supports the popular notion that women are antagonistic and born troublemakers.

4. A cry for help, that is, informing others of wrongs one is suffering, aims to involve outsiders in one's affairs in order to embarrass one's own people into addressing the problem. This form of resistance undermines indirectly a woman's standing, the more so the more people get involved: honorable people take care of their problems themselves.

For example, a woman who has been beaten may choose to go to the public bathhouse where her bruises will tell her story without a word from her. The news will spread to her father who may then decide to have a word with her husband, usually with as little noise as possible. In another example, a young woman in Deh Koh, who had married into a small town from elsewhere, one day was briefly wailing loudly in the courtyard of her husband's family. Her neighbors heard her, and although nobody intervened directly, a few days later her father came with several relatives from afar, threatening to take her home unless her complaints were redressed. In both cases, as in most others of this kind, the success of the strategy rests on the willingness of other men in positions of authority vis-à-vis the woman to back her. Her plea for help leads to power negotiations between men. Although cries of protest as pleas for help, such as wailing, shouting, crying loudly, throwing tantrums, having hysteric fits, may successfully engage a woman's social network and are thus effective power tools, they too lead to loss of face of the woman and the man involved. They contribute to the negative notions about women's weakness and unreliability that are taken to justify strong male supervision and control.

These examples suggest that resistance as a source of power for women is considered destructive to self and to others in Iran. Resistance supports the stereotyping of women's power as an inherently dangerous force that must be controlled. Women's resistance is taken by men and women (in what Wright calls the 'dominant model' for behavior and attitudes)[14] as proof of women's inherent weaknesses, their unreliability, recalcitrance, childishness, and antagonism. Although all of these have to be feared as dangerous to the social and moral order, the fear is not a wholesome one, but rather leads to distrust and further curtailment of movement and options for women. Yet, despite its limited, at best short-range, benefits and high costs, resistance is the single most frequently used tactic of power, the most popular 'weapon of the weak' that women use when they feel wronged. Social developments in the Islamic Republic have neither led to equal access to resources for women and men nor to equal opportunities for self-determination and personal autonomy. Given the government's social and gender philosophy, gender equality is not even a sociopolitical agenda. Women therefore can be expected to continue to try to use traditional means to create power, such as resistance, in conducting their lives, even to intensify these power tactics when other sources of power are curtailed.

Work as Power

Women's participation in the labor market is generally taken as an indicator of the status of women, especially in developing countries, and employment of women is considered a means, even a necessity, for women's emancipation. True as this view might be in the long-range processes of women's liberation, my observations in Iran suggest that a woman's labor contribution is not in itself a reliable indicator of a woman's autonomy and power (let alone her status), at least not among the lower classes. This is especially true for manual labor, which generally is regarded as demeaning drudgery. But even clerical work has this connotation, at least among people in the lower classes. Hegland reports from a village in southwest Iran that 'employment outside the home was considered an indication of low socio-economic position and a source of shame both for the women involved and for their relatives.'[15] Such women often find it necessary to assert that they don't *have* to work, that they are well taken care of and chose employment.

The work women do, be it in- or outside of the home, can be tapped by women as a source of power under certain conditions: (1) The work creates dependencies that the woman can exploit; (2) the work creates resources that the woman can control; (3) the work creates skills that enable the woman to access other sources of power and creates in her the self-confidence to shrewdly exploit them. I will briefly discuss these three conditions.

Dependencies

Within the family, it is easy for a woman to make others, for example, her children, husband, and aged parents-in-law, dependent on her services. A woman in a traditional rural household, by refusing to cook or to milk animals, for example, might force her husband to negotiate with her for better treatment. (This, however, happens at the cost of reinforcement of the negative stereotype of women as nags, or, in extreme cases, the threat of divorce.) On the other hand, as a willing, cooperative, and competent housekeeper, a woman can gain considerable manipulative power. She can gain control over most of the household resources (including even control over a co-wife).[16] By wisely using her resources, she will build up her husband and earn the respect of relatives and others in her social circle, which in turn will empower her to have input in others' and her own affairs. In this way she will also accumulate knowledge about others, which she can incorporate into a power base that includes political as well as economic and emotional resources, and provides many angles for arranging her circumstances to the benefit of herself and her protégés. Hegland reports that the village women she observed used 'their verbal and intellectual skills in gathering information, spying, persuading, taunting, berating, threatening, shaming, discussing, interpreting, encouraging'[17] in order to manipulate their power base. One result of such successful manipulation is the 'powerful' wife-mother figure of popular culture and folklore: the woman who knows everything, who controls children and relatives, who makes and breaks people, who keeps her sons on short emotional reins, and whom everybody loves and fears at the same time. A competent woman in this sense is using her talents, connections, and services—all her assets—to build up her husband (or sons) and herself simultaneously. The most successful will continue to give the impression of overt deferral to male authority, because it is important for the maintenance of 'face' (*aberu*) that her husband's dominance should not be challenged overtly. This pretense of submission in turn has to be accepted by the husband at face value along with his wife's manipulations which, after all, he recognizes as advantageous for himself.[18] This is a power game which so-called successful couples seem to be playing all over the patriarchal world, and which, because of its success, makes other ways of assertion by women, including attempts at emancipation in a western sense, seem superfluous, even foolish, to many men and women in these systems.

In economically depressed post-revolutionary Iran, the household, the kin group, large families are more important than before in structuring the lives of people; the social life as well as economic assistance flow in the kind of close-knit social networks in which women operate very well. Thus, chances for wielding the kind of power that comes from cleverly creating and using dependencies have increased in importance for women.

Women-controlled resources

A salary or wage is a major power source for a woman only if she retains control over it. If she has to give her earnings to her father or husband to manage, her power is reduced to threats of refusal to work.

For example, a professional woman in Esfahan, married to a rich man and controlling her own income, used her own money to get her son out of the country during the Iran–Iraq war—an enormously expensive undertaking—against the will of her husband and her in-laws. Short of making a public scandal, which would have hurt him and his wife personally and professionally, the husband had no way to intervene. Control over her money not only gave the woman financial power but also the power to assert her will. Similarly, on a much smaller, rural scale, an elderly widow I know in Deh Koh who had supported herself for many years by weaving locally-used flatweave storage bags paid her own way to Mashhad, the site of the most important shrine in Iran, over the loud objections of her children.

She, too, converted financial independence into the power of self-determination.[19]

Most working married women I have met in Iran over the years in low-paying jobs (such as teachers, midwives, secretaries, domestic servants), who do not control their salaries and have little say in how their income is spent, have either left their jobs after a few years or said they wanted to quit. They complain about ill health and the double burden of running a household and working outside the home—complaints rarely heard from women who keep control of their wages and salaries. They see their work as exploitation, not liberation, and take their husbands' assertion of spending their salaries for the benefit of the whole family as thinly veiled dispossession.

Not surprisingly, in the Islamic Republic, ideologues proclaim household work as ideally suited for women, home-making and taking care of husband and children as a woman's most important responsibility. Since this work is not remunerated, the issue of financial independence of women is avoided. Jobs that are open, even pushed, for women, are mostly low paid and appeal to young, unmarried women. (Fathers, it seems, are not likely to regard their daughters' income as their own.)

For example, the labor of rug weaving in the government-organized carpet cottage industry for women is paid so low that the wages do not pose a threat to the power hierarchy within or outside of the family.

In the traditional village economy, few women-created products were actually controlled by women: yarns and rugs manufactured by women, as well as milk products such as cheese and butterfat, were marketed by men who disposed of the income as they saw fit. Not surprisingly, few women involved in the traditional agricultural economy seem concerned about the recent decline in demands for their textiles, or resent their husbands' selling of the herds to be free to do other work.[20]

Self-confidence and skills

Work can be a source of power for women inasmuch as it instills self-confidence, builds skills (including social skills), and leads to self-reflection. These qualities make women more daring in resisting unreasonable burdens and in demanding help and consideration, and more successful in manipulating the few resources available to them.

For example, the first woman in Deh Koh who asked for a divorce and fought for it successfully and alone in court was a teacher. It was also a woman teacher, in a different village, who successfully petitioned a mullah-judge to force her husband to send his father away who had inflicted himself on her and her husband because he did not get along with his wife.

Formal education can also increase a woman's critical assertiveness. In Iran, educated young women are often said to be 'troublemakers.' Not surprisingly, the majority of girls in the villages are sent to school for only three or five years now—'too much' education, it is said, will make them insubordinate wives and daughters-in-law.[21]

Despite the potential benefits of paid work for women, in the pro-natal atmosphere of the Islamic Republic[22] working outside the home places an enormous burden on most women, at least poor and rural ones (who constitute the majority of women in Iran), because caring for many children requires great effort and energy under difficult economic circumstances and often from a mother who is in poor health.[23] Instead of desiring to work outside the home, mothers of large families treat their labor in raising their children as a source of self-worth, even self-righteousness. They often use their hard work, their worries, and their own ill health and fatigue to drive home the message, 'I am a good mother but get nothing but troubles for it.' They play the role of martyr. They make doing the right thing as a wife-mother look unjust, and use their hardships to manipulate their social network into providing help or compensatory favors. Although using a guilt-trip tactic feeds the familiar stereotype of woman as complainer, it is strongly reinforced in Iran and often creates considerable manipulative power for the woman.

Mothers tend to use their children, especially their daughters, as sources of cheap labor and information about other people. Although mothers have no legal rights over their children beyond an early age under Islamic family laws, they find children easy to manipulate and to cultivate as their supporters. And although stories of sons and daughters who neglect their aging mothers abound, every woman sees the work she does for her children as an investment in her future. Thus, in the absence of other possibilities to use work as a source of power, women in the Islamic Republic now more so than before can be expected to try to use their household duties and household resources, including children, in this way. Despite the hardships, having many children is viewed as one way—for many women the only way—to establish themselves as actors in their own rights.

Religion as Power

Religion can empower women insofar as the religious idiom can provide the means, justifications, and rationalizations for independent actions. Religious concepts thus can be and are used as manipulative devices.

For example, during the revolution, many Iranian women participated in demonstrations against the Pahlavi regime. Hegland reports that the women (and the men who allowed them to do so) saw protest as a religious rather than a political activity: women were giving testimony to Islam by supporting Khomeini.[24]

The paucity of occasions for women in the Islamic Republic to congregate legitimately outside their homes seems to be one of the reasons for the rapid increase in women's participation in graveyard visitation parties on Thursday afternoons. During these visits, women socialize while ostensibly fulfilling a pious obligation. Likewise, *rowzeh* gatherings and *sofreh*s (parties given in honor of a saintly personage) are used extensively for what is elsewhere called women's networking.[25]

Likewise, pilgrimages to saints' shrines are popular among women as religiously motivated social activities. Women consider visits to a neighborhood shrine to be like informal visits to a relative,[26] close to home and easily fit between chores. Pilgrimages to distant, important shrines, however, involve considerable expense and logistical problems, which make male approval, support, and escort necessary for women. Indeed, a woman very likely must use her manipulative powers to make her husband or son take her on a pilgrimage. Frequently a woman can keep her vow to pay a visit to a saint only after she is widowed or has found a separate source of funding for the travel.

For example, an old widow in Deh Koh, an herbalist who had been living precariously on her own for many years, wanted to make the pilgrimage to Mashhad, but was very concerned about the possible impropriety in going alone. On the bus to Mashhad she met a mullah with his eight-year-old son and contracted a temporary, non-sexual marriage with the boy. This allowed her to make the journey as a well-chaperoned married woman. Thus, she used the combination of control over her finances and two religiously sanctioned customs to gain the autonomy to venture into an otherwise inaccessible world. Temporary marriage, which can be taken to demean women,[27] in this case became a source of power that enabled a woman to realize her wish.

Women can use expressions of piety as a manipulative strategy.

Since about 1983, a code of piety has developed in Iran, a politically-piously correct way of talking, dressing, reading; a politically correct body of knowledge and phrases that one can use to one's personal advantage.

For example, a young woman (or man for that matter) seeking acceptance at a university or promotion at work will avoid the slightest hint of resistance to the dress code. In public, she will wear the plainest outer garments, correct low-heeled shoes, and a dark scarf pulled over her forehead, completely covering her hairline. She will accept a scholarship to a special Quran course in the summer, no matter how boring she might find it. She will not tell others that at home she is looking at American videos smuggled in from Kuwait. She will pray and observe the fast ostentatiously. She will not be seen with men (other than close family members) in public, and will discourage male attention. Her impeccable behavior will be noted by those who report on her morality, and this will increase her chances for advancement. The restrictive code is thus turned into a tool with which she can manipulate her career.

In the Islamic Republic many women, especially those in the middle class and the former elite, have perfected the art of dissimulation and the use of the code of piety to the extent that their private and public personae are almost totally different.

Since the war, the status of 'Mother of a Martyr' has become a potential source of power for women who have lost a son in the war. The government has given these women the moral right to demand respect and consideration from other people. These women are given preferential treatment in the allocation of subsidized appliances, and they are enlisted as watchers over the correctness of their neighbors' behavior. Some of these women, especially those with limited access to other sources of power and respect, use their position as informer to the point where conversation in a room falters when they enter. These women are seen by others as using a government-bestowed power to the detriment of other women.

In a more traditional religious domain, the prestige of a successful pilgrimage to certain shrines (expressed in the titles *haji*, *karbela'i*, *mashhadi)* and that of a descendant of the Prophet Mohammad (*sayyed*) carry respect and are thus a potential source of power for women.[28] A *sayyed* woman often is sought out as a mediator in disputes or as a peacemaker.

For example, in Deh Koh, a man whose wife had fled to her father after a fight enlisted the help of a *sayyed* woman to persuade his father-in-law to send back his wife. Although the young woman's family had vowed they would let her go only if her husband agreed to a list of demands, they found it impossible to resist the *sayyed*, whose invocations of piety, morality, and peace were strengthened greatly by her illustrious descent. In effect, this *sayyed* used her own male-derived powers (from her ancestor, the Prophet) to undermine the protest action of another woman who, as a young wife, had very little power over her fate.

Government as Source of Power

Women in Iran have the right to vote. Yet although voting gives women a voice in political matters equal to men, not all women, especially not rural ones, consider it a source of power. A woman's vote is often regarded as her husband's or father's second vote: he will determine how she is to vote.

Similarly, women do not regard law and the courts as sources of power and rarely use them, even if in a particular instance the law would indeed be on their side. Involving the court in one's affairs is taken as a sign of failure of the informal, traditional, honorable ways of dealing with problems and thus is easily seen as shameful, especially for women. Furthermore, few women have the economic and strategic-assertive resources to go to court alone and plead their case, especially against a male relative.

For example, when in a small town a young woman's husband died, his relatives sent her back to her father without her two infant children. Although the law gave her the right to keep her children at least for a specific time, and although she missed her children badly and fell into serious depression, her father decided not to press the issue in court to avoid the embarrassment of a public fight. The woman felt completely unable to deal with the problem herself, especially over the objection of her father. For similar reasons, women who are denied their legal share of the inheritance by their brothers usually 'pardon' it rather than face a court battle with them.

As mentioned before, politically correct demeanor helps a woman with professional aspirations. In this regard, one could say the government provides a script for women who want to attain power positions, be it as a school principal, a medical professional, an elected member of a village or town council, a Revolutionary Guard, an informer in an office, or an employee of an intelligence agency.

In the last three instances, 'successful' women use their government-bestowed powers against other women in the interest of the male dominants, thereby supporting women's domination. Thus, the government makes it possible for some women to advance individually without emancipation.

Quotas for admission to scarce places in public universities are other examples of government-derived potential access to power for some women, especially women in small towns and villages who did not have this access before. In the former merit-based admissions policy of universities, women without access to the intellectual culture and to the good high schools of the cities had virtually no chance to compete successfully with their urban middle-class sisters on the difficult entrance examinations. Now, the quota system assures a certain percentage (which varies annually) of rural women high-school graduates a place in a university. However, the increase in admissions of rural and lower-class women, laudable as it is, happens at the cost of denial of a placement to other, often better qualified women from the urban middle classes.[29]

A final example of a government-generated source of potential power for women comes from an unexpected and controversial circumstance: the mandatory sex-segregation in schools. Although motivated by a restrictive code of sexual morality that otherwise works against women, sex segregated schools have the advantages of all-women's groups in general: they provide young women with an environment where they are not harassed, restricted, challenged, or intimidated by male teachers and male classmates. In such environments women can express themselves freely, they have more opportunity to practice leadership and intellectual skills than they would have if men were present, and they can develop confidence even in such subjects as mathematics and the sciences which in some societies are said to be the domain of men.[30]

Summary

When legitimate sources of power for women become increasingly scarce in an androcentric, male-dominated society such as the Islamic Republic of Iran, and women's realm of action and influence becomes more restricted, women can be expected to intensify their use of the 'weapons of the weak,' that is, manipulation of resources and resistance to restrictive rules to exert control over issues important to them. Both strategies potentially lead to a reinforcement of the popular Iranian stereotype of women's negative character traits, from childishness to outright evil, and reinforce the cycle of antagonism and distrust characteristic of such power constellations. Women who use this system 'well,' that is, in such a way that men feel secure in their claim to control and superiority (regardless of how manipulated or subverted they may be) or else feel that their women's strategies and tactics are advantageous for them, can derive power to the extent that the dominant–subordinate constellation may even seem reversed. Such women are viewed not only as 'powerful' but as de facto rulers of the house. Women who control other women in the interest of dominant authority, either within the family or in public, do so to the detriment of women in general and cannot easily derive autonomy over their own lives from this position. In both cases, that of the successful wife-mother and the wielder of male-derived power, however, the existing hierarchy of domination remains not only unchallenged but is stabilized, and the gendered system of super- and subordination is cemented.

Appendix I
The Legal Status of Women in the Family in Iran

Sima Pakzad

The purpose of this study is to discuss some legal issues relating to the Iranian family's female members and to highlight the contrast between the legal rights of men and women in the family. These issues will be reviewed in two parts. The rights of women as daughters in the parental home will be discussed in the first part, while the rights of women living with their spouses will be taken up in the second part.

Part One: Woman as Daughter

In her first family role, woman as daughter appears already in an inferior position since she will not be able to retain and propagate her family name once she becomes married. The Note to Article 41 of the Law of the Registration of Vital Statistics, enacted in 1976, stipulates that: 'The family name of the child shall be that of the father.' Thus, the mother cannot, even with her husband's consent, bestow her maiden name on her child. The law is both a reason for and a reflection of the fact that in most Iranian families a male child is held in higher regard and that the ultimate wish of most fathers is to have a son who will be the bearer and guardian of their name.

Marriage

According to Article 1041 of the Iranian Civil Code: 'Marriage is forbidden before the age of majority.' The minimum age of majority as defined in Note 1 to Article 1210 of the Civil Code is 15 lunar years for boys and nine lunar years for girls. Two points must be underlined in this regard.

1. With the consent of his or her guardian, a minor may be permitted to marry before reaching the age of majority. The Note to Article 1041 of the Civil Code thus specifies: 'With the consent of the guardian,

marriage of the dependent child may be permitted even before the age of majority, provided that the best interest of the said child is taken into account.' There is no reference to the mother's right or responsibility in this matter.

2. The marriage of a girl, even after she has reached the age of majority, depends on the consent of her father or her paternal grandfather. However, if the father or the paternal grandfather refuses, without justifiable cause, to grant his permission the girl may, presenting full particulars of the prospective groom and the terms of the proposed marriage and the nature of brideprice, ask the special civil tribunal to notify her father or paternal grandfather of the said particulars and terms. Fifteen days after said notification is made and in the absence of any justifiable response, the tribunal may issue a marriage authorization for the applicant (Civil Code, Article 1043).

Inheritance

The word 'inheritance' means the property left behind by the deceased. In legal terminology, however, it refers to involuntary transfer of the property of the deceased to his or her surviving inheritors. A woman's inheritance in the family takes two forms: (1) the daughter's inheritance from her father or mother; (2) the father or mother's inheritance from their daughter.

1. Daughter's inheritance from her father or mother. According to Article 907 of the Civil Code, if the deceased is survived by only one offspring, whether son or daughter, the whole estate will be inherited by said offspring. If the deceased is survived by more than one offspring, his or her inheritance will be equally divided among them, provided all are of the same sex. However, if some of the surviving offspring are sons and some daughters, each son's share of the inheritance will be twice that of each of the daughters. This rule applies whether the deceased is the father or the mother; a son's share of inheritance is, in any case, twice as much as a daughter's. Also, according to Article 915 of the Civil Code, the father's favorite ring as well as his Quran, clothing and sword shall be inherited by his eldest son, unless the property of the deceased is limited to the said items, in which case the general provisions of the law apply.

2. Parents' inheritance from their daughter. A daughter's death may result in a number of different cases.

Case 1. If the deceased daughter has no children or grandchildren, her sole surviving parent, whether the father or the mother, will inherit the whole estate. The same rule applies in the case of the deceased being a son with no surviving children or grandchildren.

Case 2. If the deceased, whether a son or a daughter, has no surviving children or grandchildren but is survived by both of his or her parents, two-thirds of the inheritance shall be inherited by the father and one-third by the mother.

Case 3. If the deceased has no surviving children and is survived by his or her parents, and if the mother's right to inheritance is legally restricted, her share shall be one-sixth and that of the father five-sixths of the estate. According to Section B of Article 892 of the Civil Code, the said restriction, reducing the mother's share from one-third to one-sixth of the estate, is activated, under certain conditions, when the deceased has several brothers or sisters. It is interesting to note that the sisters or brothers who, in this case, cause the reduction of the share of their own mother will not themselves inherit any share of the estate since it is the father who will inherit the shares taken away from the mother. The said rule applies only to the mother and not the father, and regardless of whether the deceased is a son or a daughter.

Case 4. If the deceased (whether daughter or son) is survived by any children or grandchildren, each of the surviving parents will inherit one-sixth of the estate. This is the only case where the father and the mother inherit equal shares, regardless of whether the deceased is a son or a daughter.

Citizenship

Citizenship, according to the Iranian legal system, is granted on the basis of one's paternal status. Section 2 of Article 976 of the Civil Code specifies that those born in and outside Iran and whose fathers are Iranian shall be considered Iranian citizens. However, according to Section 5 of Article 976 if only the mother of the child is Iranian the child will be granted Iranian citizenship provided that the child: (1) has been born in Iran, and (2) has resided at least one more year in Iran immediately after reaching the full age of 18. If a man applies for Iranian citizenship and his application is approved his minor children shall also become Iranian. However, if a woman becomes a naturalized Iranian citizen, her minor children shall not be considered, ipso facto, Iranians.

Part Two: Woman as Wife

In this part, the family rights of a woman as a legally married wife shall be examined.

Marriage

Marriage, according to the current Iranian law, consists of two kinds: permanent and temporary. In permanent marriage, as the name indicates, no duration is specified in the marriage contract. Temporary marriage, also known as *sigheh*, on the other hand, can, according to Article 1075 of the Civil Code, last only for a specific period of time. In permanent marriage, a wife enjoys a higher degree of security and respect within the family. In temporary marriage, on the other hand, matrimonial relations are considered terminated and the wife must leave the husband's residence as soon as the specified period is over or if the husband waives his right to the remaining portion of the said period. In addition, while in permanent marriage the husband is legally responsible for supporting his wife, in temporary marriage the wife is not entitled to such support. Furthermore, in temporary marriage neither the husband nor the wife inherit from the other.

Following the conclusion of the marriage contract, whether permanent or temporary, legal matrimonial relations will automatically exist between the parties, in which, according to Article 1105 of the Civil Code, the husband will exercise his exclusive rights as the head of the family.

Financial Support

In return for her submission to the 'head' of the family, the wife is entitled to receive financial support. As defined in Article 1107 of the Civil Code, the husband's financial obligations include payment for such expenses as dwelling, clothing, food, and furniture, commensurate with the wife's social status, and hiring of a maid if the wife is accustomed to one or if she needs one due to illness or a physical handicap. Article 1108 of the Civil Code specifies that: 'If the wife refuses to fulfill her nuptial obligations without justifiable cause she shall not be entitled to financial support.' Only in the case where the husband contracts a venereal disease after the marriage act can the wife refuse, according to Article 1127 of the Civil Code, to have sexual relations with him without losing the right to receive financial support from her husband. If the husband refuses to provide financial support for his wife, the latter may file a complaint before the Special Civil Tribunal which shall compel the husband to provide such support. If the husband cannot be compelled to provide financial support or if he is otherwise financially unable to do so, he shall be compelled, upon the wife's request, to divorce her.

Following the act of marriage, the wife must reside in the dwelling that the husband designates. By leaving her husband's residence in order to live in another dwelling, including her father's, the wife shall lose the right to financial support. There are two exceptions to this rule: (1) when the husband has granted the wife the right to choose her residence (Civil Code, Article 1114) and (2) if the presence of the wife and the husband in the same dwelling involves the risk of bodily or financial harm to the wife, or demeans her honor, she can choose a separate residence, in which case she shall be entitled to financial support as long as she is justified in refusing to return to the original dwelling, provided she has proved her case in court (Civil Code, Article 1115).

Wife's Financial Affairs

A married woman is not required to obtain her husband's permission or heed his advice in disposing of her possessions, whether such possessions have been acquired prior to or during her marriage.

Marrying a Non-Muslim of Foreign Nationality

According to Article 1059 of the Civil Code, marriage of a Muslim woman with a non-Muslim man is prohibited, that is, a Muslim woman may only marry a Muslim man. There is no such limitation on the marriage of a Muslim man. According to Article 1060 of the Civil Code, the marriage of an Iranian woman with a foreign national requires, even in the absence of any legal bar, the special permission of the Iranian government. According to Article 17 of the Marriage Law, enacted in 1931, any foreign national who marries an Iranian woman without receiving the required official permission shall be subject to imprisonment from one to three years.

In this area, too, the restrictions on Iranian men are less severe than those placed on women. According to Article 1061 of the Civil Code, the government may require certain government officials or government-sponsored students to obtain special permission prior to marrying a woman of foreign nationality. An Iranian man, therefore, need not in general acquire special official permission to marry a foreign national unless the marriage specifically requires such permission. It must be noted that the said restriction applies only when the man is a government official or a government-sponsored student. The marriage of Iranian diplomatic envoys with a woman of foreign nationality, for example, requires prior authorization of the Iranian Ministry of Foreign Affairs.

Domicile

Every person, whether real or legal, must have a domicile. Domicile is the place where a person lives and conducts his or her main business affairs. If the place of residence of a person is different from the principal center of his or her business affairs, the latter shall be considered as his or her domicile. According to Article 1005 of the Civil Code, the domicile of a married woman is the same as that of her husband. However, when the husband has no known domicile or when the wife has acquired, with her husband's permission or court sanction, a separate residence, she may have a separate domicile.

Citizenship

Citizenship is the legal and political bond that ties a person to a specific country. In this area, too, the Iranian legal system treats men more favorably than women. Section 6 of Article 976 of the Civil Code grants Iranian nationality to any woman of foreign nationality who marries an Iranian man. However, if an Iranian woman marries a man of foreign nationality, not only her husband shall not be accorded Iranian citizenship but also she herself may be, depending on the nationality laws of her husband's country of nationality, compelled to acquire the same nationality as that of her husband, in which case she will lose her Iranian citizenship.

Employment

A married woman may, without needing her husband's permission, be gainfully employed. However, if the nature of her occupation is not compatible with the family's interests or dignity, the husband may prevent his wife from engaging in such an occupation, provided he can prove such incompatibility in the Special Civil Tribunal.

Polygyny

There are a number of articles in the Iranian Civil Code which implicitly permit a man to have several wives. Article 942, for example, states: 'If there is more than one wife, the fourth or eighth part [of the inheritance], which belongs to the wife, shall be divided equally among them.' Although no specific limits for polygyny are set for men in Iranian legal codes, Islamic jurisprudence, which constitutes the source of the laws of the Islamic Republic of Iran, does not permit a man to have more than four permanent wives. There are, however, no limits to the number of temporary wives that a man is permitted to have. In Islamic law polygyny is permitted only if the husband is able to be equally fair to all his wives. The Civil Code has designated the husband himself as the sole judge of whether he can be equally fair to two or more wives.

Travelling Abroad

To leave Iran, a married woman needs her husband's written permission. In cases of emergency, and in the absence of such permission, the wife may present to the public prosecutor her reasons for wishing to travel abroad and request permission to leave the country.

Brideprice

Brideprice is the property given by the husband to the wife for agreeing to marry him. It is one of the required conditions for a permanent marriage. According to Iranian laws, in permanent marriage, a woman must receive a brideprice in order to be able to marry, even if it is as little in value as a gold coin. Immediately following the act of marriage, the wife is entitled to possess her brideprice and dispose of it in any way she desires, provided there has been no agreed-upon timetable or installment plan for the possession of the brideprice by the wife. If the husband divorces his wife before the marriage has been consummated, the wife shall be entitled only to half of the brideprice and shall return half of the brideprice if she has already received it in full.

Legal Relations between Mother and Child

There are two important issues involved in the legal relations between mother and child: (1) raising and guardianship of the child; and (2) administering the child's estate.

1. Guardianship and raising of the child, called *hezanat* in Islamic jurisprudence and the Iranian Civil Code, is the common responsibility of both parents as long as they are not separated. According to Article 1168 of the Civil Code, raising and educating their offspring is both

the right and the obligation of the parents, for which they are expected to utilize all the possibilities at their disposal. But who is entitled to be the guardian of the child if the child's parents are separated? Article 1169 of the Civil Code specifies that: 'The mother shall have the preferential right to the custody of her child in the first two years of the child's life, after which the father shall have the custody unless the child is a girl in which case she will remain under the mother's custody until she reaches the age of seven.' The mother loses this minimal right of custody over her children as soon as she remarries. In case one of the parents dies, the custody of the children shall, according to Article 1171 of the Civil Code, belong to the surviving parent even if the deceased parent is the father and even if he has designated a third person as guardian. Child support shall be borne by the child's father and, in the case of the father's death or financial inability, by the child's paternal grandfather. In the absence of the paternal grandfather or in case of his financial inability, the child's mother shall be responsible for her child's support. It is interesting to note that, according to Article 1176 of the Civil Code, the mother is not obligated to nurse her child unless it cannot be fed otherwise. In the case where the mother demands payment for nursing her child, the father shall pay her for nursing the child or hire another woman to nurse the child, or provide for dried or cow's milk.

2. The child's guardian need not necessarily be the person who is charged with the administration of the child's estate, for, according to Iranian laws, these are two completely distinct categories. According to Article 1180 of the Civil Code: 'The minor shall be under the guardianship of his or her father or paternal grandfather.' The father and paternal grandfather, therefore, have certain inherent rights regarding their child or grandchild, respectively, which require no additional confirmation by legal or government authorities. The father and the paternal grandfather have the same legal standing in terms of their right to guardianship of the child. In the Iranian legal system this right may under no circumstances be waived or abrogated. Even in the case where the natural guardian commits a felony in the administration of the estate of the child, or becomes incapacitated due to old age or illness, he cannot be removed as the guardian of the child. In the said case, the public prosecutor shall designate a trustee who will, jointly with the legal guardian, administer the child's estate.

According to Article 1188 of the Civil Code: 'Either the father or the paternal grandfather may, following the death of the other, appoint an executor for the children under his guardianship who shall attend to the upbringing and education of the children and administer their estate.' It is thus evident, on the one hand, that the legal guardianship of the father and the paternal grandfather is not only inviolable during their lifetime (even if they prove to be incompetent or betray their trust) but also survives after their death. On the other hand, not only the father and the paternal grandfather have legal priority over the mother for the guardianship of the child, but also any other person who is appointed as the executor can supersede the mother, who is left without any authority in administering her child's estate, including the property that she herself might have given to her child. If the child does not have a legal guardian (that is, father, paternal grandfather or a guardian appointed by either of them), the Special Civil Tribunal shall, upon the recommendation of the public prosecutor, appoint an executor to administer the child's estate. The main difference between the court-appointed executor and the legal guardian is that the executor must perform his or her duties under the supervision of the public prosecutor and submit to him an annual fiscal report, whereas the legal guardian acts freely and independently in administering the ward's estate. The mother of the child, if competent, has priority over others for becoming the executor of her child's estate, provided that she has not remarried. If the mother has remarried she shall have no priority over other relatives of her child and her appointment as the executor is, therefore, at the discretion of the court which may appoint another person as the executor and authorize the mother only to act as the guardian of her child.

According to Article 1233 of the Civil Code: 'The wife cannot accept guardianship without the consent of her husband.' Thus, if the mother requests to become the guardian of her child the court may only agree to her request if she has acquired her husband's consent.

Divorce

According to Article 1133 of the Civil Code: 'The husband may divorce his wife whenever he wishes to do so.' In the case where the husband wishes to divorce his wife—and the wife raises no objection—the couple may go to the notary public, declare their agreed-upon terms of separation and be considered officially divorced. If the wife does not agree to be divorced, the husband may take his case to the Special Civil Tribunal. The tribunal shall try to reconcile the couple by appointing one or more arbiters. If the husband refuses to reconcile with his wife and insists on divorcing her, the tribunal shall permit the husband to do so.

According to Article 1129 of the Civil Code, in the case where the husband refuses, or is unable, to provide support for his wife, the latter may sue for divorce in the Special Civil Tribunal. Article 1130 of the Civil Code was amended in 1982 in such a way as to increase the number of instances where the wife has the right to sue for divorce. According to the amended Article, the wife may sue for divorce if the continuation of the marriage causes undue hardship. Instances of undue hardship have not been specified in the law. Determination of such instances has been left to the judgement of the court, which has, therefore, expanded the range of the wife's right to sue for divorce. In general, any unsavory development or occurrence such as the husband's drug addiction, his association with unsavory characters, his contraction of a serious contagious disease, or his imprisonment may be considered as a source of undue hardship for the wife.

It must be noted that the husband and wife may agree to include in the marriage contract a proviso that the realization of a particular condition—such as the marriage of the husband to a second wife, his abandonment of the home for a specific period, or his becoming an addict—would empower the wife to divorce the husband, provided that the materialization of the specified condition is confirmed in a binding judicial verdict.

Divorce concerns only the permanent marriage. The dissolution of the temporary marriage, as was indicated before, occurs when the specified period is over or when the husband waives the remainder of the period.

Inheritance in Permanent Marriage

In permanent, and not temporary, marriage the husband and the wife inherit from each other and their respective shares of the estate are as follows.

1. The husband's share from the wife's estate: If the wife is survived by any children or grandchildren, from any marriage, her husband's share shall be one-quarter of the estate. The husband's share shall be one-half of her estate, if his wife is not survived by any children or grandchildren. If the wife is survived by no consaı guineous relative, her husband, as her sole survivor, shall inherit the whole estate, including movable and immovable property.

2. The wife's share from the husband's estate: If the husband is survived by any children or grandchildren, from any marriage, his wife's share shall be one-eighth of his estate. The wife's share shall, however, be one-quarter of the estate, if her husband is not survived by any children or grandchildren. If the husband is survived by no consanguineous relatives, his wife, as his sole survivor, shall only inherit one-quarter of his estate, in which case the rest of the estate shall be deemed as intestate and therefore public property. In case of a polygynous husband, the wives shall equally share their one-quarter or one-eighth of the estate whichever may be the case. While the husband's share of the inheritance covers all the wife's property, the wife's share of the estate, according to Article 946 of the Civil Code, shall only be from: (a) movable property of any kind; and (b) buildings and trees.

Personal Status of Non-Shiite Women

The foregoing covered the legal status only of Shiite women. According to 'The Law on the Legal Standing of Non-Shiite Individuals,' enacted in 1933, in all instances related to personal status and inheritance rights of an individual belonging to one of the officially recognized religions, the court shall, except in cases involving public order, apply the rules and generally accepted traditions of the religion professed by said individual. Thus in cases involving marriage and divorce the religion of the couple, in cases of inheritance the religion of the deceased, and in cases of adoption the religion of the adoptive mother or father shall constitute the respective applicable law.

The officially recognized religions in Iran are the four main sects of Sunni Islam (*Shafi'i, Hanbali, Hanafi,* and *Maleki*), Zoroastrianism, Judaism, and various Christian sects such as Catholic, Protestant and Gregorian.

Appendix II
The Islamic Penal Code of the Islamic Republic of Iran: Excerpts Relating to Women

Pursuant to Article 85 of the Constitution of the Islamic Republic, the Islamic Penal Code was passed by the Judiciary Committee of the Islamic Consultative Assembly on 8 Mordad 1370 (30 July 1991) and was subsequently approved by the Council on the Determination of the Regime's Welfare (*Majma'-e Tashkhis-e Maslehat-e Nezam*) on 7 Azar 1370 (28 November 1991) and was received on 30 Azar 1370 (21 December 1991) by President Akbar Hashemi Rafsanjani for implementation.

The Code contains four basic sections: general, *hodud* (punishment prescribed in religious law; singular, *hadd*), *qasas* (retribution), and *diyeh* (money paid in lieu of criminal damage). Article 12 of the Code establishes criminal punishments as follows.

Punishments established by this law are of five kinds: (1) *Hodud*; (2) *Qasas*; (3) *Diyat*; (4) *Ta'zirat*; (5) Prohibitive punishments.

Each category is then defined. *Hadd* is a punishment whose kind, extent, and quality are defined in the *shari'a* (religious law). *Qasas* is a punishment that is inflicted on the condemned criminal and must be equal to the crime committed. *Diyeh* is the amount of money or property that the religious law-giver has determined for the crime. *Ta'zir* is a punishment the kind and extent of which are not defined in the law and therefore are left to the judge's discretion. Prohibitive punishments are punishments established by the government against civil and other wrong-doings for the purpose of maintaining peace and social tranquility.

Crimes that require *hadd* punishments include adultery, male homosexuality, lesbianism, sexual procurement, accusations of adultery or homosexuality, use of alcoholic beverages, fighting, corruption on earth, and robbery. *Qasas* is used in cases of homicide or damage to bodily organs. *Diyeh* is used when a crime against life or a bodily organ has been committed. The Code details the extent, amount, and conditions of *qasas* and payment of *diyeh* in relation to practically all parts of the human body.

This section contains articles and sub-articles in the code that specifically concern women. The materials presented are representative rather than inclusive.

Hodud

Article 63. Adultery is the act of intercourse, including anal intercourse, between a man and a woman who are forbidden to each other, unless the act is committed unwittingly.

Article 64. Adultery shall be punishable (subject to *hadd*) when the adulterer or the adulteress is of age, sane, in control of his or her action and cognizant of the illicit nature of his or her act.

Article 65. Only the adulterer or the adulteress who is cognizant of the illicit nature of his or her act shall be punished for adultery.

Article 66. If either the adulterer or the adulteress claims ignorance of law or fact, he or she shall not be punished for adultery if his or her claim is presumed to have *prima facie* validity, even if no witnesses to verify said claim are produced.

Article 67. If either the adulterer or the adulteress claims to have been under duress while committing the act of adultery, he or she shall not be punished if his or her claim is not otherwise clearly disproved.

Article 68. If a man or a woman repeats his or her confession of adultery four times before the judge, he or she shall receive the designated punishment, but if he or she repeats his or her confession fewer than four times, the punishment shall be at the judge's discretion.

Article 73. Pregnancy of an unmarried woman shall not by itself be the cause of punishment unless relevant evidence, as defined in this code, proves that she has committed the act of adultery.

Article 74. Adultery, whether punishable by flogging or stoning, may be proven by the testimony of four just men or that of three just men and two just women.

Article 75. If adultery is punishable only by flogging it can be proven by the testimony of two just men and four just women.

Article 76. The testimony of women alone or in conjunction with the testimony of only one just man shall not prove adultery but it shall constitute false accusation which is a punishable act.

Article 81. If the adulterer or the adulteress repents prior to confessing to the act of adultery, he or she shall not be punished (subject to *hadd*). If, however, he or she repents following his or her confession the punishment for adultery shall apply.

Article 82. The penalty for adultery in the following cases shall be death, regardless of the age or marital status of the culprit: (1) Adultery with one's consanguineous relatives (close blood relatives forbidden to each other by religious law); (2) Adultery with one's stepmother in which the adulterer's punishment shall be death; (3) Adultery between a non-Muslim man and a Muslim woman, in which case the adulterer (non-Muslim man) shall receive the death penalty; (4) Forcible rape, in which case the rapist shall receive the death penalty.

Article 83. Adultery in the following cases shall be punishable by stoning: (1) Adultery by a married man who is wedded to a permanent wife with whom he has had intercourse and may have intercourse when he so desires; (2) Adultery of a married woman with an adult man provided the woman is permanently married and has had intercourse with her husband and is able to do so again.

Note. Adultery of a married woman with a minor is punishable by flogging.

Article 84. Old married adulterers and adulteresses shall be flogged before being stoned.

Article 85. Revocable divorce shall not relieve the husband or wife from the bond of marriage during the waiting period whereas irrevocable divorce shall do so.

Article 86. Adultery of a permanently married man or a permanently married woman who does not have access to his or her spouse, due to travel, incarceration or similar impediments, shall not require stoning.

Article 88. The punishment for an unmarried adulterer or adulteress shall be one hundred lashes.

Article 90. If a man or a woman has committed the act of adultery several times and has been punished after each act, he or she shall be put to death following his or her fourth act of adultery.

Article 91. An adulteress shall not be punished while pregnant or in menstruation or when, following birth and in the absence of a guardian, the newborn's life is in danger. If, however, the newborn becomes the ward of a guardian the punishment shall be carried out.

Article 92. If the flogging of a pregnant woman or a woman nursing her child poses risks to the unborn or to the child respectively, the execution of the punishment shall be delayed until the said risk is no longer present.

Article 93. If an ailing woman or a woman in menstruation has been condemned to death or stoning, the punishment shall be carried out. If, however, she is condemned to flogging, the punishment shall be delayed until she is recovered or her menstruation period is over.

Article 100. The flogging of an adulterer shall be carried out while he is standing upright and his body bared except for his genitals. The lashes shall strike all parts of his body—except his face, head and genitals—with full force. The adulteress shall be flogged while she is seated and her clothing tightly bound to her body.

Article 102. The stoning of an adulterer or adulteress shall be carried out while each is placed in a hole and covered with soil, he up to his waist and she up to a line above her breasts.

Article 119. Testimony of women alone or in conjunction with that of a single man shall not prove sodomy.

Article 127. Lesbianism consists in genital sexual acts carried out between women.

Article 128. Evidence for proof of lesbianism and sodomy is the same.

Article 129. The punishment for lesbianism is a hundred lashes for both parties to the act.

Article 130. Punishment for lesbianism applies only to the person who is of age, sane, in control of her actions and who has been a willing party to the act of lesbianism.

Note. In the application of the penalty for lesbianism there shall be no distinction as to whether the culprit has been passive or active or as to whether she is a Muslim or non-Muslim.

Article 131. If the act of lesbianism has been repeated three times and punishment has been carried out each time, the death penalty shall apply if the act is committed a fourth time.

Article 132. If the perpetrator of the act of lesbianism repents prior to the testimony of witnesses, the penalty of *hadd* shall not apply. Repentance following the witnesses' testimony, however, shall not bar *hadd* punishment.

Article 133. If the act of lesbianism is proved through confession and the culprit repents afterwards, the judge may ask the supreme jurist (*vali-ye amr*) for waiver of punishment.

Article 134. If two women, who are not consanguineous, go under the same bed cover while nude and without justification, they shall be given fewer than one hundred lashes. In case of repetition of the act for a third time each shall be given one hundred lashes.

Article 138. The penalty for procurement is in the case of a male procurer 75 lashes and banishment between three months and a year and in the case of a female procurer only 75 lashes.

Article 140. The penalty for false accusation is 80 lashes regardless of the gender of the culprit.

Article 145. Any insult that causes indignation to the victim but which does not constitute false accusation of adultery or male homosexuality, such as when a husband tells his wife: 'You were not a virgin,' is punishable by up to 74 lashes.

Article 150. If the husband falsely accuses of adultery his deceased wife who is survived only by a child from him, no punishment shall apply. If, however, the said deceased wife is survived by inheritors other than the said child, the penalty shall apply.

Article 164. The right to demand punishment for false accusation belongs to all survivors except the husband and the wife. Any one of the survivors may demand the application of said punishment even if other survivors waive their right.

Article 174. The punishment for intoxication is 80 lashes for both men and women.

Article 176. When flogging is carried out, the man being flogged shall be in a standing position and be bared except for his genitals, whereas the woman being flogged shall be seated and her clothing tightly bound to her body.

Note. The face and head and genitals of the condemned shall not be struck by the lashes during flogging.

Qasas

Article 209. If a Muslim man commits first-degree murder against a Muslim woman, the penalty of retribution shall apply. The victim's next of kin, however, shall pay to the culprit half of his blood money before the act of retribution is carried out.

Article 210. If a non-Muslim commits first-degree murder against another non-Muslim, retribution shall apply even if the culprit and his or her victim profess to two different religions. In the said case, if the victim is a woman her next of kin shall pay the culprit half his blood money before retribution is carried out.

Article 237. (1) First degree murder shall be proven by testimony of two just men; (2) Evidence for second-degree murder or manslaughter shall consist in the testimony of two just men, or that of one just man and two just women, or the testimony of one just man and the sworn testimony of the accuser.

Article 243. The claimant [in the case of murder] may be either a man or a woman but in either case he or she must be one of the victim's inheritors.

Article 248. In case of doubt, first-degree murder may be proved by the sworn testimony of 50 men who must be sanguineous relatives of the claimant.

Note 2. If the number of the sworn testimonies does not reach 50, any of the male testifiers may repeat his oath as many times as it is necessary to constitute 50 testimonies.

Note 3. If the claimant cannot present any of his sanguineous male relatives to provide sworn testimony in support of his or her claim, the claimant may repeat the sworn testimony 50 times, even if she is a woman.

Article 258. If a man murders a woman, the woman's next of kin may ask for retribution if he pays the murderer half of his blood money or they may agree to a settlement whereby the murderer pays him an amount less or more than the victim's blood money.

Article 261. Only the inheritors of the victim of a murder shall have the option of retribution or pardon. The victim's husband or wife, however, shall have no say in either retribution, pardon or execution of the punishment.

Article 262. Retribution shall not be carried out against a pregnant woman. In said case, if post-delivery retribution endangers the newborn's survival it shall be delayed until such time as the child's life is no longer in danger.

Article 273. In retribution for injury to, or loss of, bodily organs men and women shall be treated equally. Thus, a male culprit who has maimed a woman or otherwise caused her bodily injury shall be subject to commensurate retribution unless the blood money for the lost organ is a third or more than a third of the full blood money, in which case the female victim shall pay the culprit half of the blood money for said organ.

Diyeh

Article 300. The blood money for the first- or second-degree murder of a Muslim woman is half of that of a murdered Muslim man.

Article 301. The blood money is the same for men and women except when it reaches a third of full blood money, in which case a woman's blood money shall be half of a man's.

Article 441. Defloration of a virgin by insertion of a finger that results in incontinence shall entitle the victim to her full blood money plus a sum equal to her potential dowry.

Article 459. In case of disagreement between the culprit and the victim, the testimony of two just male experts or that of one male expert and two just female experts asserting unrecoverable loss of sight or loss of sight for an indeterminate period shall entitle the victim to blood money. In the said case, the blood money is due the victim if the eyesight is not recovered at the time predicted by the experts, or if the victim dies before his or her eyesight is restored, or if someone else gouges his or her eye.

Article 478. If a man's reproductive organ is severed from the circumcision line or lower he shall be entitled to his full blood money, otherwise the amount of blood money shall be proportional to the size of the severed part.

Art. 479. If a woman's genital is totally severed she shall be entitled to her full blood money and if only half of her genital is severed half of her blood money is due her.

Article 483. Compensation for injury to hand or foot caused by spear or bullet shall be 100 dinars if the injured party is male and commensurate with the injury if the injured party is female.

Article 487. Section 6. Blood money for the aborted fetus which has taken in the human spirit shall be paid in full if it is male, one-half if it is female, and three-quarters if its gender is in doubt.

Article 488. If the fetus is destroyed as a result of its mother's murder its blood money shall be added to the blood money of its mother.

Article 489. If a woman aborts her fetus at any stage of pregnancy she shall pay its full blood money and no share of the blood money shall go to her.

Article 490. Separate blood monies shall be paid for each aborted fetus if more than one is involved in an abortion.

Article 491. Blood money for loss of limb of, or injuries to, the fetus shall be proportionate to its full blood money.

Article 492. The blood money for the aborted fetus in cases involving deliberate intent shall be paid by the culprit, otherwise by the fetus's next of kin.

Notes

1. Mahnaz Afkhami: Women in Post-Revolutionary Iran

Author's note: I wish to thank Guity Nashat, Miriam Cooke, Shahla Haeri and Seyyed Vali Reza Nasr for reading an earlier version of this paper. Their comments have been of great help to me.

1. Feminism has been defined and argued differently not only at different times in different cultures, but also by men and women at the same time in the same culture. A representative set of essays on feminism in the West is contained in Alice S. Rossi (ed), *The Feminist Papers: From Adams to de Beauvoir* (Boston: Northeastern University Press, 1988), first published in 1973. See also, *inter alia*, Catherine Belsey and Jane Moore (eds), *The Feminist Reader: Essays in Gender and the Politics of Literary Criticism* (New York: Basil Blackwell, 1989); Gloria Bowles and Renate Duelli Klein (eds), *Theories of Women's Studies* (London and New York: Routledge and Kegan Paul, 1983); Toril Mori (ed), *French Feminist Thought: A Reader* (Cambridge, MA: Basil Blackwell, 1987); Catherine A. Mackinnon, *Toward a Feminist Theory of the State* (Cambridge, MA: Harvard University Press, 1989); Chandra Talpade Mohanty, Ann Russo and Lourdes Torres (eds), *Third World Women and the Politics of Feminism* (Bloomington: Indiana University Press, 1991); and Fatima Mernissi, *The Veil and the Male Elite: A Feminist Interpretation of Women's Rights in Islam*, trans Mary Joe Lakeland (New York: Addison-Wesley, 1991). For properties of feminism used in this discussion see Karen Offen, 'Defining Feminism: A Comparative Historical Approach,' *Signs* 14 (Autumn 1988), 119–57.
2. The correspondence between Divine Law (*Jus Divine*) and Natural Law (*Jus Naturale*) is a commonplace of most religions, including the Abrahamic. For a general discussion of the essentials of Shii Islam see Allameh Sayyid Muhammad Husain Tabataba'i, *Shiite Islam*, trans S. H. Nasr (Houston: Free Islamic Literature, 1979). For a discussion of women in Islam see Morteza Motahhari, *The Rights of Women in Islam* (Tehran: World Organization for Islamic Services, 1981) part vii; John L. Esposito, *Women in Muslim Family Law* (Syracuse: Syracuse University Press, 1982).
3. The theory of *hadith*, or tradition, did not take definite shape until late

in the second century after Islam. Since its inception, its method and authority have been matters for disagreement among Muslim scholars as well as others in terms of the reliability of its raconteurs and continuity of chains of transmission. Furthermore, there has always been a conflict among the various Sunni and Shii schools. Thus, the time factor involved and the differences between the compilers on the authenticity of the sayings or the chains opens the validity of much of the *hadith* to serious doubt even among Muslim ulema. For Shiis, perhaps the most celebrated compiler of tradition is Mohammad Baqer Majlesi, a *mojtahed* of the Safavid era. For the meaning and a concise discussion of the theory and development of *hadith* see J. Robson's article in *The Encyclopaedia of Islam* (Leiden: E. J. Brill, 1971), vol 3, pp 23–9. For a brief history of imamite jurisprudence, particularly a survey of important Shii jurists, see A. A. Sachedina, *The Just Ruler in Shiite Islam: The Comprehensive Authority of the Jurist in Imamite Jurisprudence* (Oxford: Oxford University Press, 1988), pp 9–25. For a Marxist discussion see I. P. Petrushevski, *Islam in Iran* (Albany: State University of New York Press, 1985), pp 101ff.

4. Motahhari: *Rights of Women in Islam.*
5. See Yvonne Yazbeck Haddad and Ellison Banks Findly (eds) *Women, Religion and Social Change* (Albany: State University of New York Press, 1985); also chapters by Denise L. Carmody, Rosemary R. Ruether and Jane I. Smith on Judaism, Christianity and Islam respectively in Arvind Sharma (ed), *Women in World Religions* (Albany: State University of New York Press, 1987).
6. See the *Laws of Ancient Persians As Found in the Matikan-i Hazar Datastan or the Digest of A Thousand Points of Law*, trans S. J. Bulasara (Tehran: Imperial Organization for Social Services, 1976), first published by Hoshang T. Anklesaria, Bombay, 1937.
7. For women in *Shahnameh* see Khojasteh Kia, *Sokhanan-e Sezavar-e Zanan dar Shahnameh-ye Pahlavani* (*Words Deserving of Women in the Epic Shahnameh*) (Tehran: Nashr-e Fakhteh, 1371). For a comparative rendition of Iranian and non-Iranian female character see Saidi Sirjani, *Sima-ye Do Zan* (*A Portrait of Two Women*) (Tehran: 1367), where an Iranian and non-Iranian woman as portrayed in Nezami's *Khamseh* are compared.
8. See A. Perikhanian, 'Iranian Society and Law,' in *The Cambridge History of Iran*, vol 3 (2), ed. Ehsan Yarshater (Cambridge: Cambridge University Press, 1983), particularly pp 646–55.
9. Judith Baskin, 'The Separation of Women in Rabbinic Judaism,' in Haddad and Findly: *Women, Religion and Social Change*, pp 3–18 and Denise L. Carmody in Sharma: *Women in World Religions*, p 192.
10. Rosemary R. Ruether in Sharma: *Women in World Religions*, p 209.
11. Muslims generally agree that, as a wealthy independent woman who married and nurtured the Prophet Mohammad, Khadija's moral and financial support was essential for the development of the Prophet's social standing and his ability to withstand the Qorayshi aristocratic pressures. Aysha, for her part, played a pivotal role in Muslim politics

during the latter part of the Prophet's life and after his death. See Mernissi: *The Veil and the Male Elite*, pp 4–7 and throughout the book. Ayesha is particularly important to Shiis for her opposition to Ali, the first Shii Imam. For a general discussion of women in early Islam see Jane I. Smith, 'Women, Religion and Social Change in Early Islam,' in Haddad and Findly: *Women, Religion and Social Change*, pp 19–35.

12. Hind Bint 'Ubta is recognized as the moving force behind Abu Sufiyan and other members of Meccan aristocracy in fighting Mohammad. She was instrumental in the killing of the Prophet's uncle, Hamza, in the Battle of Uhud, in which she and other women participated. For a short account see *Encyclopaedia of Islam*, vol 3, p 455.
13. Majlesi as quoted in Adele K. and Amir H. Ferdows, 'Women in Shii Fiqh: Images Through the *Hadith*,' in Guity Nashat (ed), *Women and Revolution in Iran* (Boulder: Westview Press, 1983), p 59.
14. Major theories of Social Contract were developed by Thomas Hobbes in *Leviathan, the Matter, Form and Power of a Commonwealth Ecclesiastical and Civil* (1651), John Locke in *The Second Treatise on Civil Government* (1689) and Jean-Jacques Rousseau in *Le Contrat Sociale* (1762). For a feminist interpretation see Kate Millett, *Sexual Politics* (New York: Simon and Schuster, 1969), chs 1 and 2.
15. For these and other feminist essays see Rossi: *Feminist Papers*.
16. See Jamshid Behnam, 'Dar Bareh-ye Tajaddod-e Iran' ('On the Modernization of Iran') I and II in *Iran Nameh*, vol 8, no 3, pp 347–74 and vol 8, no 4, pp 507–40. The articles are in Persian with abstracts in English. Amin Banani, *The Modernization of Iran: 1921–1941* (Stanford: Stanford University Press, 1961), ch 1; Roger Savory, 'Social Development in Iran During the Pahlavi Era,' in George Lenczowski (ed), *Iran Under the Pahlavis* (Stanford: Stanford University Press, 1978), pp 85–127.
17. This tension was picked up by a small number of extraordinary women. Tahereh Qorrat al-Ayn, a brilliant student of Shiism and arguably the most interesting woman in Iran's history, for example, professed her ideas as a revolutionary religious thinker, whereas, on the other side of the scale, Taj al-Saltaneh, Naser al-Din Shah's daughter, expressed her concern not only for women's condition, but also for the country under men's rule in her memoirs. On Qorrat al-Ayn see Farzaneh Milani, *Veils and Words: The Emerging Voices of Iranian Women Writers* (Syracuse: Syracuse University Press, 1992), pp 77–99. For Taj al-Saltaneh, see Mansureh Ettehadieh, *Khaterat-e Taj al-Saltaneh* (*Taj al-Saltaneh's Memoirs*) (Tehran: Nashr-e Tarikh-e Iran, 1371); Fereydun Adamiyat and Homa Nateq, *Afkar-e Ejtema'i va Siyasi va Eqtesadi dar Athar-e Montasher Nashodeh-e-Dowran-e Qajar* (*Unpublished Political, Social and Economic Thought of the Qajar Era*) (Tehran: Agah Press, 1356), pp 155–63.
18. See Janet Afary, *Grassroots Democracy and Social Democracy in the Iranian Constitutional Revolution, 1906–1911* (unpublished PhD dissertation, University of Michigan, 1991). Also, *inter alia*, Ahmad Kasravi, *Tarikh-e Mashruteh-e Iran* (*History of Iranian Constitutionalism*) (Tehran: Amir Kabir, 1349); Badr al-Moluk Bamdad, *From Darkness into Light: Women's*

Emancipation in Iran, trans F. R. C. Bagley (Hichsville, NY: Exposition Press, 1977), Nikkie R. Keddie, *Roots of Revolution: An Interpretive History of Modern Iran* (New Haven: Yale University Press, 1981), particularly pp 33–6.

19. Bamdad: *From Darkness into Light*. See also Guity Nashat, 'Women in Pre-Revolutionary Iran: A Historical Overview,' in Nashat: *Women and Revolution in Iran*, pp 5–36.
20. Between 1967 and 1976, the Women's Organization of Iran (WOI) grew into an extensive network of 350 branches and 113 centers, offering literacy and vocational training classes, birth control and abortion information, job and legal counseling and childcare as well as youth programs and discussion groups. There were other organizations such as the University Women's Association, the Association of Women Journalists, the Association of Women Lawyers that were independent, autonomous organizations working in their area of interest. Members often had multiple affiliations with the WOI and other women's groups. There were 51 other organizations and interest groups which held a loose affiliation with WOI.
21. In 1975 there were three women undersecretaries (labor, mines and industries and education), one cabinet member (Minister of State for Women's Affairs), six representatives to the Majles, two senators, one governor, one ambassador. Twenty-four women were elected to the boards of the provincial councils. Of the members elected to the provincial councils, 11.9 per cent were women. The percentage of women in the paid labor force was 12.6. Even though the level of participation of women in decision-making in all spheres of public life was very limited, the trend was decidedly and strongly upward. In 1978 more women passed the entrance examination for medical schools than men. Over 42 per cent of children in school in the first six grades were girls. WOI suggested and lobbied successfully for the passage of a package of laws and regulations which greatly enhanced participation of women in employment. The package included paid maternity leave up to seven months, choice of half-time work with full-time benefits for up to three years after the birth of a child, and childcare on the work premises for all working mothers.
22. In the area of women's legal rights within the family, the Family Protection Law as revised in 1975 gave women the right to file for divorce on the same grounds and conditions as men; left decisions regarding child custody and alimony up to a special family court, recognized the mother as the legal guardian of her child in case of the death of the father, practically eliminated polygyny by stipulating exceptional conditions including the permission of the first wife, and at any rate limited legal marriages to two wives, and increased the minimum age of marriage to 18 for women and 21 for men. Abortion was made legal with the consent of the husband. Unmarried women were able to obtain abortion on demand up to the eighth week of pregnancy.
23. This was accomplished by a variety of means and methods. Women in

high office, such as Queen Farah and Princess Ashraf, were briefed regularly and familiarized with the newest activities and thinking concerning women's rights in Iran and in the region. They were asked to lobby with the Shah for support of particular measures such as the change in the passport law which required the husband's permission for the wife to leave the country and Article 179 of the penal code which allowed extreme leniency for crimes of passion involving a man's honor. (See Mahnaz Afkhami, 'A Future in the Past: the Prerevolutionary Women's Movement in Iran,' in Robin Morgan [ed], *Sisterhood Is Global: An International Women's Movement Anthology* [New York: Doubleday, 1984], pp 330–38.) High government officials and opinion-makers were educated about women's rights by being coopted into various multisectoral committees, where they would interact recurrently with women leaders and receive sustained encouragement to see and study the condition of women from the women's perspective. In one such committee meeting, where an article of the Family Protection Law concerning the right of the husband to oppose his wife's employment if his honor were involved was being discussed, an interesting argument developed between Mr Sadegh Ahmadi, Minister of Justice and a traditional scholar, and Abdol Majid Majidi, Head of the Plan and Budget Organization, whose emancipated wife was Iran's first opera virtuoso and an influential member of Iran's Ministry of Culture. See Shahla Haeri and Mahnaz Afkhami's forthcoming Oral History Autobiography.

24. The important factor here is the replacement of a model of humanism, democracy, and progress as the ideal with a model derived from Islam as interpreted by Muslim clerics in pre-modern times. The essentials of the new model were contained in the Islamic Repubic's constitution, particularly in parts referring to *velayat-e faqih* (rule of the religious jurist), hierarchy of guiding values, and women.
25. Iranian women's first massive post-revolutionary demonstration for freedom and rights was held on Women's Day on March 8, 1979, less than a month after the revolution. Since then, women have remained at the center of the regime's ideological and political concerns, as any casual reading of any of Tehran's daily newspapers at any given time will show. For a recent study of women's condition in universities see Shahrzad Mojab, 'Control-e Dowlat va Moqavemat-e Zanan dar Arseh-ye Daneshgahha-ye Iran' ('State Control and Women's Resistance in Iranian Universities'), in *Nimeye Digar* 14 (Spring 1991), pp 35–76.
26. See, for example, Hamid Naficy's discussion of films and Azar Naficy's discussion of literary development in contemporary Iran in this volume. For women in education see Mojab: 'Control-e Dowlat va Moqavemat-e Zanan . . .'
27. Even now such arguments are raised in the West by the Catholic church and until recently by the Anglican church to oppose women's ordination as priests.
28. The Left's ideological use and misuse of women's issues is not confined to Iran. 'The "marriage" of marxism and feminism has been like the marriage of husband and wife depicted in English common law: marxism

and feminism are one, and that one is marxism.' Heidi Hartmann, 'The Unhappy Marriage of Marxism and Feminism: Towards a More Progressive Union,' in Lydia Sargent (ed), *Women and Revolution: A Discussion of the Unhappy Marriage of Marxism and Feminism* (Boston: South End Press, 1981), p 2. The Left in Iran, of course, received both its ethos and pathos through the Soviet intermediary, which gave it a peculiarly 'underdeveloped' flavor.

29. Ashraf Pahlavi, *Faces in a Mirror* (Englewood Cliffs, NJ: Prentice-Hall, 1980), p 25.
30. See, for example, Oriana Fallaci, 'The Mystically Divine Shah of Iran,' *Chicago Tribune*, December 30, 1973, sec 2, p 1.
31. A time-honored practice of structural dissimulation by the Shiis to withstand stronger opponents. The Islamic Republic leaders, however, do not look favorably on *taqiyyah*.
32. I realize that these terms are problematic. The function of a global discourse is to define and clarify the concepts invoked by these terms in a way that is suitable to the requirements of an equitable system of gender relations in the twenty-first century, if not earlier in the so-called 'new world order.' For a critique of approaches to feminism, patriarchy, and Islam see Deniz Kandiyoti, 'Islam and Patriarchy: A Comparative Perspective,' in Nikkie R. Keddie and Beth Baron (eds), *Women in Middle Eastern History: Shifting Boundaries in Sex and Gender* (New Haven: Yale University Press, 1991), pp 23–42.
33. For a relevant critique see Christine Delphy, 'Protofeminism and antifeminism,' in Moi: *French Feminist Thought*, pp 80–109. See also Linda Kauffman (ed), *Gender and Theory: Dialogues on Feminist Criticism* (New York: Basil Blackwell, 1989).
34. For some possibilities of what might constitute a discourse that has a chance of transcending fixed sexual polarities see Julia Kristeva, 'Woman's Time,' in Belsey and Moore: *The Feminist Reader*, pp 198–217.
35. What appear as obstacles to the development of a global approach to a feminist social and literary criticism, namely, the contemporary emphasis in universities on cultural relativism, on one hand, and on textual and deconstructionist analysis, on the other, may prove a positive force for the future involvement of Third World women in the construction of a global discourse. The transition from parochial/relativistic to a global approach is already taking place as more and more feminist positions are advanced mutually through intellectual representatives of western and non-western cultures.
36. Nupur Chaudhuri and Margaret Strobel (eds), *Western Women and Imperialism: Complicity and Resistance* (Bloomington: Indiana University Press, 1992).

2. Patricia J. Higgins and Pirouz Shoar-Ghaffari: Women's Education

Authors' note: We wish to thank Sohrab Behdad and Hooshang Amirahmadi for assistance with access to recent statistical data.

1. Unless stated otherwise, statistical data are taken from the following sources: *Summary of Educational Statistics for the Academic Year 2535–2536* (Tehran: Ministry of Education, 1977); *National Census of Population and Housing, Ostan Reports* (November 1976) (Tehran: Statistical Center of Iran, 1980); *National Census of Population and Housing, Selected Tables: Total Country* (October 1986) (Tehran: Statistical Center of Iran, 1990); *Iran Statistical Yearbook 1369* (March 1990–March 1991) (Tehran: Plan and Budget Organization, 1992).
2. For example, Jalal Matini, 'The Impact of the Islamic Revolution on Education in Iran,' in Adnan Badran (ed), *At the Crossroads: Education in the Middle East* (New York: Paragon House, 1989), pp 43–55; Golnar Mehran, 'Socialization of Schoolchildren in the Islamic Republic of Iran,' *Iranian Studies* 22, 1 (1989), pp 35–50; 'Ideology and Education in the Islamic Republic of Iran,' *Comparative Education Review* 20, 1 (1990); pp 53–65; M. Mobin Shorish, 'The Islamic Revolution and Education in Iran,' *Comparative Education Review* 32, 1 (1988), pp 58–75.
3. Mehran, 'Ideology'; Bahram Mohsenpour, 'Philosophy of Education in Postrevolutionary Iran,' *Comparative Education Review* 32, 1 (1988), pp 76–86.
4. 'Educational Reforms and Innovations, Part II,' *Echo of Iran* 6, 2 (1986), p 20; Mehran, 'Ideology,' p 57.
5. Hammed Shahidian, 'The Education of Women in the Islamic Republic of Iran,' *Journal of Women's History* 2, 3 (1991), pp 11–12.
6. Hamid Algar (trans), *Constitution of the Islamic Republic of Iran* (Berkeley: Mizan Press, 1980).
7. Mehran, 'Ideology,' p 60; see also Mohsenpour, 'Philosophy,' p 85.
8. Mehran, 'Ideology,' p 57.
9. Robert Looney, 'War, Revolution, and the Maintenance of Human Capital: An Analysis of Iranian Budgetary Priorities,' *Journal of South Asian and Middle Eastern Studies* 25, 1 (1991), p 4.
10. Ibid, p 9.
11. Ibid, p 14.
12. Ibid, pp 2–3.
13. A. Reza Arasteh, *Education and Social Awakening in Iran, 1850–1968* (Leiden: E. J. Brill, 1969).
14. Shahidian, 'Education,' p 30.
15. Hooshang Amirahmadi and Farhad Atash, 'Dynamics of Provincial Development and Disparity in Iran, 1956–1984,' *Third World Planning Review* 9, 2 (1987), p 30.
16. Here, 'ethnic,' 'mixed,' and 'Persian' provinces are distinguished by the proportion of the population able to speak Persian, according to the 1986 census. While a more useful measure would be the proportion of the population whose native language is other than Persian—a question not asked on any recent census—the ranking of provinces based on the proportion of the population knowing Persian conforms fairly well to other rankings in the scholarly literature. See Akbar Aghajanian, 'Ethnic Inequality in Iran: An Overview,' *International Journal of Middle East Studies* 15 (1983), pp 211–24; Hooshang Amirahmadi, 'A Theory

of Ethnic Collective Movements and Its Application to Iran,' *Ethnic and Racial Studies* 10, 4 (1987), pp 363–91; and Nikki R. Keddie, 'The Minorities Question in Iran,' in Shirin Tahir-Keli and Shaheen Ayubi (eds), *Old Weapons, New Conflicts* (New York: Praeger, 1983), pp 85–108.
17. Khosrow Shobe, 'Education in Revolution: Is Iran Duplicating the Chinese Cultural Revolution?' *Comparative Education* 18, 3 (1982), p 276.
18. Valentine M. Moghadam, 'The Reproduction of Gender Inequality in Muslim Societies: A Case Study of Iran in the 1980s,' *World Development* 19, 10 (1991), p 1340.
19. Ibid, p 1341.
20. Shahidian, 'Education,' p 18.
21. Marzieh Goli Rezai-Rashti, 'Iran,' in Gail P. Kelly (ed), *International Handbook of Women's Education* (New York: Greenwood Press, 1989), pp 455–71, 467.
22. Shahidian, 'Education,' p 18.
23. Shahin Gerami, 'Privatization of Woman's Role in the Islamic Republic of Iran,' in Gustavo Benavides and N. W. Daly (eds), *Religion and Political Power* (Albany: SUNY Press, 1989), pp 99–118, 113.
24. Moghadam, 'Reproduction,' p 1341; Shahidian, 'Education,' p 18.
25. Nader Habibi, 'Allocation of Educational and Occupational Opportunities in the Islamic Republic of Iran: A Case Study in the Political Screening of Human Capital in the Islamic Republic of Iran,' *Iranian Studies* 22, 4 (1989), p 27.
26. Ibid, pp 32–3.
27. Ibid, p 42.
28. Matini, 'Impact.'
29. Golnar Mehran, 'Social Implications of Literacy in Iran,' *Comparative Education Review* 36, 2 (1992), p 194.
30. *Iran Statistical Yearbook 1369*.
31. Mehran, 'Social Implications,' p 200.
32. Ibid, pp 207–8.
33. Ibid, p 210.
34. Ibid, p 200.
35. Roberta M. Hall and Bernice R. Sandler, *The Classroom Climate: A Chilly One for Women?* (Washington: American Association of Colleges, 1982), pp 1–2. Marlaine E. Lockheed with Susan S. Klein, 'Sex Equity in Classroom Organization and Climate,' in Susan S. Klein (ed), *Handbook for Achieving Sex Equity through Education* (Baltimore: Johns Hopkins University Press, 1985), pp 189–217; Janice Pottker, Psychological and Occupational Sex Stereotypes in Elementary School Readers,' in Janice Pottker and Andrew Fishel (eds), *Sex Bias in the Schools: The Research Evidence* (London: Associated University Press, 1977), pp 111–25; Kathryn P. Scott and Candace Garrett Schau, 'Sex Equity and Sex Bias in Instructional Materials,' in Klein (ed), *Handbook*, pp 218–32.
36. Mehran, 'Socialization,' p 37.

37. Mohsenpour, 'Philosophy,' p 84.
38. Patricia J. Higgins and Pirouz Shoar-Ghaffari, 'Sex-Role Socialization in Iranian Textbooks,' *NWSA Journal* 3, 2 (1991), p 224.
39. Mehran, 'Socialization,' pp 36–7.
40. Jacquiline Rudolph Touba, 'Cultural Effects on Sex Role Images in Elementary School Books in Iran: A Content Analysis After the Revolution,' *International Journal of Sociology of the Family* 17, 1 (1987), pp 143–58.
41. Higgins and Shoar-Ghaffari, 'Sex-Role.'
42. Hall and Sandler, *Classroom Climate*, p 3; Scott and Schau, 'Sex Equity and Sex Bias.'
43. Touba, 'Cultural Effects,' p 146.
44. Gerami, 'Privatization,' p 113.
45. Shahidian, 'Education,' p 13.
46. Habibi, 'Allocation,' p 33; Gerami, 'Privatization,' p 117.
47. Shahidian, 'Education,' p 22.
48. Mehran, 'Social Implications,' p 200.
49. Gail P. Kelly and Ann Nihlen, 'Schooling and the Reproduction of Patriarchy: Unequal Workloads, Unequal Rewards,' in Michael W. Apple (ed), *Cultural and Economic Reproduction in Education* (London: Routledge and Kegan Paul, 1982), pp 162–80; Pat Mahony, *Schools for the Boys: Co-education Reassessed* (London: Hutchinson, 1985), p 11; Janice Pottker, 'Psychological and Occupational Sex Stereotypes in Elementary School Readers,' in Pottker and Fishel (eds), *Sex Bias*, pp 111–25; Scott and Schau, 'Sex Equity and Sex Bias,' pp 218–32.
50. Hall and Sandler, *Classroom Climate*, p 5; Lockheed and Klein, 'Sex Equity,' pp 197–9; Wellesley College Center for Research on Women, *The AAUW Report: How Schools Shortchange Girls* (Washington: AAUW and NEA, 1992).
51. Mahony, *Schools*, pp 25–31; see also Lockheed and Klein, 'Sex Equity,' pp 199–206.
52. Mahony, *Schools*, p 7.
53. Ibid, pp 23–4; Kelly and Nihlen, 'Schooling.'
54. Mahoney, *Schools*, pp 16–19.
55. Barbara J. A. Gordon and Linda Addison, 'Gifted Girls and Women in Education,' in Klein (ed), *Handbook*, pp 405–7.
56. Mahony, *Schools*, pp 21–2.

3. Akbar Aghajanian: The Status of Women and Female Children

Author's note: The preparation of this chapter was partially supported by a grant from the Rockefeller Foundation.

1. For a detailed discussion of the concept of the status of women see Karen Mason, 'The Impact of Women's Social Position on Fertility in Developing Countries,' *Sociological Forum* 2 (Fall 1987), pp 718–45.
2. Frank R. C. Bagley, 'The Iranian Family Protection Law of 1967:

Milestone in the Advance of Women's Rights,' in C. E. Bosworth (ed), *Iran and Islam* (Edinburgh: Edinburgh University Press, 1971) pp 47–64; Ali Banani, *The Modernization of Iran: 1921–1941* (Stanford: Stanford University Press, 1961); Cheryl Bernard, 'Some Reflections on the Experience in Iran,' *Journal of South Asian and Middle Eastern Studies* 4 (Winter 1980), pp 10–26; Patricia Higgins, 'Women in the Islamic Republic of Iran: Legal, Social, and Ideological Changes,' *Journal of Women in Society and Culture* 10 (Spring 1985), pp 477–94; Ali-Akbar Mahdi, 'Women of Iran: A Bibliography of Sources in the English Language,' *Review of Iranian Political Economy and History* 4 (Fall 1980), pp 59–86; Kate Millet, *Going to Iran* (New York: Coward, McCann, and Geoghegan, 1982); Farin Mirvahabi, 'The Status of Women in Iran,' *Journal of Family Law* 14, 3 (1975), pp 383–404; Valentine Moghadam, 'Women, Work and Ideology in the Islamic Republic,' *International Journal of Middle East Studies* 20 (May 1987), pp 221–43; Guity Nashat, 'Women in the Islamic Republic of Iran,' *Iranian Studies* 13 (March 1980), pp 22–30; Nesta Ramazani, 'Behind the Veil: Status of Women in Revolutionary Iran,' *Journal of South Asian and Middle Eastern Studies* 4 (Winter 1980), pp 27–36; Simin Royanian, 'A History of Iranian Women's Struggles,' *Review of Iranian Political Economy and History* 3 (Spring 1979), pp 17–29; Eliz Sanasarian, *The Women's Rights Movement in Iran: Mutiny, Appeasement, and Repression* (New York: Praeger, 1982).

3. Constantina Safilios-Rothschild, 'Socio-Economic Development and Status of Women in the Third World,' Population Council, Working Paper no 112 (New York: Center for Policy Studies, 1985).
4. Akbar Aghajanian, 'Evaluation of the Iran Fertility Survey,' Working Papers (Honolulu: East–West Center Population Institute, 1992).
5. Janet Bauer, 'Poor Women and Social Consciousness in Revolutionary Iran,' in Guity Nashat (ed), *Women and Revolution in Iran* (Boulder: Westview Press, 1983), pp 141–69; Erika Friedl, 'State Ideology and Village Women,' in Nashat (ed), *Women and Revolution*, pp 217–30; 'Division of Labor in an Iranian Village,' *MERIP Reports* 95 (March–April 1981), pp 12–18; Mary Elaine Hegland, 'Traditional Iranian Women: How They Cope,' *Middle East Journal* 36 (Autumn 1985), pp 477–94; Susan Wright, 'Prattle and Politics: The Position of Women in Doshman-Ziari,' *Anthropological Society of Oxford Journal* 9, 2 (1978), pp 98–112.
6. Alaka M. Basu, 'Is Discrimination in Food Really Necessary for Explaining Sex Differentials in Childhood Mortality?' *Population Studies* 43, 2 (1989), pp 193–210.
7. *Iran Statistical Yearbook 1984* (Tehran: Statistical Center of Iran, 1985).
8. Statistical Center of Iran, *The Population Growth of Iran* (Tehran: Statistical Center of Iran, 1977).
9. Population Reference Bureau, *World Population Data Sheet* (Washington: Population Reference Bureau, 1991).
10. Lincoln C. Chen, Aladin Chowdhury, and Sandra L. Huffman, 'Seasonal Dimensions of Energy-Protein Malnutrition in Rural Bangladesh: The

Role of Agriculture, Dietary Practices, and Infection,' *Ecology of Food and Nutrition* 8 (1979), pp 175–87.

11. Statistical Center of Iran, *National Census of Population and Housing, 1986*, Total Country (Tehran: Statistical Center of Iran, 1988).
12. The regression method is the Multiple Classification Analysis. This technique shows the mean score for each category of the independent variable and how it deviates from the grand mean of the sample. See *SPSS/PC+ Base Manual* (Chicago: SPSS Inc, 1988).
13. Karen Mason, 'Status of Women and Fertility,' *Sociological Forum* 1 (1986), pp 284–300; Yasmin L. Mossavar-Rahmani, 'Family Planning in Post-Revolutionary Iran,' in Nashat (ed), *Women and Revolution*, pp 253–62.
14. Statistical Center of Iran, *National Census of Population and Housing, 1986*, Selected Tables (Tehran: Statistical Center of Iran, 1990).

4. Haleh Esfandiari: The Majles and Women's Issues

This chapter is based primarily on two sources. One major source is the debates in the Assembly of Experts that in 1979 approved the text of the Constitution of the Islamic Republic. These debates were published in three volumes under the title of *Surat-e Mashruh-e Mozakerat-e Majles-e Barresi-ye Naha'i-ye Qanun-e Asasi-ye Jomhuri-ye Islami-ye Iran* (*Proceedings of the Assembly for the Final Consideration of the Constitution of the Islamic Republic of Iran*), published by the Majles of the Islamic Republic, Tehran, 1364/1986, and cited in the notes below as *Debates*. A second primary source is the debates on bills pertaining to women's issues in various sessions of the first and second parliaments in the years 1980–84 and 1984–8. The official record of the Majles debates can be found in *Ruznameh-ye Rasmi-ye Jomhuri-ye Islami-ye Iran: Mashruh-e Mozakerat-e Majles-e Showra-ye Islami* (*Official Gazette of the Islamic Republic of Iran: Proceedings of the Islamic Consultative Assembly*) and cited in the notes as *Majles Proceedings*.

1. *Debates*, vol III, p 1509.
2. *Debates*, vol I, p 439.
3. *Debates*, vol I, p 189.
4. Ibid.
5. *Debates*, vol III, p 1724.
6. *Debates*, vol I, p 188.
7. *Debates*, vol I, p 191.
8. *Debates*, vol I, p 439.
9. *Debates*, vol I, p 440.
10. *Debates*, vol I, p 444.
11. *Debates*, vol I, p 615.
12. *Debates*, vol I, p 628.
13. *Debates*, vol III, p·1403.
14. *Debates*, vol III, p 1506.
15. *Majles Proceedings*, 3 Esfand, 1361.
16. Ibid.
17. *Majles Proceedings*, 8 Esfand, 1361.

18. *Majles Proceedings*, 21 Farvardin, 1362.
19. Ibid.
20. *Majles Proceedings*, 12 Azar, 1364.
21. Ibid.
22. *Majles Proceedings*, 28 Bahman, 1364.
23. *Majles Proceedings*, 20 Khordad, 1364.
24. *Majles Proceedings*, 1 Mehr, 1363.
25. *Majles Proceedings*, 22 Farvardin, 1364.

5. Fatemeh E. Moghadam: Commoditization of Sexuality and Female Labor Participation in Islam

Author's note: I would like to thank Mahnaz Afkhami, Erika Friedl, and Hamideh Sedghi for their helpful suggestions and comments.

1. Gary Stanley Becker, *The Economics of Discrimination*, 2nd edn (Chicago: University of Chicago Press, 1971); *A Treatise on the Family* (Cambridge, MA: Harvard University Press, 1981); 'Human Capital, Effort, and the Sexual Division of Labor,' *Journal of Labor Economics* 3 (January 1985), pp 533–58; Heidi I. Hartman, 'Capitalism, Patriarchy and Job Segregation by Sex,' *Signs* 1 (1976), pp 137–69; Jacob Mincer and Solomon Polachek, 'Family Investments in Human Capital: Earnings of Women,' *Journal of Political Economy* 82, (1974), pp S76–S108; Francine D. Blau, 'Gender' in John Eatwell, Murray Milgate, Peter Newman (eds), *The New Palgrave: A Dictionary of Economics*, vol 2 (New York: Stockton Press, 1987), pp 492–8.
2. Esther Boserup, *Women's Role in Economic Development* (New York: St Martin's Press, 1970); Patricia Stamp, "Women in Development" as a Field of Inquiry: Issues and Conceptual Problems,' (paper prepared for the IDRC Project, Toronto, 16–19 May 1988); Patricia Maguire, *Women in Development: An Alternative Analysis* (Amherst: Center for International Education, University of Massachusetts, 1984).
3. Jane Parpart, 'Introduction,' in Parpart (ed), *Women and Development in Africa: Comparative Perspectives* (Lanham: University Press of America, 1989), pp 1–18; Gita Sen and Caren Grown, *Development, Crises, and Alternative Visions* (New York: Monthly Review Press, 1987).
4. Fatima Mernissi, *Beyond the Veil: Male–Female Dynamics in Modern Muslim Society* (Bloomington: Indiana University Press, 1975).
5. Shahla Haeri, *Law of Desire: Temporary Marriage in Shi'i Iran* (Syracuse: Syracuse University Press, 1989).
6. Hamid Bagh-Shomali and Syrus Elahi, 'Motale'e-ye Tatbiqi-ye Vaz'-e Eqtesadi va Ejtema'i-ye Zanan-e Shaghel dar Shahrha-ye Tehran, Qazvin, Kashan' ('A Comparative Study of the Socioeconomic Conditions of Working Women in Tehran, Qazvin, and Kashan') (Tehran, 1977), pp 5–21; Mitra Baqerian, 'Eshteghal va Bikari-ye Zanan az Didgah-e Towse'eh' ('Employment and Unemployment of Women from the Perspective of Development'), *Zanan* 1 (February 1992), pp 4–10; Valentine Moghadam, 'Women, Work, and Ideology in The Islamic Republic,' *International Journal of Middle East Studies* 20 (May 1988), pp 221–43.

7. Haleh Afshar, 'Women, Marriage, and the State in Iran,' in Haleh Afshar (ed), *Women, State and Ideology: Studies from Africa and Asia* (Albany: SUNY Press, 1987); Guity Nashat (ed), *Women and Revolution in Iran* (Boulder: Westview Press, 1983); Hamideh Sedghi, 'Women in Iran,' in Lynne B. Iglitzin and Ruth Ross (eds), *Women in the World: A Comparative Study* (Oxford: Clio Books, 1976), pp 219–28; Hamideh Sedghi and Ahmad Ashraf, 'The Role of Women in Iranian Development,' in Jane Jacqz (ed), *Iran: Past, Present and Future* (New York: Aspen Institute for Humanistic Studies, 1976), pp 201–10; Hamideh Sedghi, 'An Assessment of Works in Farsi and English on Iran and Iranian Women: 1900–1977,' *The Review of Political Economics* 12 (1980), pp 37–41; Azar Tabari and Nahid Yeganeh, *In the Shadow of Islam: Women's Movement in Iran* (London: Zed Press, 1982); Eliz Sanasarian, *The Women's Rights Movement in Iran* (New York: Praeger, 1982); G. Mehran, 'The Education of a New Muslim Woman in Postrevolutionary Iran,' *Muslim Education Quarterly* 8 (1991), pp 5–12.
8. Blau, 'Gender,' p 492.
9. Becker, *Treatise.*
10. Donald J. Treiman and Heidi I. Hartman (eds), *Women, Work, and Wages: Equal Pay for Jobs of Equal Value* (Washington: National Academy Press, 1981).
11. Blau, 'Gender,' pp 492–7.
12. Parpart, 'Introduction,' pp 3–18.
13. Stephen Breyer and Paul W. MacAvoy, 'Regulation and Deregulation,' in Eatwell et al (eds), *New Palgrave*, vol 4, p 128. Note that regulation has been defined and theorized in a variety of ways by economists. In this chapter, I have used the most popular definition.
14. Yahya Ben Adam, *Kitab al-Kharaj* (*Taxation in Islam*), trans and ed A. Ben Shamesh (Leiden: E. J. Brill, 1968).
15. *Qur'an-e Majid* (The Holy Quran), trans from Arabic to Persian, Abdol-Majid Ayati (Tehran: Soroush Publishers, 1988), verses 2: 236, 237; 4: 4, 24; 4: 4.
16. Quran, verses 2: 228; 4: 34; 65: 7.
17. Quran, verse 2: 223.
18. The Islamic injunction concerning the treatment of co-wives with justice, *adl*, has been interpreted by some as meaning equal treatment of co-wives. See Leila Ahmed, 'Early Islam and the Position of Women: The Problem of Interpretation' in Nikki R. Keddie and Beth Baron (eds), *Women in Middle Eastern History* (New Haven: Yale University Press, 1991), pp 58–9. It is argued that had this injunction been included in Islamic law, the institution of polygyny would have been undermined. In fact, however, none of the major Islamic sects has incorporated this concept—with the interpretation of equality—into Islamic law.
19. Quran, verse 2: 226–32.
20. Quran, verse 4: 20, 21, 24.
21. Quran, verse 4: 3, 20, 23.

22. The advice to treat women with justice has been interpreted by some to imply monogamy. It has been argued that it would be impossible for a man to treat co-wives equally, and that therefore the Quran is indirectly advising men to be monogamous. See Leila Ahmed, *Women and Gender in Islam* (New Haven: Yale University Press, 1992), p 88. However, the word *adl* means justice. Justice and equality are not synonymous. Furthermore, the Quran explicitly states that men may marry by ones, twos, threes and fours. The Prophet Mohammad himself practiced polygyny.
23. Quran, verse 4: 34.
24. In court, two female witnesses are considered equal to one male. This can be interpreted to mean that women are not qualified for the legal profession.
25. Quran, verse 4: 34.
26. No doubt there is a great deal more to marriage than the sale of female sexuality. However, this issue is central to our analysis.
27. Ahmed, *Women and Gender*, pp. 44–6.
28. Ibid, p 91.
29. Ibid, p 83.
30. Ibid, pp 88–101. She argues that the position of women in Islam is a matter of interpretation. To a limited extent this point is accurate. However, the examples Ahmed uses are unrepresentative. She refers to the practices of the early Sufis and Qarmatians as evidence of equal spiritual treatment of women in Islam. In their methodology of spiritual practices, the Sufis have borrowed from eastern religions. Thus, their method is distinct from that of the more popular—and Quran-based—Muslim practices. The spiritual equality women can obtain is derived from the methodology of spiritual practice, and not from the belief in Islam. The Quarmatians can hardly be regarded as typical Muslims. Their general beliefs were derived from Ismaili Shiism. They did not say the Islamic prayers and did not fast. In their stronghold in Bahrain they did not have a mosque. See N. V. Pigulevskaya, A. V. Yakubovsky, L. V. Petrushevski, L. V. Striyeva, A. M. Belintski, *Tarikh-e Iran az Dowreh-e Bastan ta Payan-e Sadeh-e Hezhdahom* (*The History of Iran from Ancient Times to the End of the Eighteenth Century*), 2 vols, trans from Russian to Persian K. Keshavarz (Tehran, 1967), pp 212–13. Thus, neither group can be considered representative of Islamic interpretations. Despite the differences, however, the commoditized and regulated treatment of women in the four major orthodox schools as well as in popular unorthodox Shiism is similar.
31. Quran, verse 2: 228–33.
32. Quran, verses 24: 31, 60; 33: 33, 59.
33. Quran, verse 33: 53.
34. For an examination of the subject, among others, see Nikki R. Keddie, *Roots of Revolution* (New Haven: Yale University Press, 1981); Fatemeh Moghadam, 'An Historical Interpretation of the Iranian Revolution,' *Cambridge Journal of Economics* 12 (1988), pp 401–18.

35. Hamideh Sedghi, 'Women in Iran', pp 222–6.
36. The report was designed to provide guidelines for the anticipated sixth development plan which was not implemented because of the revolution. See Sazman-e Barnameh va Budgeh, 'Negareshi Novin beh Eshteghal-e Zan dar Iran' ('A New Outlook on Female Employment in Iran') (Tehran: Mo'avenat-e Barnameh Rizi, Daftar-e Jam'iyat va Niru-ye Ensani, 1976, unpublished).
37. Markaz-e Amar-e Iran, *Kholaseh-e Sarshomari-ye Sal-e 1365* (*Summary of the Population Census for 1986*) (Tehran, 1986, unpublished).
38. Markaz-e Amar-e Iran, *Salnameh-e Amari-ye Keshvar: 1369* (1990) (Tehran, 1991), pp 62–3.
39. Bank Markazi, *Daramad-e Melli-ye Iran* (*The National Income of Iran*) (Tehran, 1973).
40. Baqerian, 'Zanan,' pp 4–10.
41. Markaz-e Amar-e Iran, *Kholaseh*.
42. Baqerian, 'Zanan,' pp 4–10.
43. Ibid. Also note that the percentage of women students in the total population of ten years and older has increased. However, the relative share in urban areas has declined, a factor that may be explained by the decline of female university students (see Table 5.1).
44. Baqerian, 'Zanan,' pp 4–10; *New York Times* (14 March 1992), p 2.

6. Shahla Haeri: An Islamic Discourse on Female Sexuality

Author's note: An earlier version of this paper was published in *Social Research* 59 (Spring 1992). I am grateful to Talal Asad, Kaveh Safa-Isfahani, Mahnaz and Gholam Reza Afkhami, Mohamad Tavakoli-Targhi, David Powers, Susan C. Rogers, Seyyed Vali-Reza Nasr, Afsaneh Najmabadi, Mina J. Bissell, Mary Hebert, and Erika Friedl for their helpful comments. Unless otherwise stated, all translations from Persian to English are mine.

1. Reprinted in *Zan-e Ruz* 1294 (1990), p 55.
2. Ibid.
3. Such beliefs are not exclusive to Shii Muslim men. Greek belief in this matter closely resembles the Persian. In Bürgel's words, a 'man's abstinence from sexual intercourse as a rule results in his becoming melancholic, as soon as the putrid matter of the retained semen reaches his head' (J. C. Bürgel, 'Love, Lust, and Longing: Eroticism in Early Islam as Reflected in Literary Sources,' in Afah L. S. Marsot (ed), *Society and the Sexes in Medieval Islam*, (Malibu, CA: UNDENA Publications, 1979), p 89.
4. *Zan-e Ruz* 1294 (1990), p 55.
5. Mullah is a general term for men who receive religious education and training. A mullah is a member of the ulema (clergy), particularly the Shii ulema. The term also implies low rank within the hierarchy of Shia Islam.
6. *Zan-e Ruz* 1294 (1990), p 55.
7. Ibid, p 4.
8. Ibid.

9. *Kayhan* (17 December 1990), p 5.
10. The Persian language carries no gender distinction. The sex of a subject may be understood within the context. From the text under consideration, it is evident that he is primarily talking about males.
11. *Kayhan* (16 December 1990), pp 6, 12.
12. *Kayhan* (11 December 1990).
13. See Mohamad Tavakoli-Targhi, *The Formation of Two Revolutionary Discourses in Modern Iran: The Constitutional Revolution of 1905–1909 and the Islamic Revolution of 1978–1979* (PhD dissertation, University of Chicago, 1988) p 35.
14. Afsaneh Najmabadi, 'Sharm-e Zaban-e Ayan va Hujb-e Paykar-e Uryan' (unpublished, 1991).
15. For an interpretation of the Sunni view, see Fatimah Mernissi, *Beyond the Veil: Male–Female Dynamics in a Modern Muslim Society* (Cambridge, MA: Schenkman, 1975). Fatna Ait Sabbah, *Women in the Muslim Unconscious*, trans Mary Jo Lakeland (New York: Pergamon Press, 1983).
16. Several provisions in Shii Islamic law may be construed as aspects of discourse on female sexuality: that girls should be married off before the onset of their menses, or that married women have the right to sleep with their husband every fourth night, *haqq-e hamkhabegi*, and to have intercourse with him once every four months, *haqq-e vatye.* Legally, these provisions have less to do with female sexuality than with their implications for men. First, fathers are encouraged, though they are not required—it is not a right—to arrange their daughter's marriage early to ensure that his and her honor remain unsoiled. Secondly, the right of sleeping with a husband every fourth night is within the confine of Islamic marriage, which legally permits a man to have four wives simultaneously. A woman does not, however, have the right to demand intercourse—a right reserved exclusively for her husband. *Haqq-e vatye* is more complex than the other two. This right allows a woman to sue her husband if he refrains from having intercourse with her less than every fourth month. However, it has little, if anything, to do with female sexuality as such. It is, rather, an occasion to allow a woman to conceive, since the objective of permanent marriage is procreation.
17. It is related from Ayesha, the beloved wife of the Prophet Mohammad that there were at least four forms of marriages before Islam. For details of the pre-Islamic form of temporary marriage see William Robertson Smith, *Kinship and Marriage in Early Arabia* (Boston: Beacon Press, 1903). See also I. K. A. Howard, 'Mut'a Marriage Reconsidered in the Context of the Formal Procedures for Islamic Marriage,' *Journal of Semitic Studies* 20 (1975), pp 82–92; Sachiko Murata, 'Temporary Marriage (Mut'a) in Islamic Law,' *Alserat* 13 (Spring 1987). For an ethnography on the subject, see Shahla Haeri, *Law of Desire: Temporary Marriage in Shi'i Iran* (Syracuse: Syracuse University Press, 1989).

18. Rubin Levy, *Introduction to the Sociology of Islam* (London: Williams and Norgate, 1933), vol 2, p 149; *'Mut'a,'* *Encyclopedia of Islam* (Leiden: E. J. Brill, 1927) vol 3, pp 773–6; C. Snouck Hurgronje, *Mecca in the Latter Part of 19th Century*, trans J. H. Monahan (London: Luzac, 1931), pp 12–13.
19. 'And those of whom ye seek content (by marrying them), give unto them their portions as a duty. And there is no sin for you in what ye do by mutual agreement after the duty (hath been done). Lo! Allah is ever Knower, Wise.' Trans M. M. Pickthall, *The Meaning of the Glorious Koran* 4:24. The Imam Ja'far Sadeq was asked: 'And, did the Messenger of God practice *mut'a*?' He replied: 'Yes.' Cited by Murata, 'Temporary Marriage', p 72.
20. For a review of the dispute between the Sunnis and Shiis, see Murata, 'Temporary Marriage', pp 51–73; Haeri, *Law of Desire*, pp 61–4.
21. It may be noted here that the term brideprice in *mut'a* marriage is *ajr* (reward, wage), whereas that of permanent marriage is *mehr*. Each term has specific legal implications, and their structural differences and similarities have been disputed by Shii and Sunni ulema. See Haeri, *Law of Desire*, pp 36–8, 53–4.
22. The period of abstinence in temporary marriage is 45 days or two menstrual cycles, while that of divorce is three months or three menstrual cycles.
23. Socially, however, the status of children born of a temporary marriage depends very much on how their father relates to them. If he recognizes them as his own and treats them like his other children, they will not suffer the stigmatization that otherwise often awaits children of temporary marriages.
24. For primary sources on temporary marriage, see Shaykh Abu Ja'far Mohammad Tusi, *An-Nahayeh*, trans from Arabic to Persian by Mohammad Taqi Danesh Pazhuh (Tehran: Tehran University Press); Najm al-Din Abu al-Qasem Ja'far Muhaqqeq Hilli, *Sharay' al-Islam* (*Islamic Law*), trans from Arabic to Persian by A. Ahmad Yazdi and M. T. Danesh Pazhuh (Tehran: Tehran University Press), p 2; Ayatollah Ruhollah Khomeini, *Towzih al-Masa'el* (*Book of Exegesis*) (Tehran: n.p., n.d.); and 'Non-Permanent Marriage,' in *Mahjubeh* 2, 5 (1982), pp 38–40; Ayatollah Morteza Motahhari, *Nezam-e Huquq-e Zan dar Islam* (*The Legal Rights of Women in Islam*), 8th edn (Qom: Sadra Press, 1353/1974). For a detailed comparison between permanent and temporary marriages see Haeri, *Law of Desire*, pp 33–72.
25. The clerics and the more religious-minded Iranians see no contradiction between supporting the institution of temporary marriage and the cultural value of virginity simultaneously as long as they are the beneficiaries of both. They may think differently about it if their own unmarried daughters decide to contract a temporary marriage. Since customarily the female clientele of temporary marriages have been divorced or widowed women, virginity was not a major issue. The Islamic regime's public support for the use of the institution by young people, however, may have reinforced some individuals' own support of it, or else

added more ambiguity in the minds of others. Yet others may feel ambivalence regarding this practice for women, but nevertheless support the institution in principle because it is Islamic. See Haeri, *Law of Desire*, pp 153–97.

26. See Morteza Motahhari, 'The Rights of Women in Islam: Fixed Term Marriage,' part 3, in *Mahjubeh* (October/November 1981), pp 52–6; and Allameh Sayyed Mohammad Husayn Tabataba'i, 'Mut'a ya Ezdevaj-e Muvaqqat' ('*Muta'a* or Temporary Marriage') in *Maktab-e Tashayyu'* 6, (1343/1964), pp 10–20; Allameh Sayyed Mohammad Husayn Tabataba'i et al, *Ezdevaj-e Muvaqqat dar Islam* (*Temporary Marriage in Islam*) (Qom: Imam Sadeq Press, n.d.).
27. Interviews with Iranian women and men carried out in Iran in 1978 and 1981 by the author. See Haeri, *Law of Desire*, pp 153–97.
28. Ibid, pp 105–52.
29. Although it was Reza Shah who issued the unveiling edict, the concept of veiling and the phenomenon of the veil had come under attack in various intellectual and political circles earlier. See Mohamad Tavakoli-Targhi, 'Zani Bud, Zani Nabud' ('There was a Woman, a Woman was Not'), *Nimeye Digar* 14 (1991), pp 77–110.
30. Olive Suratgar, *I Sing in the Wilderness* (London: E. Stanford, 1951), p 132.
31. For a symbolic comparison between walls and veils see Shahla Haeri, 'Law, Women, and Social Change,' in Jane I. Smith, *Women in Contemporary Muslim Societies* (Lewisburg, PA: Bucknell University Press, 1980), pp 215–16; see also Farzaneh Milani, *Veils and Words* (Syracuse: Syracuse University Press, 1992).
32. As part of the overall package of reform, or the 'White Revolution,' Mohammad Reza Shah Pahlavi granted women the right to vote and to be elected to public office. However, the active lobbying of women and their struggle to affect the consciousness of the state and the public deserve belated attention.
33. Earlier, in 1951–2, some women apparently demanded to have the right to vote. Their demand, which had some state support, led to so much opposition by the clergy that it had to be withdrawn until an opportune moment in 1963. Mohamad Tavakoli-Targhi, personal communication, July 1991.
34. Afkhami was also the Secretary-General of the Women's Organization of Iran (1970–79). Some of my observations here are based on several discussions I have had with her regarding the relationship between the state, the clergy, and women's representatives. She has not always agreed with my interpretations. I am most grateful for her generosity in discussing the circumstances surrounding the sociopolitical activities of women in Iran during the time she held office.
35. Haeri, *Law of Desire*, pp 33–72.
36. Ibid, p 222; see also Mernissi, *Beyond the Veil*.
37. Personal observations, summer 1973, Tehran.
38. See Afsaneh Najmabadi, 'Contested Veils, Veiled Contestations: Power and the Public Female' (paper presented at the conference on 'Women,

Work and Power in the Middle East', University of California at Los Angeles, 12–13 April, 1991).

39. Mahnaz Afkhami, personal communication.
40. These remarks are taken from our ongoing project on her life history and her activities during the period of 1969–79 when she was the Secretary-General of the Women's Organization of Iran and the Minister for Women's Affairs.
41. This magazine was published during the Pahlavi regime, but after the revolution it changed hands. Although it is now published under the same name, its ideological framework is different from that of its predecessors. Significantly, more substantive issues are being pursued presently in this magazine than were before.
42. See *Zan-e Ruz* from 1967 to 1969 for a series of arguments between various readers and Ayatollah Morteza Motahhari regarding these issues. The regime in power allowed the religious leaders, particularly figures of the stature of Ayatollah Motahhari in Tehran and Makarem Shirazi in Qom, an appreciable freedom of expression, particularly on matters relating to family and personal law.
43. Hujjat al-Islam Mohammad Ja'far Bahonar et al, *Ta'limat-e Dini* (*Religious Education*) (Tehran: Davarpanah Press for the Ministry of Education, 1360/1981).
44. *The Legal Rights of Women in Islam* by Morteza Motahhari was originally published in 1974 and has been reprinted several times. The quotes here are from the Tehran 1982 edition.
45. Ibid, p 52.
46. Motahhari, 'The Rights of Women,' pp 52–3.
47. It is interesting to note here that Ayatollah Motahhari took full notice of Bertrand Russell's reference to temporary marriage in his book *Marriages and Morals*, suggesting a variation of that as an ideal form of marriage for young people in the modern world. Russell's acknowledgement of the relevance of temporary marriage to modern society is continuously referred to by the religious establishment, and is held as a westerner's admission of the institution's superiority to its western counterparts, and of its universal relevance.
48. This was not the first time Mr Rafsanjani had talked about temporary marriage. Occasionally, he discussed temporary marriage in his Friday sermons, in his capacity as the Friday Prayer leader. Even then he was promptly challenged by women from *Zan-e Ruz*. See *Zan-e Ruz* 1050 (1985), pp 4–5, 52–3, 58.
49. See *Zan-e Ruz's* earlier editorials regarding their objections to Rafsanjani's support for temporary marriage and plural marriages: 1985: 1044, p 3; 1045, p 3; 1046, p 3; and 1047, p 3.
50. Such opposition has been voiced by some women and men inside and outside the country. In Iran, *Zan-e Ruz* has been more vocal than others, but is not the only forum. Other women's magazines, even some daily newspapers, have raised objections to state support for the widespread use of temporary marriage.

7. Azar Naficy: Images of Women

1. The theme of women's 'guile,' especially in Middle Eastern cultures, needs to be treated separately and in much greater detail. It is one of the best examples of the ambiguous and contradictory attitude toward women prevalent in patriarchal societies.
2. I agree with Vladimir Nabokov that the term 'reality' should be used in quotations unless its context is clarified.
3. See Northrop Frye's definition in *The Anatomy of Criticism* (Princeton, 1975).
4. Adorno well exposes the nature of such writer–reader relationships in the 'committed' works of art:

   > The notion of a 'message' in art even when politically radical, already contains an accommodation to the world: the stance of the lecturer conceals a clandestine entente with the listeners, who could only be rescued from deception by refusing it.
   >
   > The type of literature that, in accordance with the tenets of commitment but also with the demands of philistine moralism, exists for man, betrays him by traducing that which could help him, if only it did not strike a pose of helping him. ('Adorno on Brecht,' *Aesthetics and Politics* [London, 1977], p 193.)

5. This is not to say that a novel cannot be based on monologue. But even a novel like Beckett's *Malone Dies* creates an audience and a dialogue with that audience; Malone's monologues echo the external world, as well as his inner feelings and thoughts. Also, see Bakhtin's arguments in favor of the novel's polyphonic nature and the need for the characters' 'voices' to be independent of the novelist's ideology. (Mikhail Bakhtin, *Problems of Dostoevsky's Poetics* [Manchester, 1984].)

8. Hamid Naficy: Veiled Vision/Powerful Presences

Author's note: An earlier version of this chapter appeared in *The American Journal of Semiotics*, 8 (1991), pp 1–2.

1. On the term *hejab* (cover) and its various interpretations, see Morteza Motahhari, *The Islamic Modest Dress*, trans Laleh Bakhtiar (Albuquerque, NM: Abjad, 1989).
2. Ruhollah Khomeini, *Seda va Sima dar Kalam-e Emam Khomeini* (Tehran: Sorush, 1984), p 147.
3. For a detailed analysis of the institutionalization of veiling practices in cinema during these three phases see Hamid Naficy, 'Zan va Mas'aleh-ye Zan dar Sinema-ye Iran-e Ba'd az Enqelab,' *Nimeye Digar*, 14 (Spring 1991), pp 123–69.
4. 'For the Sake of Women's Image,' *Mahnameh-ye Sinema'i-ye Film* 117 (Day 1370/February 1991), p 3 of the English section. For more on this film, see the interview with the director in Hamid Reza Sadr, 'Doshvariha-ye Bipayan-e Sakhtan-e Filmi Bara-ye Zanan-e Faramushshodeh,' *Zan-e Ruz* (Aban 1370/1991), pp 32–3.

5. Women have directed both feature-length narrative and short films (narrative, documentary, and animated), with the latter often acting as a stepping stone in their career. Some have directed both types of films. To give a sense of the diversity as well as linkages, a list of the short films screened at the Fajr Festival is provided below. The features shown there are listed in Table 1 in this chapter. Both the following Persian and English titles are from: *9th Fajr International Film Festival Catalog* (Tehran: Ministry of Culture and Islamic Guidance, 1369/1990): *Abgineh va Marammat* (*Mirror and Maintenance*) directed by Ludmilla Tavana; *Ariyeh* by Ozra Inche Dargahi; *Arz-e Hal* (*Petition*) by Farzaneh Haydarzadeh; *Az Tehran ta Tehran* (*From Tehran to Tehran*) by Nafiseh Riahi; *Cheragh va Pesarak* (*The Boy and the Lamp*) by Farzaneh Haydarzadeh; *Dar Abi-ye Aseman, dar Sepidi-ye Parandeh* (*In the Blue of the Sky, in the Whiteness of the Bird*) by Mahvash Ardeshiri; *Haft Ruz-e Hafteh* (*Seven Days of the Week*) by Qamartaj Makui; *Hasir* (*Straw*) by Farzaneh Haydarzadeh; *Nani az Gel* (*Bread from Mud*) by Farideh Shafai; *Parastu* (*The Swallow*) by Feryal Behzad; *Qessehha va Andarzha* (*Tales and Advices*) by *Feryal Behzad; Rangin Kaman* (*Rainbow*) by Qamartaj Makui; *Reza Kuchulu* (*Little Reza*) by Mina Taqva'i; *Sana'i-ye Chubi-ye Kordestan* (*Kordestan's Wood Industries*) by Puran Derakhshandeh; *Tamarkoz* (*Overpopulation*) by Rakhshan Bani-E'temad.
6. To this list, of course, must be added an increasing number of women who direct documentary films and television programs for Voice and Vision of the Islamic Republic. A few directors, such as Puran Derakhshandeh, make not only feature films but also documentary films and television serials. Her latest documentary series about drug addiction is called 'Shokaran' (1991). There are also a number of women directors who are making feature films in exile. For these, see Hamid Naficy, 'The Aesthetics and Politics of Iranian Cinema in Exile,' *Cinemaya* (Fall 1990), pp 4–8.
7. Puran Derakhshandeh, 'A Gentle Look at a Harsh World,' *Cinemaya* 10, pp 14–16.
8. Ahmad Talebinezhad, 'Afsaneh-ye Ah, Andar hekayat-e Qodrat-e Taksir,' *Mahnameh-ye Sinema'i-ye Film* 66 (Azar 1370/1991), pp 66–7.
9. 'Olgu-ye Ensani?' *Mahnameh-ye Sinema'i-ye Film* 10 (Shahrivar/August 1371/1992), p 8.
10. For details, see Naficy, 'Zan va Mas'aleh-ye Zan . . .'
11. The private core self is jealously guarded from contamination by the outside but in such a way that reciprocal and symbiotic group relations are maintained. The interior self is generally positively valued, and its expression is demanded at appropriate times. On the other hand, the exterior is the locus of contact with the Other(s), is generally negatively valued, and its expression is circumspect. See William Beeman, *Language, Status, and Power in Iran* (Bloomington: Indiana University Press, 1986).
12. Sigmund Freud, *The Standard Edition of the Complete Works of Sigmund Freud* (24 vols), trans James Strachey (London, 1953–73) vol 3, p 307.
13. See Lila Abu-Lughod's study of the links that exist between status,

social honor, and the patterns of women's veiling in an Egyptian Bedouin community: Lila Abu-Lughod, *Veiled Sentiments: Honor and Poetry in a Bedouin Society* (Berkeley: University of California Press, 1986). Of course, veiling is not limited to women; men engage in it as well but for different reasons. Murphy explores the use of the veil for Tuareg men as an index of social distance and social status: Robert F. Murphy, 'Social Distance and Veil,' *American Anthropologist* 64 (1964), pp 1257–74.

14. A few caveats are in order: (1) Many of the Iranian cultural, social, and psychological categories and practices to which I refer here are not new but pre-date the Islamic revolution of 1979. Some of them have been intensified since the revolution and many are present also in other Islamic and Third World societies. (2) Although the case study for this analysis is the Iranian post-revolutionary cinema and culture, much of what is said here applies to pre-revolutionary Iranian cinema as well. (3) Even though for the sake of analysis I am assuming here that psychic life is to a large extent universal and I am using western theories cross-culturally, I do not intend to westernize the psyche or the unconscious or to posit any inferiority or superiority. Instead, I will pay attention to the play of differences and sameness across cultures and cultural discourses.
15. For an extensive analysis of the dynamics of veiling and voicelessness and unveiling and speech in women's literature in Iran, see Farzaneh Milani, *Veils and Words: The Emerging Voice of Iranian Women Writers* (Syracuse: Syracuse University Press, 1992).
16. In the film, *Madreseh'i keh Miraftim* (*The School We Went To*, 1980–89), director Dariush Mehrju'i highlighted Iranian hermeneutics and deconstructive strategies as well as the play of difference between the interior and the exterior, which he uncannily reversed. The locus of the film is a high school for boys in Tehran, where a student organizes a group of boys to stage a play. The assistant principal forbids the play, which sets the scene for a major confrontation. Authorized by a sympathetic teacher of literature, the boy writes a critical article in the school's wall newspaper, in which in a reversal of Iranian psychology he compares the differences between the front and back yards of the school. The front yard (the exterior), he declares, is filled with justice, friendship, and work while the backyard (the interior), which is hidden from outsiders, is filled with lies and injustice—where no freedom is allowed. This causes the confiscation of the paper, which in turn motivates students and instructors alike to take action. The ethical center of the film is the school librarian who sympathizes with the students and whose own exterior and interior coincide, that is, are in balance. With much humor, a sharp eye for the child's world view and a keen ear for their dialogue, Mehrju'i explores the nature of repressive authority through the eyes of youngsters who prove to be very adept at deconstructing the world of adults who say one thing and do another. In this sense the diegesis of the film can be taken as a metaphor for post-revolutionary Iran, where things are not always what they seem.

17. The concept of the veil as a lure or masquerade can profitably be discussed through Lacan's theories: Jacques Lacan, *The Four Fundamental Concepts of Psycho-Analysis*, ed Jacques-Alain Miller, trans Alan Sheridan (New York: W. W. Norton, 1981). For a relevant application of these to cinema see Mary Anne Doane, *The Desire to Desire: The Women's Films of the 1940s* (Bloomingdale: Indiana University Press, 1987).
18. Shahla Haeri, *Law of Desire: Temporary Marriage in Shi'i Iran* (Syracuse: Syracuse University Press, 1989), 229.
19. See Michel Foucault, *Discipline and Punish: the Birth of the Prison*, trans Alan Sheridan (New York: Vantage, 1979).
20. Furthermore, although the other dualities of religiously related/not related (*mahram/namahram*), inside/outside (*baten/zaher*), religiously allowed/forbidden (*halal/haram*) are structured psychically and socially, they are not only porous but also invite transgressive pleasures. In addition, although the veil restricts women, it can also empower them through anonymity. Margaret Mills, for example, found that women in Afghani folktales engage less in disguising themselves as men than do men as women. The reasons she formulated are relevant to the potential empowerment that the veil may afford women:

    Many conservative women do not favor 'going public' by adopting male behavior, because in doing so they forfeit the power of anonymity, a power they have learned to exploit to give themselves mobility, and certain ways of manipulating the public, masculine sphere as well . . . [M]en, socialized to regard only the public sphere of male–male relations as 'significant,' and having little real privacy in the domestic world, fantasize more about manipulation and concealment of sexual and other identity. (Margaret Mills, 'Sex Role Reversals, Sex Exchanges, and Transvestite Disguise in the Oral Tradition of a Conservative Muslim Community in Afghanistan,' in Rosan Jordan and Susan Kalicik (eds), *Women's Folklore, Women's Culture* [Philadelphia: University of Pennsylvania Press, 1985], p 211.)

21. For the politics and symbolism of veiling during the anti-Shah revolution of 1979 see Anne Betteridge, 'To Veil or Not to Veil,' in Guity Nashat (ed), *Women and Revolution in Iran* (Boulder: Westview Press, 1983), pp 109–28.
22. Hamid Naficy, 'The Development of an Islamic Cinema in Iran,' *Third World Affairs* (London: Third World Foundation, 1987), pp 447–63. That is not to say, of course, that women in Islamic Iran are not treated like commodities. They are, especially in various forms of marriage exchanges. For more, see: Haeri, *Law of Desire*, and Moghadam in this volume.
23. Hamid Naficy, 'Islamizing Film Culture in Iran,' in Samih Farsoun and Mehradad Mashayekhi (eds), *Iran: Political Culture in the Islamic Republic* (London: Routledge and Kegan Paul, 1992), pp 173–208.
24. Mas'ud Purmohammad, 'Ebteda Sangha-ye Kuchak,' *Mahnameh-ye*

Sinema'i-ye Film, 66 (Azar 1366/1987), p 8. Of course, underrepresentation of women as 'heroes' in films made in the US is a serious and much discussed matter also. The specific reasons for underrepresentation of women in American and post-revolutionary Iranian cinema may be different; however, the global reasons, patriarchy and phallocentrism, are the same.

25. A post-revolutionary film director underlines these practices by saying that women in Islamic performing arts should be shown seated at all times so as to avoid drawing attention to their 'provocative walk,' thereby allowing the audience to concentrate on the 'ideologies' inherent in the work. 'Honarpishegan-e Zan az Film Hazf Shodeh' and *Kayhan* (London) (26 September 1985), p 11.
26. See Hamid Naficy, 'Zan va Mas'aleh-ye Zan . . .'
27. Same-sex or cross-sex role exchanges as both a cultural practice and a literary tradition is not unknown in Islamic cultures as Mills's study of the oral narratives of a Muslim community in Afghanistan shows. The weak point implies male-to-female role switching not only through its use of generic cinematic formulas but also, following Mills's formulation, by positioning the captive as the vulnerable one. See Mills, 'Sex Role Reversals', p 196.
28. Annette Kuhn, *Women's Pictures: Feminism and Cinema* (New York: Routledge and Kegan Paul, 1982), p 58.
29. In much of Iranian secular poetry and in religious discourses, the gaze is likened to an arrow that has irretrievably left the bow: it is direct, powerful, and aggressively aimed at a victim, the love object.
30. Quoted in Naficy, 'Zan va Mas'aleh-ye Zan . . .' p 149.
31. Abol-Hasan Bani-Sadr, the first post-revolutionary president, claimed in a speech that a woman's hair gives off certain powerful 'rays' that transform the men and must therefore be contained by a veil or a scarf. Meanwhile, this has become the butt of jokes.
32. Motahhari, *Islamic Modest Dress*, p 13.
33. Laura Mulvey, 'Visual Pleasure and Narrative Cinema,' reprinted in *Visual and Other Pleasure* (Bloomington: Indiana University Press, 1989), pp 14–26; E. Ann Kaplan, 'Is the Gaze Male?,' *Women and Film: Both Sides of the Camera* (New York: Methuen, 1983), pp 23–35.
34. Gaylyn Studlar, *In the Realm of Pleasure: Von Sternberg, Dietrich, and the Masochistic Aesthetics* (Urbana: University of Illinois Press, 1988).
35. Gilles Deleuze, *Masochism: An Interpretation of Coldness and Cruelty* (New York: George Braziller, 1971).
36. Abbasali Mahmudi, *Zan dar Eslam* (Tehran: Nehzat-e Zanan-e Mosalman, 1360/1981), p 117.
37. Slavoj Zizek, 'Looking Awry,' *October* 51 (1990), pp 30–55.
38. Paul Willemen, 'Voyeurism, The Look, and Dworkin,' reprinted in Philip Rosen (ed), *Narrative, Apparatus, Ideology: A Film theory Reader* (New York: Columbia University Press, 1986), pp 210–18.
39. Sayyed Abolqasem Musavi Kho'i, *Resaleh-ye Towzih al-Masa'el* (n.p.: Entesharat-e Javidan, 1395/1975) Ruhollah Khomeini, *Towzih al-Masa'el Ba Ezafat va Masa'el-e Jadid* (n.p.:n.d.).

40. On the subject of photography there are divergent opinions. For example, Khomeini states that it is not forbidden for a man to take pictures of an unrelated woman (*Towzih al-Masa'el*, p 266), while Kho'i declares that a man must not only not take pictures of an unrelated woman but also must not look at her picture if he knows her (*Resaleh-ye Towzih*, pp 310–11). At any rate, the idea that certain looks are religiously allowed (*halal*) or forbidden (*haram*) based on one's familial relationship and the dual constitution of the self, affects the process of photography and archiving. As a young boy, for example, the older women in my family (my grandmothers and aunts) would either not permit me to take their picture or would permit me only if they were covered by their veil. Their reason was that although the photographer was a related man, the men at the photography shop who would develop the negatives were not, thus causing a transgression of the rules of modesty and gender segregation. I myself had to engage in a game of veiling and unveiling with them by either pretending that I was not taking their picture (while I actually did) or snapping their picture when they were not aware. At any rate, because of the complications involved in taking pictures of women, there is a definite underrepresentation of older women in family photographic albums.
41. This behavior of averting one's gaze fits the tenets of the Quran which warns Muslims against the danger of the direct gaze. In Sura of Nur it states: 'Say to the believing men to cast down their glance and guard their private parts' (24:30). And: 'Say to the believing women to cast down their glance and guard their private parts' (24:31). (Quoted in Motahhari, *Islamic Modest Dress*, pp 47–8.)
42. Zizek, 'Looking Away,' p 34.
43. Personal interview, Los Angeles, April 1988. The actress wishes to remain anonymous.
44. Personal interview, Los Angeles, April 1990.
45. Christian Metz, *The Imaginary Signifier: Psychoanalysis and the Cinema*, trans Celia Britton, Annwyl Williams, Ben Brewster, and Alfred Guzetti (Bloomington: Indiana University Press, 1982).
46. Mohsen Makhmalbaf, *Yaddashtha'i dar Bareh-ye Qessehnevisi va Namayeshnevisi* (Tehran: Howzeh-ye Andisheh va Honar-e Eslami, 1360/1981), pp 136–7.
47. *Zan-e Ruz* (25 Esfand 1369/1990), p 45.
48. Homa Kohlari, 'Az Eshq ta Ebtezal,' *Kayhan Hava'i* (20 February 1991), p 21.
49. For an analysis along this line, see the special cinema issue of the *Sureh* magazine, (Spring 1379/1991), pp 4–9.
50. Mohsen Makhmalbaf, 'Tasvir-e Makhdush-e Man dar Matbu'at-e Dakheli,' *Zan-e Ruz* (25 Esfand 1369/1990), pp 46–7.
51. It must be noted that the binary positioning of female qualities such as 'chaste,' 'modest,' 'revolutionary,' and 'indigenous' versus 'lewd,' 'corrupted,' 'anti-revolutionary,' and 'westoxicated' creates both an erroneously rigid opposition between these terms and the impression that they are fixed and permanent attributes. In reality, of course,

attributes and qualities are much more fluid. However, a revolution which replaces one political regime with its opposite also necessitates similar binary shifts in other domains. Iranians immediately after the 1979 revolution focalized on inflexible binaries in the interest of replacing one quality (lewd) with the other (modest).

52. Mulvey, 'Visual Pleasure,' p 25.

9. Erika Friedl: Sources of Female Power

Author's note: This paper is based on nearly six years of qualitative anthropological fieldwork in Iran, conducted between 1965 and 1992, including, but not limited to, the village I have studied intensively and which I call Deh Koh. Field research at various times was supported by grants from the Social Science Research Council, the National Endowment of the Humanities, the Wenner Gren Foundation for Anthropological Research, and Western Michigan University.

1. Fatna Ait Sabbah, *Woman in the Muslim Unconscious* (New York: Pergamon, 1984); Adele K. Ferdows and Amir H. Ferdows, 'Women in Shi'i Figh: Images through the Hadith,' in Guity Nashat (ed), *Women and the Revolution in Iran* (Boulder: Westview Press, 1983).
2. Ülkü Bates, 'Women as Patrons of Architecture in Turkey,' in Lois Beck and Nikki Keddie (eds), *Women in the Muslim World*, (Cambridge and London: Harvard University Press, 1978); Lois Beck, *The Qashqai of Iran* (New Haven and London: Yale University Press, 1986), p 192; Shusha Guppy, *The Blindfold Horse: Memories of a Persian Childhood* (Boston: Beacon Press, 1988), p 18; Susan Wright, 'Prattle and Politics: The Position of Women in Doshman-Ziari,' *Journal of the Anthropological Society of Oxford* 9, 2 (1978), p 102.
3. James C. Scott, *Weapons of the Weak: Everyday Forms of Peasant Resistance* (New Haven and London: Yale University Press, 1985); *Domination and the Arts of Resistance* (New Haven and London: Yale University Press, 1990).
4. Etymologically, the word 'power' is linked to the notion of 'being able to do.' Definitions of 'power' according to *Webster's New Collegiate Dictionary* (Springfield: Merriam, 1973) include the concepts of control, efficacy, capacity, and right. In vernacular English, 'power' has the connotation of power to limit, control, even destroy, others. These definitions and connotations put the term power into an aggression-oriented, androcentric discourse. It is, however, not an ethnocentric one: the Farsi terms *qodrat, zur, harf* which are used in the local gender discourse, correspond fairly well to our terms power, force, and say (in the sense of verbal input, as in: 'I have no say in this matter'), respectively.
5. For recent discussions on different theoretical ramifications of resistance of women in Middle Eastern countries, see Lila Abu-Lughod, 'The Romance of Resistance: Tracing Transformations of Power through Bedouin Women,' *American Ethnologist* 17 (February 1990), pp 41–55; and Arlene E. Macleod, *Accommodating Protest: Working Women, the*

new Veiling, and Change in Cairo (New York: Columbia University Press, 1991). .

6. Information supporting generalizations and conclusions comes from my own observations in Iran· both before and after the revolution, and from the literature. Examples and illustrations not credited to others are my own and come from various localities in Iran. For reasons of confidentiality, I decided not to identify locations other than large cities, and to omit particularities of circumstances of the people whose cases are described in this paper.
7. The most helpful discussion of this topic is Scott, *Weapons*, and *Domination*.
8. For a detailed discussion of the psychological aspects of this process, see Jean Baker Miller, *Toward a New Psychology of Women* (Boston: Beacon Press, 1986), especially p 11.
9. Janet Bauer, 'Poor Women and Social Consciousness in Revolutionary Iran,' in Nashat (ed), *Women and Revolution*, p 152.
10. Lois Beck, 'Women among Qashqai Nomadic Pastoralists in Iran,' in Beck and Keddie (eds), *Women*, p 345; Mary Elaine Hegland, personal communication.
11. For a general discussion of wife-beating see Mary Elaine Hegland, 'Wife Abuse and the Political System,' in Dorothy Ayers Counts, Judith K. Brown, and Jacquelyn C. Campbell (eds), *Sanctions and Sanctuary* (Boulder: Westview Press, 1992). Statistical data on domestic violence in the Islamic Republic are unavailable. However, increases in wife-beating are reported by health workers in towns and villages. For the purposes of this paper, the number of cases is less important than the explanation given locally for their occurrence, that is, reaction to challenges to the traditional power hierarchy within the family.
12. Another example is given by Susan Wright, 'Prattle,' p 98. Writing about Doshman Ziari women, she says: 'The concepts which structure that [dominant] model [for behavior and attitudes] are accepted by the women, but by employing the obverse implications of their meaning and their interlinking, women obtain a degree of freedom of action and influence in social affairs from which the dominant model theoretically excludes them.'
13. Ibid, p 110.
14. Ibid, p 98.
15. Mary Elaine Hegland, 'Aliabad Women: Revolution as Religious Activity,' in Nashat (ed), *Women and Revolution*, p 173.
16. Guppy, *Blindfold Horse*, p 18.
17. Mary Elaine Hegland, 'Political Roles of Aliabad Women: The Public–Private Dichotomy Transcended,' in Nikki R. Keddie and Beth Baron (eds), *Women in Middle Eastern History* (New Haven and London: Yale University Press, 1991), p 225.
18. About the Shahsevan, Tapper writes: 'Women control the daily affairs of the household and men willingly accept their judgment in this sphere, but leadership in all relations outside and inside the family is held to be a male prerogative.' Nancy Tapper, 'The Women's Subsociety

among the Shahsevan Nomads of Iran,' in Beck and Keddie (eds), *Women*, p 377.

19. This case is described in Erika Friedl, *Women of Deh Koh: Lives in an Iranian Village* (New York: Penguin, 1991), pp 160–82.
20. Erika Friedl, 'The Division of Labor in an Iranian Village,' *MERIP Reports* 95 (March–April 1981), p 16.
21. See also Wright, 'Prattle', p 110f on teachers in this sense.
22. Since 1991, family planning has become a priority in the government's efforts to improve the economy. Even if these efforts turn out to be successful, their effects on family size will not be felt until several years hence.
23. In the province of Kohgiluye Boir Ahmad, for example, local administrators in 1989 declared the birth rate to be 5 per cent. Generally, throughout western Iran, I found that people considered seven children to be a 'good' number for a woman in 1989, compared to four children in 1975.
24. Mary Elaine Hegland, 'Women and the Iranian Revolution: A Village Case Study,' *Dialectical Anthropology* 15 (1990), p 189.
25. Anne H. Betteridge, 'The Controversial Vows of Urban Muslim Women in Iran,' in Nancy Auer Falk and Rita M. Gross (eds), *Unspoken Worlds: Women's Religious Lives in Non-Western Cultures* (San Francisco: Harper and Row, 1988), p 143.
26. Anne H. Betteridge, *Ziarat: Pilgrimage to the Shrines of Shiraz* (PhD dissertation, University of Chicago, 1985).
27. Shahla Haeri, *Law of Desire: Temporary Marriage in Shi'i Iran* (Syracuse: Syracuse University Press, 1989).
28. Tapper, 'Women's Subsociety', p 382.
29. For families with money, several new universities that charge tuition now provide an alternative to the traditional, tuition-free universities.
30. For a discussion of this phenomenon, see Higgins and Shoar-Ghaffari in this volume. All-women's groups, be they comprised of kinswomen or organized in other ways, tend to have this effect. Among themselves, women develop group dynamics with commensurate psychological-emotional benefits different from those they develop in mixed groups. In the Middle East, such groups are not studied and not well understood.

Index